Contents at a Glance

Table of Contents

About the Author

Stephen O'Brien is an Australian-born writer and entrepreneur currently residing in Sydney after too many years in Silicon Valley. He has previously written 27 books across multiple editions with publishers such as Prentice-Hall and Que, including several best-selling titles. He also founded Typefi, the world's leading automated publishing system, and in his spare time he invented a new type of espresso machine called mypressi. He has been playing Minecraft since its earliest days and remains astounded at the unparalleled creativity it engenders.

The Ultimate Player's Guide to
MINECRAFT

Stephen O'Brien

800 East 96th Street,
Indianapolis, Indiana 46240 USA

The Ultimate Player's Guide to Minecraft

Copyright © 2014 by Que Publishing

ISBN-13: 978-0-7897-5223-9
ISBN-10: 0-7897-5223-9

Library of Congress Control Number: 2013946682

Printed in the United States of America

Second Printing November 2013

Trademarks

All terms mentioned in this book that are known to be trademarks or service marks have been appropriately capitalized. Que Publishing cannot attest to the accuracy of this information. Use of a term in this book should not be regarded as affecting the validity of any trademark or service mark.

Minecraft is a trademark of Notch Development AB.

Warning and Disclaimer

Every effort has been made to make this book as complete and as accurate as possible, but no warranty or fitness is implied. The information provided is on an "as is" basis. The author and the publisher shall have neither liability nor responsibility to any person or entity with respect to any loss or damages arising from the information contained in this book.

Bulk Sales

Que Publishing offers excellent discounts on this book when ordered in quantity for bulk purchases or special sales. For more information, please contact

U.S. Corporate and Government Sales
1-800-382-3419
corpsales@pearsontechgroup.com

For sales outside of the U.S., please contact

International Sales
international@pearsoned.com

Editor-in-Chief
Greg Wiegand

Executive Editor
Rick Kughen

Development Editor
Rick Kughen

Managing Editor
Sandra Schroeder

Project Editor
Seth Kerney

Copy Editor
Gill Editorial Services

Indexer
Ken Johnson

Proofreader
Jess DeGabriele

Technical Editor
Timothy L. Warner

Publishing Coordinator
Kristen Watterson

Book Designer
Mark Shirar

Compositor
Bronkella Publishing

Dedication

To Mika, who at age nine taught his dad to laugh hysterically at the sight of a pig riding up a mountain in a minecart. Laughs and love always, dear boy.

Acknowledgments

It's an author's dream to work with a talented team, and I feel like I'm having a better dream than most. After 12 years away from Que working on entrepreneurial projects, I was incredibly fortunate to step straight back into the fold of a fantastic group. I'd like to thank Rick Kughen for his outstanding project direction, polished editorial efforts, and always gentle prompting even as I started to run behind schedule. Rick, it's such a true pleasure to work with you again. Seth Kerney, thank you for so smoothly shepherding this book through the numerous stages of the publishing process. Karen Gill, I appreciate your thorough, precise copyediting and constantly joyful feedback. Mark Shirar, you created a fantastic cover and page design. And Tim Warner, thanks for a technical edit that truly left no block uncovered, no cobblestone unturned.

Writing a book always feels a long leap into the dark, with the only light often being close family and friends. I thank you all, in particular my dad, Tony; my siblings, Justin, Adele, and Siobhan; my dear friend Laura; and everyone else who gave me no end of encouragement, best wishes, and a chorus of variations on the very Australian "goodonya."

Last, but by no means least, thank you, Amy, for your constant love, support, and encouragement.

We Want to Hear from You!

As the reader of this book, *you* are our most important critic and commentator. We value your opinion and want to know what we're doing right, what we could do better, what areas you'd like to see us publish in, and any other words of wisdom you're willing to pass our way.

We welcome your comments. You can email or write to let us know what you did or didn't like about this book—as well as what we can do to make our books better.

Please note that we cannot help you with technical problems related to the topic of this book.

When you write, please be sure to include this book's title and author as well as your name and email address. We will carefully review your comments and share them with the author and editors who worked on the book.

Email: feedback@quepublishing.com

Mail: Que Publishing
ATTN: Reader Feedback
800 East 96th Street
Indianapolis, IN 46240 USA

Reader Services

Visit our website and register this book at quepublishing.com/register for convenient access to any updates, downloads, or errata that might be available for this book.

Introduction

Imagine waking one morning thrust from your soft, cozy bed into a strange new world. A square sun crosses the sky. You have no tools or weapons—nothing but your bare, knobby hands. You briefly survey the landscape. Hills and forests surround you. A cow lows in the distance.

On a hunch you look for a Horn of Plenty—anything that may deliver something useful. Every other RPG you've played has plenty of stuff lying around. But it's a fruitless search with no cache in sight. Curiously, though, one of your random clicks does dig a hole in the ground. Interesting. But how does it help? You try again. Another hole. Hmmm.

You continue your reconnaissance, admiring the varied terrain, soaring cliffs, verdant forests, and clear blue lakes. It certainly is pleasing to the eye, but this universe seems to work by unfamiliar rules. The sun is moving far too briskly across the sky, and nightfall now looks like it's mere minutes away.

That can't be good.

You start a kind of random flail, clicking everything in sight. The trunk of a tree looks promising. Aha! A block of wood falls to the ground. But what to do with it? You have to figure that out later.

Darkness descends, and with it comes an unearthly groan. Strange figures appear in the distant gloom, lurching toward you. A slithering slurp shrieks into your senses from behind. A cold finger of fear trips down your spine.

You run for the base of the nearest cliff. If your back's against the wall, it might as well be a sturdy one. Wait a moment. Is that the mouth of a cave? Perfect! A final quick dash sees you safely inside.

The darkness turns to an inky black. You stumble down a ledge putting more distance between you and the horrifying creatures outside. Stop, breathe, look around.

You hear the briefest hiss, like a burning fuse. Frantically spinning to find the source, you catch a glimpse of a ghastly green face. It's the last you'll see before a gigantic explosion claims your life.

Welcome to Minecraft and a typical experience for the millions of players who buy this game in ever-increasing numbers on every major platform. Minecraft is, without doubt, one of the most interesting open-ended games ever produced. It's also one of the most vexatious.

From the first moment I started playing this game, back in the beta, to today's extraordinary experience, Minecraft has developed into a tour de force of absolutely splendid gameplay, but one that is not easily accessible.

Before I even thought about writing this book I found it popping up more and more frequently in random conversations among all age levels—everyone from my nine-year old's best friends going on up...way up. Minecraft's unique open-endedness offers an equally open-ended fascination to people of all ages. Fifty million of them, and counting.

Clearly, Minecraft was enjoying unparalleled success for an independent production, but there was something strange going on. The game still lacked an in-depth tutorial or documentation of any sort. And while there is no paucity of online resources, how do you explain a game where every block bends to your will; where the terrain can dance to your tune; where an electrical system can do a crazy range of things including simulating its own computer; and where other elements such as casting enchantments, brewing potions, and finding a way to get to and defeat the final boss require some curiously specific, obtuse steps and strategies?

The online community has stepped into that breach admirably, going to the point of decompiling the code to understand and document specific game mechanics, but the essentials are often buried among hundreds of thousands of random Minecraft videos or tucked in with other encyclopedically detailed documentation. And, among all that, there are literally thousands of junk sites trying to trick you into clicking on ads or installing malware.

This book fills the gap, bringing together all the key information you need in a single place. Written from the player's perspective, it takes you through the essentials and then far beyond with all the background information, crafting recipes, strategies, and ideas you need to make your Minecraft world truly your own. It covers everything from first-night survival to hosting your own Multiplayer server.

If you are a parent wondering if Minecraft is suitable for your own kids, consider it to be as far from a consumption-only experience as old-school rote learning is from an active education filled with exploration and discovery. Minecraft will inspire great feats of imagination and a thirst for understanding how its many facets enmesh and evolve. Best of all, it's like one of those great movies or books that are marketed toward kids but entertain adults on a whole other level. Play it together—even turn off the monsters through its creative or peaceful modes—and enjoy your time playing together with kids as young as four or five. But I warn you, it's addictive. Please remember to give them a go now and then.

No matter who you are or how you play, you'll find Minecraft to be an endlessly fascinating, wonderful, enjoyable world. It's going to be quite the journey!

What's in This Book

Survive and thrive in Minecraft with 13 chapters of detailed step-by-step guides, tips, tricks, and strategies. Each chapter in this book focuses on a key aspect of the game, from initial survival to building an empire. Make the most of your Minecraft world today:

- Chapter 1, "Getting Started," will walk you through the steps needed to download and install Minecraft, and start a new game, optionally using seeds to control the world generation.

- Chapter 2, "First-Night Survival," is an essential strategy guide to one of the most challenging times in Minecraft. You'll learn to craft essential tools and build your first mob-proof shelter, all in less than 10 minutes of gameplay.

- Chapter 3, "Gathering Resources," will fill out the skills you need to build a permanent base of operations, create better tools, store resources, and find food to stave off hunger. I also show you how to use the built-in GPS so you can always find your way home, even after extended forays into the wilds.

- Chapter 4, "Mining," unlocks some of Minecraft's deepest secrets. I'll show you the best tunneling plan to uncover the most resources in the shortest possible time, the essential tools required, and the layers you should dig to uncover everything from basic iron ore to diamonds.

- Chapter 5, "Combat School," will get you ready to tackle any mob, including the creeper. From sword-fighting techniques to armor, this chapter has you covered. You'll also learn the essential perimeter protection techniques for your home.

- Chapter 6, "Crop Farming," will help you become completely self-sufficient, ensuring the hunger bar stays full, constantly boosting your health. Learn to hydrate 80 blocks of farm land with a single water block, and automate your harvests at the touch of a button.

- Chapter 7, "Taming Mobs," is all about Minecraft's passive animals, the chickens, pigs, cows, horses, and more that populate its world and provide you with valuable resources. Learn to breed animals, tame Ocelots to scare off creepers, and gallop across the world on horseback.

- Chapter 8, "Creative Construction," will help you unleash your inner architect. From grand constructions to inventive interiors, learn about the decorative ways you can use Minecraft's blocks and items to build the perfect abode.

- Chapter 9, "Redstone, Rails, and More," empowers your world with a host of automated devices. Control redstone power, automated doors, send minecarts on missions, and build stations, stopovers and more.

- Chapter 10, "Enchanting, Anvils, and Brewing," will have you brewing up a storm. Cast spells, improve your weapons and armor, and fall from great heights with grace.

- Chapter 11, "Villages and Other Structures," is your key to interacting with the other non-playing characters. Trade your way to better goods, and learn the secrets of the game's temples.

- Chapter 12, "Playing Through: The Nether and The End," is the strategy guide you'll need to get through these tricky sections of the game. Find a fortress fast, get what you need, and then prepare for the Ender Dragon. It's easy when you know how.

- Chapter 13, "Mods and Multiplayer," will show you how to customize the game, from new character skins to mods that add a host of functionality. And along the way you'll also learn how to access multiplayer games and set up a permanent world on your own server for family and friends.

How to Use This Book

Throughout this book, you'll see that I have called out some items as Notes, Tips, and Cautions—all of which are explained here.

NOTE

Notes point out ancillary bits of information that are helpful but not crucial. They often make for an interesting meander.

TIP

Tips point out a useful bit of information to help you solve a problem. They're useful in a tight spot.

CAUTION

Cautions alert you to potential disasters and pitfalls. Don't ignore these!

Crafting Recipes

You'll also see that I've included crafting recipes throughout this book. I've included the actual ingredients in the text, so just match the pattern you see to create the item, as shown here for a wooden pickaxe. It's easy, and you'll be surprised how quickly you can whip them up after just a few uses.

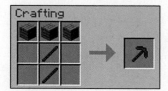

There's More Online...

In addition to the information packed between the covers of this book, I've put together a complete guide to all the crafting recipes online. Feel free to download! Visit http://www.quepublishing.com/register to register your book and download your free PDF copy.

Getting Started

In This Chapter

- Register, purchase, and install Minecraft on your platform of choice.
- Like your monsters plentiful and deadly, or do you prefer a more peaceful existence? Minecraft has a gameplay mode for you.
- Become a terraforming titan! Control your world generation with seeds and other options.
- Confused by the controls? See the complete list.

Minecraft is an amazing place. Far more than just a game, it's a world of pixelated possibility: an incredible 3D grid of blocks, resources, creatures, monsters, and pitfalls. It features multiple gameplay styles, from the safe, free-soaring Creative mode to the challenging Survival mode and the multiplayer Adventure mode.

In this chapter, you'll learn how to register, download, and install Minecraft, get a full rundown on the different gameplay modes and options, determine the way the world generates, and learn how to control your Minecraft character.

Registering and Downloading

Minecraft offers a huge amount of fun and will no doubt occupy you for many, many hours. However, before you can immerse yourself in its world, there are just a few things you need to do first. You'll need to set up an account with its creators, Mojang, purchase a license, and, of course, install the software. This will only take a few minutes, but feel free to skip to the next section in this chapter if you already have completed these.

Before we get started, keep in mind that Minecraft is available in several different versions, including a free demo that will run for about 100 minutes, which is the equivalent of 5 Minecraft day/night cycles and is playable in your browser if you have Java installed. (If you don't, just visit http://java.com to do so.)

Minecraft: Pocket Edition is also available for iOS and Android, and *Minecraft: Xbox 360 Edition* is available through the Xbox Live Marketplace and for purchase as a regular Xbox installation disc. This book is primarily about the version you can download to your PC (v1.6.2, also known as The Horse Update) because that version provides the most complete Minecraft experience to date.

The Xbox 360 Edition is catching up fast, but lacks some features, while the Xbox One edition promises a number of improvements based on that system's more powerful hardware.

There's also a version available for the tiny Raspberry Pi computer, but it lacks most of the core gameplay functionality.

NOTE

A Few Technical Specs

I'll use the term *PC* throughout this book to refer to any personal computer running Microsoft Windows, OS X, or any flavor of Linux. The one primary hardware requirement for Minecraft on a PC is that the video card support OpenGL hardware acceleration. Because almost every video card in existence does that these days, you should find that Minecraft installs and runs pretty much perfectly, even on a laptop with integrated graphics. If you hit any problems getting the game to run, make sure you have the latest Java release installed, and update your video card driver.

CAUTION

Your Mileage May Vary with the Demo Version

Playing the demo of Minecraft 1.5x in a browser can be a little problematic depending on your PC's configuration, particularly on a Mac. These issues only relate to the demo version and not the full version download. The specific solution is beyond the scope of this book and may require some significant effort to overcome. You can find further information at www.minecraftwiki.net/wiki/LWJGL, and you'll find others with a little searching online using "Minecraft demo Mac."

Registering a Mojang Account

With the exception of the Xbox and iOS versions, you'll need to register an account with Mojang before you can play the demo version or even purchase the full game. It's a quick process, similar to registering a free account for any site. You also won't need a credit card if you just want to check out the demo. The process is a little different than a lot of other software you might purchase, so I'll take you through it step by step.

Start by visiting http://minecraft.net in your browser and click the blue **Register** link in the top-right corner of the screen, shown in Figure 1.1.

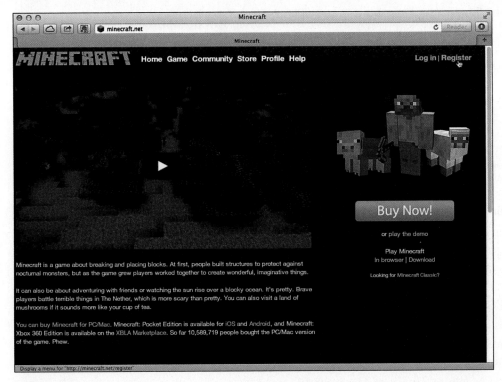

FIGURE 1.1   The first step in using the demo or download versions of Minecraft is to register with Mojang.

Provide your email address, and create a secure password. You'll also need to give your first and last name and date of birth. Then select and provide the answers to three security questions.

NOTE

Choose Your Security Questions Wisely

Choose your answers to the security questions carefully. You'll be asked one of the three questions at random the first time you log into Minecraft.net from a new PC.

> ## TIP
>
> **Don't Make Your Password Impossible to Remember!**
>
> Passwords don't need to be a confusing, impossible-to-recall mishmash of letters and numbers to be secure. A simple strategy that defeats even the most sophisticated attack is to choose two random words, an adjective and a noun, and then add a number. Then use another character to separate them. For example, red*Light29 is strong. Avoid using your own initials, a common phrase, or your date of birth. Just to be safe, also use something different from those you use for your regular email, bank access, and so on. There's no need to make it too easy for the real creepers out there to hijack your accounts.

Then check your inbox for an email from Mojang. Click the link contained in the email to confirm your email address, and you're ready to go.

In the next two sections, I'll take you through the process of purchasing and downloading Minecraft. If you've already done so, you can skip to Chapter 2, "First-Night Survival." You can also bypass this section if you just want to play the Demo version in your browser.

Purchasing Minecraft

After you've purchased Minecraft, it is permanently linked to your Mojang account. There's no need to worry about losing the install software, misplacing serial numbers, or changing PCs and needing to reinstall. Just login, download again, and install.

There is a way to download Minecraft after you've registered. But don't get too excited about seeing the download link there. You'll still need to have the actual purchase of Minecraft linked to your account before you can play. The good news is that you only need to log in once from within the Minecraft Launcher to verify the purchase. After that you can still play, even offline. And if you are online, the site will conveniently check to ensure that you have all the latest files installed, updating as it goes.

To purchase and download Minecraft:

1 Log in to http://minecraft.net with the account you set up earlier, and click the big **Buy Now** button on the right of the web page. This takes you to the Mojang store.

2 Click **Buy Minecraft for this account**. From there, the rest is standard online purchasing. Provide your credit card details and billing address, and you can complete your order.

3 When you've completed your purchase, you can return to http://minecraft.net at any time.

4 Log in if you haven't already, and you'll see the **Buy Now** button has changed to **Download Now**. Click it to move to the actual download screen shown in Figure 1.2.

These days, application and game files tend to run to hundreds of megabytes, if not giga-bytes in size, so you may be surprised at the relatively small size of the Minecraft download. It's actually just a few hundred kilobytes for Mac and Windows, and even less for Linux. That's because you aren't really downloading the game, just a utility called Minecraft Launcher. The launcher takes care of checking for updates, downloading the main Minecraft application files, and checking your account credentials. You'll always use the launcher to access the actual game.

TIP

Other Custom Launchers Available

Some enterprising developers have created their own compatible versions of Minecraft Launcher with additional features that let you easily manage mods, texture packs, and other third-party add-ons to the software. One of my favorites is *Magic Launcher*.

NOTE

Giving the Gift of Minecraft

Want to give the gift that keeps on giving? When you reach the Minecraft purchase screen, you can also choose to email a gift code to someone else or receive the gift code yourself so you can pass it on personally. You can then participate in cooperative online sessions on your local network and join sessions that are hosted on the many independent multiplayer servers available online. For more information on multiplayer servers, see Chapter 13, "Mods and Multiplayer," on page 251.

Different browsers treat downloaded files in different ways. I'll assume you are already familiar with the process of opening downloaded files for your particular computer plat-form. The following are a few notes to keep in mind:

- **Windows**—On Windows, you can save the file anywhere you prefer, perhaps in a special Minecraft folder or to your desktop.

- **OS X**—On Mac OS X, you should copy Minecraft Launcher to your Applications folder, just to keep things tidy, although I've had no problems running it from elsewhere. After you launch the game, you can attach it with a right-click to the dock.

- **Linux**—The Linux version can also run from just about anywhere, but you'll probably want to move it to your usual Applications folder as well.

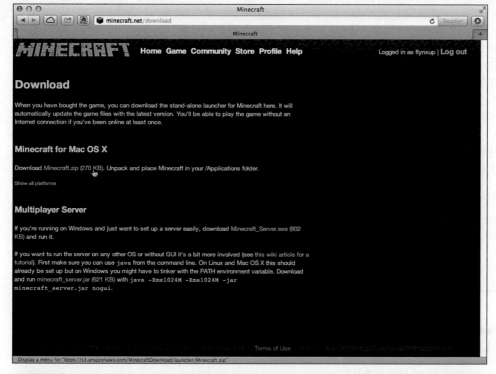

FIGURE 1.2   The download page provides links to the Minecraft download for your current platform. Click **Show all platforms** if you don't see the correct version.

Launching Minecraft

Okay, you've set up your account, and you've purchased and downloaded Minecraft. It's time to get this show on the road!

1 This first time ensure that you are online, then go to your install location and double-click the Minecraft icon. This opens the Minecraft Launcher.

2 There are just two fields to fill in:

   ■ **Username**—Enter the email you used when creating your Mojang account. Unless you have an old Minecraft account, this is the email address you used when establishing your account.

   ■ **Password**—Enter your account password.

FIGURE 1.3 The Minecraft Launcher provides the latest news, links to Minecraft-related sites, and the Twitter handles of the Mojang team.

3 Now click **Log In**. The screen shown in Figure 1.3 will become the default screen you see the next time you launch Minecraft. If you are not currently connected to the Internet, **Play** changes to **Play Offline** after a short delay, although you must have at least logged in once online from the Minecraft Launcher before this option becomes available.

4 If this is the first time you've run Minecraft, you'll need to wait while the game components download, but on a broadband connection this takes only a few minutes. The Minecraft title screen shown in Figure 1.4 is pleasantly spare. Although it's tempting to party up and hit the multiplayer mode, let's head into the single player mode first because this is the best place to learn Minecraft.

5 Click **Singleplayer**, and let's get started!

NOTE

Single and Multiplayer Terminology

Minecraft calls single player games "singleplayer" so I'll also use that spelling here. Multiplayer games are also often referred to as PvP (or "Player versus Player"), although those games can be co-operative, creative, or a faction-based mix of both.

FIGURE 1.4   The Minecraft title screen provides your launch point for single-player and multiplayer games, as well as global and language options.

1. Singleplayer offers access to the Creative and Survival modes, new games, and previously saved games.

2. Multiplayer takes you into the Adventure mode, where you can explore worlds created by others with many other players.

3. Click the World icon to change the default interface language.

4. Change the global options such as video settings; you can also change these in-game.

5. Quit to your operating system.

Starting a New Game

The Create New World screen shown in Figure 1.5 allows you to set a few essential parameters. Just follow these steps:

1 Type a name for your world in the **World Name** text box. You can use the default "New World" multiple times because Minecraft keeps the saved game files separate, but doing so can become a little confusing over time.

2 Click the **Game Mode** selector to choose between Survival, Hardcore, and Creative modes. (See "Singleplayer Game Modes" later in the chapter for more information.) For now, leave it on Survival.

3 Click **More World Options**. Ignore the **Seed** field at the top for now. You can read about it later in "Seeding Your World." Ensure **Generate Structures** is On so that Minecraft can populate the world with villages, temples, pyramids, and dungeons. This is an essential gameplay element. Leave the **World Type** as Default (see the next Note). Set **Allow Cheats** to On. We'll walk through a few of the basic cheat commands in this and the next chapter. Finally, leave **Bonus Chest** set to Off. When turned On, this option places a chest with a few random but typically useful items near your spawn point, but we're going to start from scratch.

NOTE

Cheats, Really?

Minecraft's "cheats" are a series of commands accessed by tapping the / key, or the T key. Cheats reset the time, change game modes and difficulty on the fly, allow you to set a spawn point, teleport to another location, and more. They mostly provide a host of commands that help with managing players on shared servers, but they can also save your bacon in Survival Mode. I've suggested setting cheats here so that you can explore some of the different options, but after you know the ropes, it's not a bad idea to turn them off for a survival experience that's true to form.

---

4 When you've finished, click **Create New World**. Welcome to Minecraft!

FIGURE 1.5 Change your Minecraft world name so that you can better keep track of each as you create multiple files.

Now that you're up and running, turn to Chapter 2 to start the survival tutorial, or keep reading for a little more background information.

Choosing a World Generation Style

Minecraft provides three basic world-generation styles. The default World Type provides a traditional Minecraft world, even if each of those worlds features different topology above and below ground. The two others are **Large Biomes** and **Superflat**. Usually biomes (think of them as individual ecosystems) are quite small and can be traversed easily, providing diversity of terrains and ecosystems in each world. Selecting Large Biome increases their size 16x, making for much more extensive biome traversals. A superflat world is actually completely flat except for any generated structures. If you select Superflat, you'll also gain access to new customization options and a range of presets for different types of superflat worlds.

So which biome is for you? The default setting is great for starting out. Each biome contains different resources and their smaller size in this setting makes them easy to traverse so you can move quickly from open land to a jungle, through a forest and so on, gathering all the bits and pieces you need as you go.

Large biomes open up the terrain, making it more like the real world. These worlds present a greater challenge for the intrepid explorer, with Columbus-confounding oceans that disappear over the horizon, large flat grasslands perfect for galloping across at high speed on horseback, dense endless forests, and majestic mountains. They force you to get out and see more of the world, and you'll need to be prepared for a lot of impromptu camping on the way.

The superflat world is less interesting in that sense, with nary a bump to disturb the ground, but you might prefer its blank canvas to explore different techniques in creative mode.

By the way, each block in Minecraft measures 1m per side, or one cubic meter. Each world in the PC edition has 64 million × 64 million blocks and is therefore 64,000 kilometers long by 64,000 kilometers wide. Or, to put it another way, it's massively larger than Earth itself. Happy exploring, and if you need inspiration, see *Far Lands or Bust* at http://farlandsorbust. com, where you can track Kurt and Wolfie's daily journey to the fabled Far Lands. Kurt's journeying to raise money for a children's charity and has been trekking since March 2011. He and his canine companion probably have quite a few more years to go.

The Xbox edition creates a world of just 862x862 blocks, whereas the Pocket Edition measures a much smaller 256x256.

Singleplayer Game Modes

Minecraft offers a variety of gameplay modes:

- **Survival**—This is the default mode for all new games and is the one I'll mostly focus on throughout the book. Survival mode is made up of two phases: day and night. During the day, you have a 10-minute window to gather resources, mine, build, farm—do whatever you need to do. During the first few days, this is usually made up of a few key activities, but after you've established your base, be it underground, in a walled fortress, in a building, or even in a tree house (see Chapter 8, Creative Construction," page 137, you can rest a little easier. If you spawn near sheep, you can also kill a few to quickly build a bed, even out in the open, and blissfully slumber the night away as long as no hostile mobs are present. I'll show you how in Chapter 2. Daylight is followed by 1 ½ minutes of dusk—time to get back to your base. The nighttime phase lasts 7 minutes and is a time you definitely don't want to be outside unprotected with nothing but your stumpy fists. They might be able to beat chunks out of trees, but they won't help you in a deadly scrap. Sunrise and dawn last another 1 ½ minutes and cause some hostiles, although not all, to burn up. Then it's a brand new day. Death in this mode is only temporary. You'll respawn within 20 blocks of your original spawn point and live to fight another day.

- **Hardcore**—After you've cut your teeth in the regular Survival mode and presumably made it all the way through, you may want to revisit the game in this mode. The difficulty level is set to Hard (described in the last bullet), and you get only one life: no respawning. It's quite a challenge, if you're up for it.

- **Creative**—I love creative mode. This is where Minecraft really shines after you get through the core challenge of Survival mode. Think of it as flying, not dying. At least, that's the way my 9-year-old describes it. It's also a great way to build absolutely enormous structures, intricate redstone circuits, and fantastic rail systems.

- **Adventure**—While surviving Survival is something of an adventure in itself, Minecraft's Adventure mode adds some specific challenges by limiting the destruction of blocks to specific tools. For example, you can use an axe to harvest only wood-based items, and a pickaxe to harvest only ores. Adventure mode is used most often on multiplayer servers but can be accessed from a singleplayer game by using the cheat command **/gamemode adventure**. It's also often turned on for you in downloadable Adventure maps that provide their own plot lines and challenges.

Survival mode offers four levels of difficulty, and you can switch between them at any time through the in-game **Options** window:

- **Peaceful**—All hostile mobs disappear instantly and permanently until the difficulty setting is switched to any of the other three mentioned below. Your hunger bar also remains at maximum, or the level it was when you switched to peaceful. You can still die, and therefore respawn, so be wary of long falls, lava pits, trapped temples, and other threats, but it is, eponymously, a peaceful existence.

■ **Easy**—You see hostiles, but they deliver less damage than normal. Your hunger bar does deplete, but it still leaves you with 10 health points at a minimum, or 5 hearts in the HUD. Some other mob effects, such as poison, are minimized.

■ **Normal**—As the name suggests, this is the default mode. Hostile mobs deliver normal damage (which without armor can quickly kill you), and running out of food reduces your health to just half a point, making you particularly vulnerable.

■ **Hard**—Hostile mobs cause more damage, and running out of food kills you...eventually.

NOTE

Mobs, Spawning, and Respawning

In Minecraft, any other creature besides your player and villagers (known as NPCs, or non-player characters) is called a *mob*. The term originates from "mobile entity." You'll meet three kinds of mobs in future chapters: peaceful, neutral, and hostile. The sudden appearance of any entity in the game world is called a *spawn*. Your own character will probably also die at some point. It's practically unavoidable. In any difficulty level except hardcore you'll "respawn" shortly after death. There is no limit to the number of times you can do so.

Seeding Your World

Minecraft worlds are randomly generated using an algorithm that takes a number, or *seed*, as its starting point. This seed comes from the clock that keeps track of the date and time in your PC. As time marches on the clock provides the seed for trillions of worlds, each one unique. However, you can also override this and provide your own seed. Each world created with that seed will be identical in terrain, including the location of mining resources and also generally the same in mob spawn locations. You can use just about anything for the seed, including a random set of numbers or letters such as a phrase ("Minecraft rocks!") or even your birth date. Actually, something quite fun to do is to create a Minecraft world seeded with your own real name or your unique Minecraft username. It is, essentially, a world created just for you. Try it and explore your new domain.

TIP

Sharing Seeds

Share the seed you used with a friend, and your friend can play in Singleplayer mode in a similar world to your own. Some worlds happen to be more interesting than others, so this makes for an easy way to share the better ones. If you don't know it already, you can discover the seed in-game using the Cheat command **/seed**. Some websites also provide lists of seeds that create unusual worlds. Keep in mind that Mojang, the makers of Minecraft, change the world generation algorithm now and then, which in turn changes the world that results from any particular seed. Match your Minecraft version with the seed for best results.

Controls

You don't need to memorize too many keys to start playing Minecraft. Table 1.1 lists the full set available. You can reassign all the controls through the Options menu (accessed by pressing Esc while in-game), but I'd recommend leaving them as they are for now to avoid confusion.

TABLE 1.1 Minecraft Controls

Control	Action
Left mouse button	Attack, destroy blocks, open or close doors.
Right mouse button	Place blocks, use items.
Mouse scroll wheel	Change toolbar slot.
Middle mouse button	Pick block or item adding to your current toolbar slot (Creative mode only). If your mouse doesn't have a middle button, you can reassign this control.
Keys 1 to 9	Select toolbar slot.
Mouse movement	Look around (change the direction you are facing).
Esc	Pause game (not available in multiplayer).
W	Move forward (double-tap to sprint).
S	Move back.
A	Move left.
D	Move right.
Left-Shift	Sneak forward slowly and avoid falling off ledges.
Space	Jump, fly up (Creative mode only).

Control	Action
Double space (hit spacebar twice, quickly)	Change to flying mode (Creative mode only).
Shift	Fly down (Creative mode only).
E	Open your inventory.
Q	Drop item.
T	Open chat menu in multiplayer.
L	List all players in a multiplayer world.
/	Enter a cheat command.
F1	Hide GUI.
F2	Take a screen shot.
F3	Show current data such as your avatar's coordinates, the biome, and more.
Shift+F3	Show current performance statistics, along with the standard F3 data.
F5	Switch the view from first person (the standard view) to third person following your avatar, and to an avatar-facing view.
F8	Smooth your mouse movements, which is handy if you want to capture a video, but not much use otherwise.

TIP

Mac Users Press FN key

Use a Mac? You may need to hold the function key (marked as fn in the bottom-left corner of your keyboard) while you press any of the function keys (F1, F2, and so on) listed above to access these additional commands. You can change this in your keyboard preferences so that the function keys work as assumed by default.

The Bottom Line

It's difficult to decide whether to call Minecraft a game or a creative sandbox. It straddles both in a way that has rarely been achieved before.

Although the registration and launch system are a little different to many other games, they do come with their advantages. You'll never need to worry about updating the game, because that happens automatically, and from time to time there'll be some surprises in store with continuous, steady improvements.

With a registered account, you can even change the skin of your character. Search online for Minecraft skins, and then install them through your account options on Minecraft.net. The next time you launch the game, you'll see your character in a brand new outfit. Use F5 to switch views so that you can see the result.

Minecraft world seeds also provide some useful opportunities. Not happy with how your gaming is working out? Select your old one and click **Re-Create** in the **Select World** window to automatically generate the same terrain and spawn at or close to the same point. Just keep in mind that mobs won't necessarily appear in the same locations, and there will be some other differences.

Finally, don't feel daunted by the control list. It's actually quite short compared to many other games. The key controls involve just your mouse, the WASD key set, the spacebar and the inventory key.

TIP

Controls for Lefties

If you've played any other first-person game on a computer in the last 20 years, your fingers will probably fall naturally to the WASD keys with your left hand, and to the mouse with your right. If you are left-handed and prefer to have the controls reversed, consider remapping each key under the options menu so that you use IJKL with your right-hand and the mouse with your left.

First-Night Survival

In This Chapter

- Welcome to your new world.
- Harvest your first resources and start crafting essential tools.
- Head for the hills and build a fast shelter in style.
- Cut your clicks with Inventory shortcuts.
- Bring some light into the night.
- Skip the night in seconds.

When you start a Minecraft world, your in-game character arrives with nothing but the shirt on his back, some dodgy-looking pants, and fists of fury. You've got work to do! There are many ways to end up suddenly demised in Minecraft, and you're bound to discover quite a few of them in time. But it's actually quite easy to survive your first night and get enough done to set you up for a great next day. There's no need to become spider bait, zombie fodder, or a handy target for skeleton archery practice when darkness falls and the mobs come out to play.

This chapter shows you how to pull through that first night and come out in better shape than ever.

Survive and Thrive

Your first day in Minecraft is an important one because you need to accomplish a few things quickly to prepare for the dangerous night ahead. As soon as you spawn into a new Minecraft world, take a quick look around. Just move your mouse. Your first target is trees for their wood because they provide the starting point you need for crafting tools and, frankly, it's difficult to get anywhere without them.

NOTE

Welcome to The Overworld

The Minecraft world is comprised of three dimensions. You arrive in The Overworld, the largest dimension. Over time, you'll make your way through a portal into The Nether, Minecraft's very Dante-esque "hellish" dimension, and then finally into The End, a small dimension where you'll fight the Ender dragon. That being said, most of your time will be spent in The Overworld. Chapter 12, "Playing Through: The Nether and The End" will help you move back and forth between all three, but don't worry too much about that for now.

Your second main task is to scout for a handy cliff or mound into which you can dig your first shelter or, failing that, a little bit of level ground so you can build the Minecraft equivalent of a shepherd's hut, even if it's just made from some dirt blocks.

Here, then, is a brief list of your first-day tasks:

- Find a few trees and punch their trunks to obtain wood.
- Turn the wood into plank and build a crafting bench.
- Turn some of those planks into sticks.
- Craft a wooden axe out of planks and sticks to speed up the collection of more wood.
- Craft a wooden pick to dig up stone, turning it into the cobblestone required to build a furnace.
- Craft a wooden sword, just in case.
- Dig out a basic shelter.
- Build a wooden door for your shelter, but you can also just block it off with some of the materials you've dug up if you run out of time.
- Build a furnace and smelt some wood to make charcoal.
- Use the charcoal and sticks to create torches.
- Optionally, find three sheep so you can build a bed.

That's quite a list, but it won't take you long. Think of it as survival of the quickest.

Head for the Trees

Start by heading toward the trees. You need a few, so look for a group. Use your mouse to set your direction and the **W** key to move forward, **A** and **D** to move left and right, and **S** to back up. Most biomes contain trees, so they shouldn't be too far away, and if you spawned into a jungle, forest, or taiga biome, trees are all around you. Figure 2.1 shows a spawn point by a river biome. In the interests of making the most of what you're given, I'll use this world, henceforth dubbed *Elysia*, for the remainder of the book. There is a chance you may not be so lucky. Some biomes such as the desert simply don't have trees. If that's the case, head straight for the nearest hill and jump to the top to get a good view. Press the spacebar to jump up each block while you hold down **W** to climb. If you spot any trees in the distance, make haste—the countdown to nighttime has already begun!

FIGURE 2.1 My verdant valley: trees, hills, a pleasant river, and a game of spot-the-sheep.

TIP

You Can Always Punt

If you don't spawn anywhere near a decent chunk of wood—it is possible, although rare, to spawn on a small island in the middle of a large ocean—you might want to consider abandoning the current world and creating a new one. With an infinite variety of worlds available, it's fair enough to reset your situation if you find yourself starting out in a really tough position.

When you reach those woody perennials, start swinging. That fleshy appendage you can see to the right of the HUD is your arm. Hold down the left mouse button while pointing the crosshairs at the trunk to chip away at the tree, as shown in Figure 2.2. It slowly develops a spidering of cracks as you wear it down and it will only take a few seconds to punch out the first block of wood. You'll see a smaller representation of the block fall toward the ground and float, bobbing gently up and down. Congratulations on your first harvested resource. Well done!

If you are close enough, the block is scooped up into your inventory automatically. If not, just move closer until it jumps in. Now take out the rest of the blocks, or as many as you can reach, and do the same to another two or three trees. You'll need about 15 blocks to get off to a good start. Don't worry about that mass of foliage remaining behind. It fades away, although if you do hack away at some of it, you have a good chance of getting a few saplings that you can replant in the interests of sustainability. You might also score an apple or two that you should save for later.

TIP

Lumberjacking Tips

There's an easy way to get most of the blocks from the trunk. Start by taking out the two blocks just above the one that is on the ground. Then jump onto that block and look straight up. Finish punching blocks out of the rest of the trunk above you. They'll fall on you and go straight into your inventory. When you've gone as high as you can go, look straight down and take out the block on which you are standing. You can take out most tree trunks this way. If for some reason you can't jump onto the block after you remove the two above it, you may need to clear out some foliage directly above you.

Now that you've harvested your first resources, it's time to get familiar with your inventory and crafting.

FIGURE 2.2 Punching out wood takes a little patience, but you'll build some tools shortly that speed that up quite significantly.

Using Your Inventory

The inventory screen is central to your management of resources as you start collecting and crafting various materials and items.

You've already seen part of it: those nine slots showing at the bottom of the screen represent items you've already collected, such as the wood blocks from the trees, and perhaps a sapling or two. However, this is only one-quarter of your total inventory.

Press **E** to open the inventory screen. You see the window shown in Figure 2.3 with at least the blocks of wood showing.

Let's take a closer look:

- **Armor slots**—These four slots allow you to don armor. From the top down, they represent your helmet, chestplate, leggings, and boots, and each can be made from five different materials. Initially, you'll probably start with materials made from leather or iron, because they are relatively easy to obtain. I'll show you how to craft them in Chapter 5, "Combat School." Shift-click a piece of armor to automatically place it into the correct slot.

- **Crafting grid**—Use this grid to create basic items on the run, such as torches, planks, sticks, and so on. In the next section, you'll use this to build a crafting table with a larger grid so that you can make more complex items. Figure 2.3 shows the wood blocks being crafted into wooden planks.

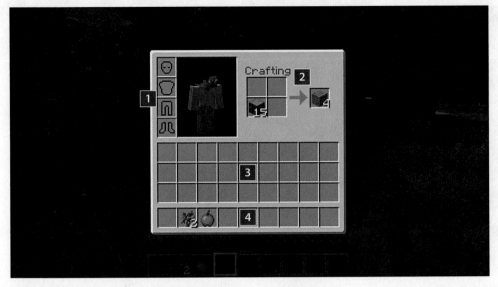

FIGURE 2.3 The inventory screen has four sections.

1. Armor
2. Crafting

3. Storage area
4. Quick access area

■ **Inventory slots**—These slots represent your full inventory.

■ **Quick access area**—The bottom row provides quick access to items either with your mouse scroll wheel or by using the 1–9 keys on your keyboard. You can use any selected item in this row with the left mouse button as the action key, or discard it with a quick press of **Q**.

■ **Storage area**—The top three rows provide storage space for items you don't immediately need but want to carry with you. This may include items you've picked up on your travels and intend to carry back to your shelter for longer-term storage or to use for construction and further crafting. Typically, you should store weapons and tools in the quick access slots, some food to quickly rebuild your health, and other vital items as you see fit. Keep the rest upstairs.

NOTE

Stacking Items

The inventory shows 36 empty slots but can store many more items than this through *stacking*. Typically, items of a similar type can stack up to 64 units high in each slot, although some items are limited to stacks just 16 units high. Tools, weapons, armor, and some other specialized items can only stack one unit high.

Minecraft has some neat tricks up its blocky sleeve that make it easier to move items between the slots in your inventory. Here's what you really need to know:

- **Pick up items**—Left-click on a slot, and you'll pick up its full stack of items. Right-click to pick up just half the items in that slot.

- **Place items**—Left-click to place all the items you are holding into a slot. If that slot is occupied, the items are swapped so that you end up holding the item or stack of items that was there initially. Right-click to place just a single item from the stack you are holding into a slot, or hold down the button and sweep through the different positions to place one each of a stack of held items in multiple slots.

- **Move items between the main storage and the quick access grids**—Shift-click a slot to transfer its items to the first available position in the other grid. Items of the same type are automatically stacked in the target grid until they reach their stack limit.

- **Distribute items evenly**—While holding a stack of items, press and hold the left mouse button and drag it across a group of slots to automatically split the stack into equal amounts across those slots. (This is particularly handy when crafting a stack of similar items at once.) If there is any remainder from the split, it stays selected and you can place it elsewhere.

- **Discard an item**—Drag and drop items from any inventory slot to the outside of the inventory window to discard them. This can discard an entire stack of items at once. You can also quickly discard any single item in a quick access slot at any time by selecting it with your scroll wheel or the 1–9 keys and pressing **Q**.

Now that you are familiar with the inventory, let's get onto crafting.

Build a Crafting Table

Why, you may be wondering, do you need a crafting table when the inventory already provides a crafting grid? It's simple really. The inventory provides a 2x2 grid, and this can build only a limited set of items. The crafting table provides a grid of 3x3 needed for more complex items such as tools and just about everything else. However you can't build a crafting table without first using the inventory crafting grid. Follow these steps to knock together your own:

1 Open your inventory screen by pressing **E**.

2 Remember those wood blocks you punched out of the tree? You need to turn those blocks into planks. Left-click on the stack of wood blocks to pick them up and drop

them into any of the four squares in the Crafting section. Bingo! A stack of four wood planks shows up in the output square to the right.

3 Click the stack of planks in the output square three times more to create a total of 16 planks.

4 Click to pick up any unused blocks left in the crafting grid and click on an empty storage slot to move them back out of the crafting grid.

5 Click on the planks in the output square to pick up the entire stack, and right-click once on each of the four squares in the crafting area. Well done! You've just created your first crafting table.

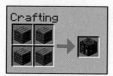

6 Click on an empty storage slot to move your unused planks back there.

7 Finally, click to pick up the crafting table and move it to one of the empty quick access slots that run along the lower edge of the inventory window.

CAUTION

Mobs Can Strike Even With Inventory Open

Don't walk away with your inventory screen open, thinking you've paused the game. Time still passes, night still falls, and you're still just as vulnerable to hostile mobs. You can easily come back to find that your character has keeled over after an attack right there in the inventory window. Remember to use the Esc key to really pause the game if you need to duck away for a while.

Okay, now the fun really begins. Let's place the crafting table and build some tools!

Use your mouse wheel to scroll until you have the crafting table selected, or press the number key that corresponds to the crafting table's quick access slot. For example, if the table is in the third slot from the left, press 3 to select it directly. Now look for a clear space to put the table, point your crosshairs down, and right-click. You can see an example in Figure 2.4.

Let's Build Some Tools

Our initial crafting list requires an axe, a pickaxe, and a sword. Building tools takes no time at all and gives your fists a bit of a break from punching.

Right-click on the table to open the crafting window. You'll notice the 3x3 grid providing more room to place crafting ingredients. We're going to use all of it!

FIGURE 2.4 You don't have to find a nice scenic spot for your first crafting, but a view doesn't hurt.

First off, craft some sticks to form the handles for your tools. Stack two plank blocks vertically using any two of the squares in the crafting grid to create four sticks. Drop these into your inventory.

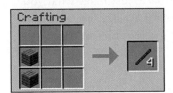

NOTE

Crafting On The Xbox and Pocket Editions

Minecraft Xbox and Pocket Editions use a simpler crafting interface that lists all the available crafting recipes and makes recipes selectable when all the required ingredients are present in your inventory. You'll still need to craft the base components, such as turning wood blocks into planks, and then those into sticks, to open up the derivative recipes, but you won't need to worry about remembering the components of each recipe or where they should be placed on the crafting grid. It's all in view. On the Xbox, press the X button to open the initial 2x2 inventory crafting area so you can build a crafting table, then use the Left Trigger to access the table's grid. Access the Pocket Edition's crafting menu with the Ellipsis (...) block in the toolbar.

Now craft an axe by placing two sticks in the middle and lower middle slots in the crafting table. Then arrange three wooden plank blocks in the upper middle, upper right, and middle right slots to build an axe.

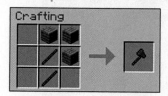

That's all there is to it. Easy, right? There are hundreds of crafting recipes in Minecraft, all with different arrangements of items in the grid using many different materials, but the actual arrangement of items usually shares some similarity with the physical object. You can see this even more so with the pickaxe and sword, and it won't take long for you to memorize the most useful recipes.

To create your first pickaxe, set another two sticks in the middle and lower middle slots. Then arrange three wooden planks across the top row.

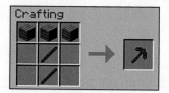

Create more sticks and planks if you need to, but don't go overboard. Just make what you need. The inventory looks like it has plenty of space right now, but it quickly fills, and while you can stack most items in piles of 64 in each inventory slot, it's more efficient to store wood in particular in its most efficient form. You see, if one wooden block can create 4 planks of wood, then converting 64 wooden blocks to planks creates 256 planks, and they'll completely fill another 4 slots. Converting all those blocks to sticks fills 8 slots! So just craft what you need when you need it.

Now create a sword using one plank block and two wood blocks using any column of three slots in the crafting grid.

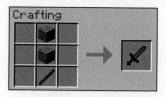

If you're enjoying crafting, also create a shovel. It's handier for digging through dirt and gravel.

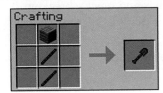

When you've finished, your inventory should look something like the one shown in Figure 2.5.

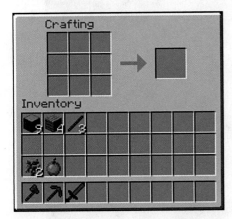

FIGURE 2.5   *Your first set of tools, but they definitely won't be your last.*

You're done for now, so switch to an empty slot in the quick access list and break down the crafting table with your fists. Walk over to it to scoop it up into your inventory so you can use it again.

Creating a Shelter

Now that you have some basic tools, it's time to prepare for the night. By far the quickest way to do this is to dig a little hideout into the side of a hill. Don't just duck into a cave, because you might get a nasty surprise.

> **NOTE**
>
> **Building an Aboveground Shelter**
>
> If you have spawned into a flat area, see Chapter 3, "Finding a Building Site," on page 63 to build an aboveground shelter.

Head toward any convenient hill, cliff, or mound and select your pickaxe. You'll be digging a space that's two blocks high, but because you also need a roof over your head, the target area should be at least three blocks high. Left-click to swing the pick and quickly break up the block in front of you at ground level, and the next one above it that's at eye level. If you are facing a terraced hill (Minecraft doesn't have any that aren't), just dig out a couple of blocks at ground level until you've created the path to a three-block-high space like you can see in Figure 2.6.

FIGURE 2.6 Tunneling into a hill is as effective as using a cliff face for a shelter.

Move forward and keep swinging that pick, because you need to carve out a little bit of room to fit your crafting table, a furnace and, potentially, a bed. A space 4×4 should do for now, although you can certainly expand it later. As you move forward, you automatically collect the blocks you're breaking. If you break out into a cave or through the hill and outside again (see Figure 2.7), open your inventory and pull some of the blocks you've collected back down into your quick access bar, select them as your active tool, point your crosshairs at the top of the block beneath the gap, and right-click to drop a new block in place.

Unfortunately, your shelter still lacks a door. In a pinch, you can just place a block in the gap and huddle in for the night, ensuring you stay out of the line of sight of the actual gap just in case a skeleton wanders by and starts firing arrows at you. But you can do a better job than that!

FIGURE 2.7   Whoops! Better fill the gap.

Place your crafting table in a corner of the room, right-click it, and then arrange two columns of wooden planks.

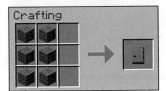

TIP

Crafting Shortcut

Crafting can seem like a lot of clicking, but one handy shortcut to remember is that you can left-click to pick up a stack of items such as wooden planks and then hold down the left mouse button as you paint them into the desired pattern in the crafting grid. Minecraft does its best to balance the number of items in each grid position as you go. When you've crafted enough of the final object, don't worry about dragging all the unused crafting elements back; just press Esc to exit the inventory, and any unused items float to the ground ready to be scooped back into your inventory.

TIP

Multi-Crafting

Crafting a bunch of the same item at once is easy. Hold down Shift while clicking the output slot, and you pick up as many of the same item as can be produced with the raw materials in the crafting slots.

Now head outside your shelter, select the door, and point your crosshairs at the ground block that is under the first section of your shelter where you have a true two-space high tunnel with a roof. Right-click to place the door. Figure 2.8 shows mine. You can then right-click to open the door, step through, and right-click once more to close it. Now we're getting more homely, but we're still missing something vital—light! There are no energy-saving bulbs in Minecraft. For light, you need a torch fashioned from a stick and a lump of coal.

CAUTION

Close the Door While You're Gone!

Always remember to close the door when you leave your shelter. Leaving it open is like leaving out the welcome mat for mobs, and you don't find want to find any lurking inside when you return.

TIP

Airlocks, Iron Doors, and More

In the Hard difficulty level, zombies can break through wooden doors. Give yourself a better chance of survival by building airlock structures using two doors instead of just one. If a zombie breaks through the first door, it will take him some time to break through the second. Hopefully, creepers aren't lined up behind. Iron doors are impervious to their attack but can only be opened with buttons or other redstone devices. Perimeter structures such as fences, moats, and lava pits also keep mobs away. See the section, "Protecting Your Perimeter," on page 153 in Chapter 8 for a few examples.

FIGURE 2.8 Shelter secured! In Easy and Normal difficulty levels, zombies still try to break down your door, and you even see some worrying cracks appear. Don't panic! Zombies give up before they break through.

CAUTION

Install Doors Properly!

Facing a door the wrong way allows mobs to attack you. Skeletons, which are always deadly accurate, can actually fire their arrows through the door. For this reason, always place doors while you are standing outside the area you want to protect.

You can find coal in the ground here and there. The blocks are patterned with flecks of black and are often visible on the sides of cave walls. But you can't dig too far or venture too deep into a tunnel complex without the lack of light becoming a problem. Fortunately, there's an easier way to make torches, and that's by using charcoal instead of coal. To make charcoal, you need a furnace, and for that you need cobblestone.

NOTE

Emergency Shelters and Pillar Jumping

Caught out exploring as night falls? You can easily survive a night in the open if you can't get back to base. Here a few techniques. First, find the most precarious ledge you can on a cliff. Hold down the Shift key as you approach cliff edges to avoid a potentially fatal fall. The cliff edge location doesn't guarantee survival, but mobs are less likely to find you, and you can improve the situation by digging into the cliff a little way, creating a corridor two blocks high. Go sideways at the end to create an L shape where you can hide out of sight. Block the lower half of the doorway with sand, dirt, or gravel—whatever you have that's handy really—and wait out the night in your nook.

Another way to protect yourself fast is to dig down three blocks in anything other than sand or gravel. Just dig down the first two blocks, jump in the hole, and dig out the last one, hoping it doesn't drop you straight into a lava pit or into the top of a deep cave. Place one block of the material you removed above your head, ensuring first it isn't sand or gravel because then you'll suffocate, somewhat defeating the purpose. Wait about eight minutes of real time, or knock out the block and replace it now and then to check for daylight before you knock out a block in front of you to create a step so you can escape into the dawn.

A final trick, which can be quite handy if you spawn in the midst of a giant desert, is to dig up about 10 blocks of sand or other ground covering and then place the first block down, climb on top, and with some careful timing jump while looking straight down to place another block directly beneath you—also known as *pillar jumping*. Repeat until you are perched on top of a pillar 10 blocks high. This keeps you well out of reach of hostile mobs. When sunrise hits, look down and left-click your mouse to dig out the blocks beneath you, easing yourself back down to the ground.

The Furnace Is Your Friend

 Furnaces are crafted from eight blocks of cobblestone, and to get that you need to mine stone. But stone is everywhere. It's the second most common element in Minecraft besides air and is usually found just one or two blocks under a layer of dirt, if not just laying around in the open waiting for you to stub an inadvertent toe. One trick to stone, though, is that you can't render it into cobblestone with your fists. You'll just pulverize it to dust instead. You'll need a pickaxe to do it properly.

Check your inventory and if you haven't yet found eight blocks of cobblestone, start expanding your shelter using the pickaxe to render any stone you find into cobblestone. Don't dig more than one block down at a time, because you won't be able to jump back up. Use a shallow staircase effect if needed, but try to just stick to the horizontal plane for now, expanding the perimeter of each interior wall rather than plowing into a long tunnel. Figure 2.9 shows a handy layer of stone that came to light just one block from the entrance.

FIGURE 2.9 Stone is plentiful in Minecraft, but remember to bring your pickaxe.

As soon as you have the blocks, head back to your crafting table and run eight blocks around the edge of the crafting grid, leaving the middle block empty.

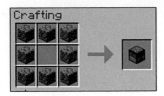

Drag the completed furnace to one of your quick access slots and then place it with a right-click next to your crafting table. It's torch time!

Let There Be Light

Light is a great way to dispel fear of the dark—in any setting. In Minecraft, light keeps hostile mobs at bay. Or, more specifically, it prevents them from spawning. There are certain rules built into the software that prevent mobs from springing into existence close to you, no matter the light level, but they also can't spawn anywhere near light. So as you expand your shelter, mine, and explore, the judicious placement of torches keeps the coast somewhat clear. Besides that, torches add that much-needed ambient touch to any home.

Right-click on your furnace. You see your inventory screen again, shown in Figure 2.10, but this time with a crafting grid containing just two slots. The lower slot holds the combustible to power the furnace, while the upper holds the object you are smelting. Place a couple of blocks of wood in each of the lower and upper slots to start making charcoal, as shown. You'll soon see the charcoal pop into the output grid. Each chunk of charcoal can make four torches.

TIP

Buckets of Lava Are the Best Fuel

You can use both coal and charcoal as sources of fuel in a furnace, and they are much more effective than most other materials, able to process eight blocks apiece. But what's the best fuel possible? A bucket of lava. You'll be able to find these easily enough later on. For now, just keep it in mind. One bucket equals 100 smelted blocks. It's like your own personal nuclear reactor.

The furnace can take a little time to do its thing, but it's also set and forget. Walk away, and the furnace keeps on burning while it has fuel and something to work on. When either runs out, the furnace just shuts down, and you can collect the results later. No need to worry about leaving the gas on or the pot boiling over.

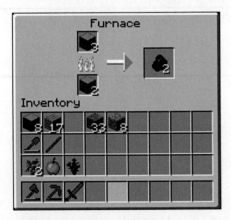

FIGURE 2.10 Burn, baby, burn. The furnace smelts objects into items more useful for crafting, building, decorating, and cooking. Keep one handy at all times.

Now you have some charcoal, press **E** to open your inventory window (or right-click your crafting table if you prefer) and place one stick in any lower position of the crafting grid and one piece of charcoal above it. Great work! You've just created four torches, and in Minecraft they're going to be some of your best friends.

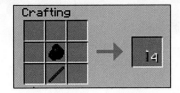

Place the torches in a quick access slot and step back a moment. Find a nice position on a wall, select the torch, and right-click the wall to attach. Torches never burn out, so you never need to replace them, although you can knock them down with a left-click, scoop them up, and place them elsewhere if your interior decorating instinct kicks in. Torches can also provide a useful homing beacon if you place a few outside your shelter. They create a nice pool of light you can spot from a distance, especially if you're making a last-minute dash for home at sunset.

Figure 2.11 shows the much-needed result in the first Elysia hidey-hole.

FIGURE 2.11   Cave, sweet cave. Safe for the night, and cozy enough to keep on crafting.

Slumber with Lumber

Beds are great because they make a house a home. They lend an aesthetic a crafting table and furnace can't really provide. But more than that, they serve a purpose that gets right down to the underlying game mechanic. A bed protects you. It provides you with a timeout through the night so you can skip to sunrise and get on with your day.

Sleeping in a bed also resets your spawn point to its location so you can venture further and further out into the world, even covering vast distances, without starting at your point of origin should you—and by should I mean will—die. However, note that if the last bed you slept in is destroyed for any reason, your spawn point reverts back to your original point of origin, so it pays to keep your bed safe.

NOTE

Time Is On Your Side

While you are sleeping, time doesn't really tick by. Sleeping is really just like typing the **/time set day** cheat code, causing an instant adjustment in the game's clock but leaving everything else in the same state before you actually went to sleep.

TIP

Spawn Point Cheat

With cheats enabled, type **/spawnpoint** to reset the world's original spawn point to your current position. If you die you'll pop up again nearby.

Building a bed is easy, but you first need to find and kill three sheep to get their wool. Later you can build shears for a more sheep-friendly experience, but for now, lamb skewers are the only option.

If you've seen sheep nearby, take your sword in hand and have at them with a few left-clicks. Keep track of your bearings, though. The sheep make a dash for it on the first attack, and you don't want to become lost as you give chase.

NOTE

Sleep Without Sheep

Sheep are the easiest way to harvest wool for a bed. If you can't find any, skip the bed-building and start on Chapter 3, "Gathering Resources," spending the night improving your tools at the crafting table. You can quietly dig up more cobblestone by expanding your shelter. Just remember to place torches every nine or so spaces to ensure you leave no dark places where a hostile mob can spawn. If there are simply no sheep anywhere nearby, look for spiders. Each drops between 0 and 2 pieces of string. Collect four of those and you can make a block of wool, so collect 12 and you'll have enough for a bed. Fair warning, though: this might take a while.

Each sheep drops one block of wool. When you've collected three, head back to your crafting table, lay three blocks of wood planks on the bottom layer and the three blocks of wool across the middle layer. Voilà! A bed is born.

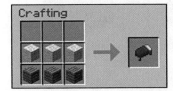

You can place the bed anywhere there is space for two blocks. Stand facing the direction you want the bed to face where the foot of the bed would be closest to you. Then right-click on the block where the foot should go, not the head. Figure 2.12 shows the placement, and Figure 2.13 shows the end result in a now very comfortable, if simple, shelter.

FIGURE 2.12 Bed placement can be a little tricky because a bed takes two blocks. Always aim for the space you plan to place the foot of the bed.

FIGURE 2.13 The bed is now tucked against the wall in the back of the shelter.

TIP

Take a Bed with You

Keep a bed in your inventory if you're trekking through the wilderness. You can place it down anywhere there's enough space, and, as long as no monsters are nearby, sleep cozily through the dark. But be ready when you awake, because you might find yourself surrounded! The bed is Minecraft's equivalent of a Get Out of Jail Free card. But this technique does have its hazards, and it really takes little effort to build a quick shelter. In other words, use at your own risk.

The Bottom Line

Surviving your first night can seem tough at first—it's a bit of a learning curve. But get through it just once, and survival becomes much easier if you need to do it again. First-night survival entails just a few simple steps: harvest wood, create a crafting table, build tools, and hollow out a shelter.

But remember, Minecraft days pass all too fast. Keep an eye out for the sun setting in the west, and make sure you can at least create a small cave in a cliff or hillside so that you are out of harm's way when night falls. When you head out again in the morning, check for hostile mobs. Their sound gives them away. Some lurk all day while others burn up in the sunlight, but be especially careful if it's an overcast day because the lower light level makes it easier for them to survive.

Now that you've had an initial taste of Minecraft, I bet you're hungry for more. At this point we've only scratched the surface of the crafting table, and while the shelter serves its purpose, Minecraft provides unlimited real estate and resources—enough to create any architectural dream. In the next chapter, you learn some essential survival tricks, including how to stave off hunger, deal with mobs, and build a few more useful tools.

Gathering Resources

In This Chapter

- Never get lost. Learn the secrets of the HUD and its hidden GPS.
- Improve your tools with more durable materials.
- Safely store your hard-earned resources.
- Learn the easy way to manage hunger.
- Build your first outdoor shelter and enjoy the view.
- Access the full Creative mode inventory.

Minecraft is filled to the brim with all manner of resources, and gathering them is the first step toward getting the most out of the game. In Chapter 2, "First-Night Survival," you put together a pack of essentials sufficient to last the first night, but this is really just the smallest prequel to the real game, and describing how to find, create, and use other types of resources forms much of this book. This chapter is about building the foundation you can use to launch into the rest of the game. Your focus is on a few key points: build an outdoor shelter, find food to stave off hunger, improve your collection of tools, and build a chest to safely store items. This solidifies your position, making your base more impervious to attack, allows you to do all sorts of Minecrafty things more efficiently, and sets yourself up for longer excursions both above and below ground.

The good news is that you already have a base, so you can explore during the day, try not to lose your way, and head back at night. However, you still need to avoid at least some of the hostile mobs that persist during the day.

Introducing the HUD

Before we start, let's take a look at the Heads-Up Display (HUD)—that collection of icons and status bars at the bottom of the screen. Figure 3.1 shows the HUD as it appears in Survival mode with all possible indicators displayed. (The Creative mode HUD only shows the Inventory bar.)

FIGURE 3.1 The HUD provides key status indications. Health is all important, but low hunger also leads to low health, so keep a close eye on both.

1. Armor bar
2. Health bar
3. Experience bar

4. Oxygen bar
5. Hunger bar
6. Inventory quick access

Each section of the HUD provides a key nugget of information about the health or status of your avatar:

- **Armor bar**—The armor bar appears when you've equipped your avatar with any type of armor and shows the current damage absorption level. Each armor icon represents an 8% reduction in the damage you'll take, so a 10/10 suit of armor reduces the damage you take by 80%, whereas a 1/10 suit absorbs only 8%. Armor becomes less effective the more damage it absorbs, although the rate at which it deteriorates also depends on its material—leather being the weakest and diamond the strongest.

- **Health bar**—You have up to 20 points of health available, represented by the 10 hearts shown. Each heart disappears in two ticks. Health and hunger have a complicated relationship. You can read more below starting at "Hunger Management."

- **Experience bar**—The experience bar increases the more you mine, smelt, cook, kill, and fish. Your current level is shown in the middle of the bar. When it's full, you move to the next experience level. Experience isn't generally important until you start enchanting and giving additional powers to items such as swords (see Chapter 10, "Enchantments, Anvils, and Brewing"). Unlike other role-playing games, experience in Minecraft is more like a currency that you spend on enchantments, so it waxes and wanes. But all experience gained counts toward the final score shown on the screen when you die. Killing a mob drops experience orbs that either fly directly toward you or float to the ground waiting for you to collect them, and you can also gain experience by smelting certain items in the furnace and carrying out other activities such as finding rare ores. Dying causes a substantial drop in your current experience level.

- **Oxygen bar**—The oxygen bar appears whenever you go underwater and it quickly starts to drop. You can probably hold your own breath for longer! As soon as your oxygen level hits zero, your health starts taking a two-point hit every second, but it resurfaces for just an instant if you hold down the jump key until you've reached air once more. Diving isn't that big of a deal in Minecraft, at least not for completing the core game, but you can use the ability to do interesting things like building an underwater base. An example is shown in Figure 3.2, and I'll show you how to build your own in Chapter 8, "Creative Construction," as well as sharing with you some other underwater breathing techniques.

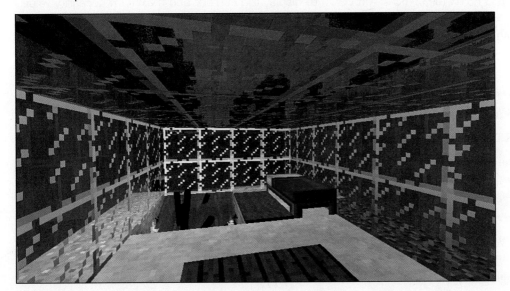

FIGURE 3.2   Underwater bases are impervious to mob attacks, even when built from glass, but you'll need to watch your oxygen bar carefully to ensure you don't run out of air while building this type of structure. By the way, the only mob that spawns underwater is the friendly, curious squid. Can you make out the one shown here? He's now part of Elysia's first private aquarium. Say hello to "Ceph."

- **Hunger bar**—You also have 20 points of hunger available, as well as a hidden value called Saturation. Like health, each hunger bar icon holds two points and can reduce by half an icon (that icon is, incidentally, a "shank," or the lower part of a leg of meat) at a time.

- **Inventory quick access**—These nine slots represent items you can select with the mouse scroll wheel or by pressing the 1–9 keys. Press **E** to access your full inventory and to change the items in these slots. The white number next to some shows that slot's count of stacked identical items. A durability bar also appears under each tool's icon in green, gradually reducing as you use them until the tool actually breaks and disappears from your inventory. You'll have some warning of this because the bar turns red when it's close to zero. See "Improving Your Tools" later in the chapter to learn more about the durability of different materials.

TIP

Showing Durability Stats in the HUD

Press F3+H (or fn+F3+H on OS X) to display the current and maximum durability value of all the tools in your inventory. The value appears in a tool tip when you hover your mouse over that item.

NOTE

HUD Changes When Mounted

The HUD changes when you ride a horse, showing the horse's health in place of your own. The experience bar also changes to the jump bar. You can learn more about horses and other mountable mobs in Chapter 7, "Taming Mobs," on page 125.

In multiplayer, your HUD also displays a chat window in the bottom-left corner. Press **T** to expand the chat window.

Toggle the entire HUD display off and on by pressing **F1**. Press **F3** with the HUD turned on to view a much more detailed HUD debug screen (see Figure 3.2.)

NOTE

Hiding the HUD in the Xbox Editions

You cannot hide the HUD in Minecraft Pocket Edition but there is an option for doing so on the Xbox edition. Press the **Start** key and open the **Help & Options** menu. Scroll down to **Settings→User Interface** and deselect **Display HUD**. Unfortunately there isn't a quicker way to do this at present.

The coordinates shown in the debug screen are based on the world's origin where x=0 and y=0. (z shows your current level above bedrock.) Take a note of the current values. If you become lost before you have had the chance to build a bed and reset your spawn point, you can always find your way back to your original spawn and, presumably, your first shelter, by facing in a direction that will bring both x and y back to those noted values. If you do sleep in a bed and reset your spawn, turn on the debug screen and write down the coordinates shown before you head out.

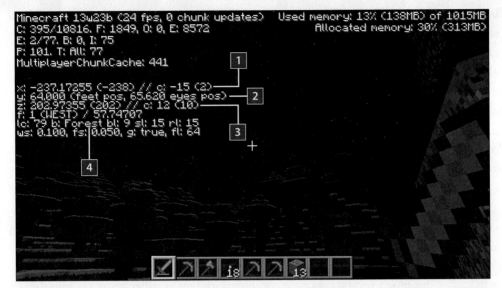

FIGURE 3.3 The Debug HUD provides a lot of cryptic information but can also help you navigate home.

1. Your location in blocks east of your original spawn point. Blocks west are shown as a negative.

2. Your current vertical height in layers above bedrock.

3. Your location in blocks south of your original spawn point. Blocks north are shown as a negative.

4. The current biome type.

When you need to return, and I should warn you that this *can* take some experimentation and a little practice, turn and take a few steps while noting the change in values of your current coordinates. Your goal is to shift those x and y values back toward the coordinates you originally recorded. You'll probably wander around a bit, but eventually you'll get there.

Improving Your Tools

Wooden tools wear out fast, so it's best to upgrade your kit as quickly as possible.

Each type of material has a different level of *durability*. Think of durability as the number of useful actions the tool can perform before wearing out completely and disappearing from the inventory. I've included the durability in parentheses after each material's description:

- **Gold (33)**—Although this is the least durable material, a gold pickaxe can break blocks out of most softer materials in the blink of an eye, and it happens to be the most enchantable material, so you can imbue it with superpowers (see Chapter 10,). But given that gold is about 5 times as rare as iron and can be used to craft many other useful items, I wouldn't recommend using it for tools.

- **Wood (60)**—It's easy to obtain, especially in an emergency aboveground, but think of wood as just a means of getting to cobblestone because, unlike the latter, wooden tools can't mine the more valuable ores such as iron, gold, diamond, and redstone. You will at least need a wooden pickaxe to mine stone because doing so with your bare hands will just break the stone down into unusable dust, but after that, switch to stone.

- **Stone (132)**—With just a touch over twice the longevity of wood, stone makes a great starting point for more serious mining and other activities. Stone tools are built from cobblestone blocks, which in turn come from stone. That may seem a little confusing, but it will seem natural enough after a while.

- **Iron (251)**—Iron will become your *go-to* material. It is found most commonly all the way from bedrock, the lowest layer of the Minecraft world, up to about 20 levels below sea level. Iron is used for building all kinds of tools, implements, and devices including armor, buckets (for carrying water, lava, and milk), compasses, minecarts, and minecart tracks. All these require at least iron ingots obtained by smelting the ore in a furnace, with each block of ore producing one ingot. Ingots and many other items are found scattered throughout the world in village chests, mine shafts, dungeons, and strongholds. You might also find them as drops from killed zombies and iron golems.

- **Diamond (1562)**—It's the strongest material of all, but also the most expensive given that diamonds are relatively rare. (You will enjoy the moment you do find your first diamond, but it's found only in the first 16 layers above bedrock, the lowest layer in the Minecraft world, and even then it's about 25 times as scarce as iron.) A diamond pickaxe is the only material that can successfully mine obsidian, a material required for creating the portal to reach The Nether region. Given diamond ore is about 25 times as scarce as iron but only 6 times as durable, you should use iron pickaxes as much as possible and only switch to diamond when you need to mine obsidian to reach The Nether. You're better off saving any diamonds you find for weapons (a diamond sword does more damage, and that combined with its increased durability will ensure it lasts much longer than any other material), armor, and enchantment tables.

NOTE

Different Materials for Different Items

Durability applies to all tools, weapons, and armor, although there are differences in the materials that can be used in each case. For example, you can craft leather armor and make stone tools, but not vice versa.

CAUTION

Don't Let Tools Wear Down to Nothing!

Try not to let a tool become so worn it actually breaks down completely and disappears. Instead, place two of the same type of worn tools in the crafting grid to combine their remaining strength into another and give it a second shot at life, or busting blocks.

The recipes for crafting tools from all materials are identical, save for the replacement of the head of the implement with the material of choice.

- To make a stone pick, you need two wooden sticks for the handle and three cobblestone blocks.

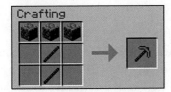

- Replace in the same way for the axe and the sword.

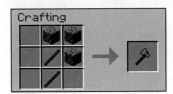 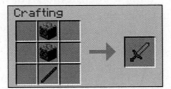

- You might also want to add a shovel to your collection, because it's about four times faster than using hands to harvest softer materials such as dirt, gravel, sand, clay, and snow, and helps some of those blocks deliver resources rather than just breaking down.

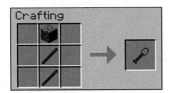

As you craft more items, you need to find somewhere to store those you don't need to use right away. You should also store other resources and food you come across on your travels. That comes next.

Chests: Safely Stash Your Stuff

Whenever you head away from your secure shelter, there is always a reasonably high risk of death. Creepers, lava pits, long falls—they can all do you in. Respawning is only a moment away, but the real danger here is that any items you've collected and carry in your character's inventory drop at the location of your untimely death and may prove impossible to retrieve in the 5 minutes you have to get back to them before they disappear forever.

Chests act as an insurance policy. Put everything you don't need in a chest before you embark on a mission, and those things will be there when you get back or after you respawn.

The natural place to leave chests is in your shelter, but you can also leave them elsewhere, perhaps as a staging point as you work away in a mine, or even outside. Mobs will leave them alone, and the only real risk you face is leaving them out in the open on a multiplayer server or getting blown up from behind by a creeper in singleplayer mode while you're rummaging around inside.

Chests come in two sizes: single and double. A single chest can store 27 stacks of items. Create a double chest by placing two single chests side by side. The double chest stores up to 54 stacks of items. Given that a stack can be up to 64 items high, that's an astonishing potential total of 3,510 blocks in a crate that takes just 2×1 blocks of floor space. If you've ever followed the Doctor Who TV series, consider chests the Tardis of storage!

Create a chest at your crafting table with eight blocks of wooden planks arranged around the outside, leaving a space in the middle.

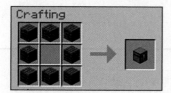

Place and then right-click the chest to open. You can then move items back and forth between your inventory and the chest. In Figure 3.4, I've transferred all the items I don't need for the next expedition.

Before you head out, there are two other things you should know: how to avoid monsters and how to deal with hunger. Read on.

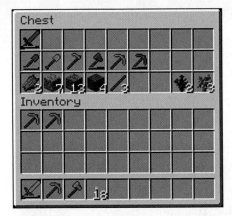

FIGURE 3.4 Chests act as an insurance policy for your items so they aren't lost if you die. Use the inventory shortcuts you learned earlier to quickly move items between your active inventory and the chest's storage slots.

THE CONNECTED CHEST

Chests are undoubtedly useful; it's difficult to survive without them. But you can't transport a chest's contents with you. Need to shift your stash of diamonds? That can make for a fairly fraught journey.

Enter the Ender chest, which is like storage in the cloud. An Ender chest isn't cheap to make. You'll need eight Obsidian blocks obtained by combining lava with water, or through regular mining and caving, and one Eye of Ender, collected from a downed endermen. So what's so good about Ender chests? All of them access the same virtual chest, sharing all contents between them. So let's say you've built multiple dwellings across your vast world, and you have some items—a few favorites—that you'd like to be able to access anywhere you go. Place an Ender chest in each of your dwellings; any items that you place in any of the chests become available in all others. It's like quantum travel without all that entanglement business.

Avoiding Monsters

There's a key difference between the Minecraft world on the first and second days. In a word, mobs: hostile ones to be specific. Mobs only spawn in dark areas, and some only during the night, so if you are outside during your first day and stay in well-lit areas, you'll be reasonably safe. By the second day, however, mobs have had a chance to build their numbers and wander about. It's not that likely you'll encounter them on day 2, but it's best to be prepared.

There are 14 types of hostile mobs in the Overworld. These are the ones you might meet on your second day outside:

- **Zombies**—Zombies burn up in sunlight but can still survive in shadows or rain, and, of course, in dark caves all hours of the day or night. They are relatively easy to defeat, and if any come after you, just head to a well-lit area and keep your distance while they burn up in the sun.

- **Skeletons**—Skeletons also burn up in sunlight unless they are wearing a helmet, and they can survive at any time in lower light conditions. They're quite deadly with a bow and arrow and best avoided until you have an iron sword and sufficient cover to avoid their line of fire.

- **Spiders**—Spiders come in two variants: large or blue. You'll probably only see the larger spiders at this stage. They are passive during the day but become hostile in shadow and can attack at any time if provoked. They'll climb, they'll jump, and they are pretty darn fast. Fortunately, they're also easy to kill with some swift sword attacks. The blue spiders are a smaller, poisonous variant called cave spiders. They live only in abandoned mine shafts underground, but in substantial numbers. If you suffer from arachnophobia, I don't have much good news for you, except that with a little time you'll get used to them and they won't seem quite so nasty.

- **Creepers**—Creepers have a well-earned reputation as the Minecraft bad guys. They are packed to their green gills with gunpowder, and they'll start their very short 1.5-second fuse as soon as they are within three blocks of you. Their explosion can cause a lot of real damage to you, nearby structures, and the environment in general. If you hear a creeper's fuse—a soft hissing noise—but can't see it, run like heck in the direction you're facing. Remember to sprint by double-tapping and holding your **W** key. With a little luck, you'll get three blocks away and the creeper's fuse will reset. Creepers are usually best dealt with using a ranged attack from a bow and arrow, but if you sprint at them with an iron or diamond sword and take a swipe at just the right moment, you can send them flying back out of their suicidal detonation range, causing the fuse to reset. Most creepers despawn around noon, leaving the afternoon generally free of their particular brand of terror.

- **Slimes**—Slimes appear in the swamp biome and in some places underground. They initially spawn as quite large Jello-like green blocks and are more than capable of causing damage. Attacking eventually breaks them up into 2–4 new medium-sized slimes. These can still attack but are relatively easily killed, only to spawn a further 2–4 tiny slimes each! These last don't cause any attack damage, but may still push you into peril if you're unlucky.

If you come across a lone spider, a zombie, or even a slime, now is as good a time as any to get in some sword practice. Just point your crosshairs at the creature and strike with the left mouse button. Keep clicking as fast as you can, and you've got a very good chance of killing the mob and picking up any items it drops before it lands too many blows. Try to avoid the other mobs for now.

TIP

Switch to Peaceful Mode to Get a Break

Getting mobbed by mobs? Click Esc to open the Options window and change your difficulty level to Peaceful. This despawns all hostile mobs and allows your health to regenerate. But do try to switch the level back to Normal as soon as you can.

So how do you avoid mobs? Use these tips to survive:

- Stay in the open as much as you can, avoiding heavily wooded areas if possible.
- Most mobs have a 16-block detection radar. If they can also draw a line of sight to your position, they will enter *pursuit* mode. (Spiders can always detect you, even through other blocks.) At that point they'll relentlessly plot and follow a path to your position, tracking you through other blocks without requiring a line of sight. Pursuit mode stays engaged much farther than 16 blocks.
- Keep your sound turned up because you'll also hear mobs within 16 blocks, although creepers, befitting their name, are creepily quiet.
- Avoid skirting along the edges of hilly terrain. Creepers can drop on you from above with their fuse already ticking. Try to head directly up and down hills so you have a good view of the terrain ahead.
- Mobs are quite slow, so you can easily put some distance between them and yourself by keeping up a steady pace and circling around to get back to your shelter. Sprint mode will leave them far behind.

CAUTION

Sprinting Makes You Hungry

Sprint mode burns up hunger points, so try to use it only in emergencies.

Hunger Management

Hunger plays a permanent role in Minecraft, much as in real life. While it's only possible to starve to death on Hard difficulty, hunger does affect your character in other ways, so it's always important to ensure you have the equivalent of a couple of sandwiches packed before heading deep into a mine or on a long trek.

Hunger is a combination of two values: the one shown in the HUD's hunger bar, as well as a hidden value called *saturation*. The latter provides a buffer to the hunger bar, decreasing first. In fact, your hunger bar doesn't decrease at all until saturation reaches 0. At that point, you see the hunger bar start to jitter, and after a short while it takes its first hit. Saturation cannot exceed the value of the hunger bar, so with a full hunger bar of 20 points, it's possible to have up to 20 points of saturation. However, a hunger level of 6 points also only provides a maximum of 6 points of saturation, and that makes you vulnerable.

You'll find some key information about the hunger system here:

- On Easy and Normal Survival modes, there is no need to worry too much about hunger because your character won't drop dead from it. If you're close to home and pottering around in your farm or constructing some building extensions, you're fairly safe, but your health starts to drop. Eat something as soon as you can to rebuild your health.

- Sprinting isn't possible when the hunger bar drops below 6 hunger points, or 3 shanks, as shown in the HUD.

- Keeping a relatively full stomach at 18 hunger points (9 shanks in the HUD) allows health to regenerate at 1 point (half a heart) every 4 seconds.

- Health depletes if the hunger bar drops to 0, increasing the risk of dying from one of the many imaginative ways Minecraft has on offer (see Figure 3.5).

- There are some limits to the amount health can drop according to the difficulty level. On Easy, health cannot deplete from hunger further than 10 points, or half the full quotient. On Normal, it drops to 1 point, which is an extreme level of vulnerability. On Hard difficulty, there are no limits; don't ignore the hunger bar, or death from starvation could be just moments away. See "Food on the Run" later in this chapter to help avoid this.

FIGURE 3.5 The effects of extreme hunger on Normal difficulty: health depletes to just one point, or half a heart.

Your Mission: Food, Resources, and Reconnaissance

Your second day is the perfect opportunity to gather food and other resources and to take a quick survey of the landscape surrounding your first shelter, in particular to find somewhere suitable for your first outdoor abode. Keep an eye out for any of the following:

- **Passive mobs**—Chickens, pigs, and cows all provide a ready source of food, or at least raw protein that can be cooked on the furnace and made more nutritious. Cows also drop leather that you can use for your first armor, and when you have an iron bucket, cows can be milked, giving you an instant cure for food poisoning. Chickens also lay eggs, so gather any that you find.

- **Natural harvest**—The harvest includes cocoa pods, apples, cactus, sugar cane, carrots and potatoes (found in villages), and seeds. Knock down tall grass to find seeds. When you plant the seeds, they mature into wheat within 5–8 day/night cycles. You can see a freshly planted wheat field in Figure 3.6. From wheat, it's easy to bake bread, one of the simplest but most effective sources of food, especially if there are no passive mobs nearby. See Chapter 6, "Crop Farming," for more on agricultural techniques.

- **Construction resources**—You can mine plenty of cobblestone quite safely by expanding your original shelter, digging into the terrain. But some other resources will definitely come in handy. Wood is always useful. If you see any sand, mine it so you can smelt it into glass blocks to let light into your shelter, and provide a view. (There's no point moving from your first cave into the outdoor equivalent of another!) Also keep an eye out for coal. You can often see it in veins on the surface of the walls of small caves or on the sides of cliffs. If you can safely get to it, make like a miner and dig it out. Use the coal to make torches and to smelt other ores.

FIGURE 3.6 Knock down grass to gather seeds to plant wheat, an easy crop to farm and turn into bread—a handy food if you're stuck with no other edible options.

TIP

Making Use of Bones

The morning sun burns up skeletons, leaving behind bones that you can craft into bone meal. Bone meal acts as a fertilizer, helping your crops grow faster. You can also use bone to tame wolves, providing you with an extra level of protection. Chapter 7, "Taming Mobs," has a lot more information on breeding and taming Minecraft's many friendly creatures.

Start early, heading out with a stone sword at the ready, just in case. If you are low on wood, swing an axe at a few nearby trees.

Move carefully so you don't lose your bearings. The sun rises in the east and sets in the west, and the clouds always travel from east to west, so you can always at least get your bearings. Following a compass cardinal point (north, south, east, or west) using the sun and clouds as a reference can lead you away and reasonably accurately back home again.

TIP

Finding Your Way

It's easy to become lost in Minecraft. Run helter-skelter from your base, chase a herd of livestock, discover a natural cave system, or take a shot across the sea like that famed Norseman, Leif Eriksson. It's all part of the Minecraft charm. But don't become Columbus in the process.

A few quick tips:

- When you are able, craft a compass. It takes some redstone and iron, and both are relatively easy to obtain with some assiduous mining. The only problem with a compass is that it always points to your original world spawn point. Think of that point as the magnetic north pole—it's not a GPS. Sleeping in a bed resets your spawn point but not your compass, so this method falls out of date as soon as you move to new dwellings and update your spawn point.

- A compass is actually more useful when crafted into a map, see Chapter 10, "Enchanting, Anvils, and Brewing" page 195.

- Don't forget that you can always use the built-in GPS available through the debug screen (mentioned under the "Introducing the HUD" section earlier in this chapter).

Food on the Run

If you are getting dangerously hungry, head to the nearest equivalent of a fast food outlet—a passive mob—sword at the ready. Your best bet is to look for cows and pigs because they each can drop up to three pieces of raw meat, with each piece restoring 3 hunger units and 1.8 in saturation. They're an excellent target of opportunity. You can also eat raw chicken, although with a 30% chance of developing food poisoning, or you can try rotten meat harvested from zombies, which is guaranteed to give you a taste of the stomach aches. But you can also cure any type of food poisoning by drinking milk obtained with a bucket clicked on a cow, and you can eat any amount of poisoned meat, gaining the restorative benefits, and curing the whole lot with one serving of milk. So keep that rotten flesh the zombies drop around! And the bucket o' milk.

That said, unless you are desperate, it is actually much better to take the time to cook all your meat first. In fact, the secondary processing of foods makes them all healthier, restoring more hunger and saturation points. It's therefore quite handy to always carry a furnace in your inventory, along with fuel. When you've finished cooking, break the furnace down with a pickaxe, and it floats back into your inventory. If you don't mind seeming like a crazed pyromaniac, you can also both kill and cook pigs, chickens, and cows in one blazing swoop by setting the ground beneath them on fire with a flint and steel (right-click on the ground, not the animal), or a little more chaotically by pouring lava from a bucket. Just take caution that you don't do this anywhere it could pose a risk, such as near that fantastic wood cabin you just spent the last three weeks building; there's no Undo key in Minecraft.

NOTE

Fishing in the Sea of Plenty

Mobs such as chicken, cows, and pigs spawn quite rarely compared to hostile mobs, so consider them a nonrenewable resource if you kill them in the wild. You're better off breeding them in a farm so they can't wander off and can be readily replaced. Fish, on the other hand, are unlimited in quantity and very plentiful. You can even fish in waterfalls! By the way, your food bar never decreases when travelling by boat, making it the perfect opportunity to get in a spot of fishing. And you can never get food poisoning from raw fish. Sushi anyone? See Chapter 7 for more information.

TIP

Let Them Eat Cake

What's the quickest way to fill your food bar? Eat cake. Unlike another well-known game, Minecraft's cake is not a lie. Cake has a quite a complicated recipe, but each full cake provides up to 6 slices, each worth 1.5 hunger points, or 9 in total, and it's less resource intensive than creating golden apples. Minecraft rewards calories, so eat as much as you like without penalty, quickly building back your full hunger bar but, as in the real world, the nutrients are lacking, so cake doesn't provide any saturation benefit. Make sure you eat some more nutritional foods such as protein as your hunger bar starts to top out to ensure you also get that extra boost. If only they added pizza!

Finally, if you simply cannot find mobs, your hunger bar has dropped to 0, and your health has plummeted to half a point, consider at least planting a wheat field and waiting it out in your shelter for three blocks of wheat to grow so you can harvest them and bake bread.

There's one final alternative, and this is a pretty neat trick. Assuming you have reset your spawn point to a bed or are still near origin, head to your shelter, place everything you carry in a chest, and then head outside and either jump off a cliff, drown in a lake, or wait for a mob to kill you. You respawn back in your shelter with full health, a full hunger bar, and all your possessions waiting for you. Get dressed, fully equipped, and head out there to try again.

Finding a Building Site

As you scout around, keep in mind that you are also looking for a new building site. This doesn't have to be fancy or even particularly large. A 6×5 space manages just fine, and even 6×4 can squeeze in the basics. You can also level ground and break down a few trees to clear space. I did this in Figure 3.7. The site is located just up the hill from the first dugout, overlooking the same lake and river system.

FIGURE 3.7   A nice, flat, elevated building site after clearing some trees and filling some holes in the ground with dirt.

I usually prefer space that's a little elevated because it provides a better view of the surroundings, but it's perfectly possible to create a protected space just about anywhere. You may even decide to go a little hybrid, building a house that's both tunneled into a hill and extending outside.

Light Those Caves

Check for any caves or tunnels close to your site's location. If they aren't too big, light them up with torches to prevent mobs spawning inside and wandering out during the day, or just block their entrance for now.

So what can we build on this site? Let me show you a basic structure. It takes 34 cobblestone blocks dug out of the first shelter and 12 wood blocks for the roof obtained by cutting down the 3 trees that were occupying the site.

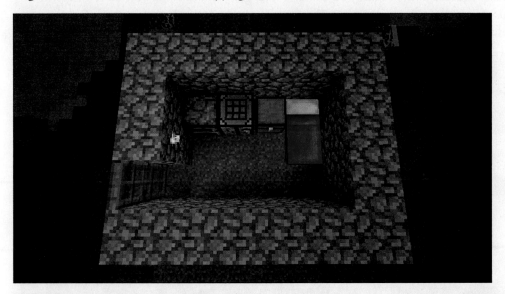

FIGURE 3.8   The layout for a small cobblestone cabin using a total of 46 blocks, roof not shown. The sharp-eyed will notice it can be reduced in width one space further, but for the sake of four blocks, that would feel a little claustrophobic.

You can build the roof from almost any handy material, including dirt, cobblestone, and wood. Avoid blocks that fall down, such as dirt, gravel, and sand. A two-block high wall keeps out all mobs except for spiders, because they can climb walls. An overhang on the wall keeps spiders out because they can't climb upside-down, but it's easier to just add a roof, especially if there are trees nearby the spiders can climb up and use as an arachnid's springboard to jump straight into your dwelling. (Yes, it's happened to me. Sent shivers up my spine.) Figure 3.9 shows the finished hut with a few torches on the outside to keep things well lit.

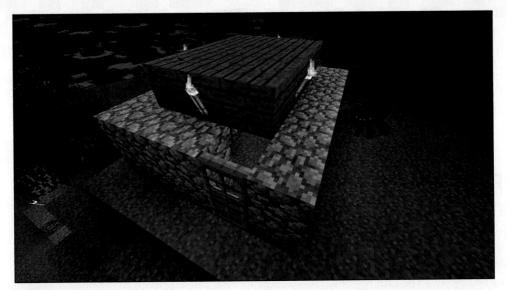

FIGURE 3.9 The finished hut—basic but serviceable. And it's spider proof. Although there is a large gap above the door, in Minecraft's geometry the door fills the entire space. Spiders are also two blocks wide, so they can't case fit through a one-block-wide gap. You could actually leave the door wide open, and spiders will just gather outside and make horrible noises, but don't do that because it's an invitation for other mobs to enter.

TIP

No Housing Codes in Minecraft

The roof in Figure 3.9 rests right on the lip of the inner wall. You can't directly build a roof like this from scratch. First place a block on top of the wall, and then attach the inner block for the roof. Remove the first block, and the inner block floats. Attach new blocks to that to build out the roof structure. It won't pass a building inspection, but it certainly works in Minecraft.

Building a wall even two blocks high can take a little bit of fancy footwork. Some basic techniques help:

- Place your walls one layer at time. Put down the first layer, and then jump on top to place the second.

- If you fall off, place a temporary block on the inside of your structure against the wall, and use this to climb back up. You can remove it when you're finished.

- Use pillar jumping if you need to go higher. While looking directly down, press the spacebar to jump and then right-click to place a block underneath you. You land on that block instead of the one below. Repeat as often as necessary. Dig the blocks out from directly underneath you to go back down.

- Hold down the Shift key as you work around the top of tall walls so you don't fall off. You can even use this technique to place blocks on the side of your current layer that are normally beyond sight.

See Chapter 8 for more building techniques and ideas.

A Resourceful Guide to the Creative Mode Inventory

Minecraft's resources fall into several primary categories. Some of them are a natural early focus as you improve your position from those gathered for first-night survival; others become more important as you get further through the game, gear up for your exploration of The Nether and The End regions, and become more creative with all that Minecraft has to offer. Here's a quick summary of the different categories. You can view all possible tools and resources by opening your inventory in Creative mode, as shown in Figure 3.10. The categories that follow correspond to the tabs running across the upper and lower sections of the Creative mode inventory.

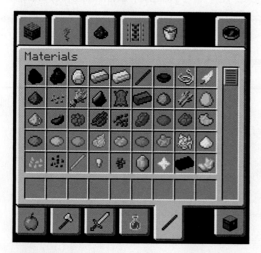

FIGURE 3.10 Creative mode inventory provides access to the full set of resources and tools.

TIP

Turn On Cheats

Turn on Cheats when you start a new world to quickly jump between different gameplay modes. Type **/gamemmode creative** and **/gamemode survival** to move between the main types. See Chapter 13, "Mods and Multiplayer," page 251.

- **Building Blocks**—Building blocks are used, as you might expect, for construction, including housing and almost anything else. Build a bridge for your redstone rail. Construct a dam. Elevate a farm above a level that won't get trampled by mobs, or put up a fence. Build a skyscraper or reconstruct a monument. Minecraft provides a large number of primary blocks—such as cobblestone, gravel, wood, and dirt—that can be harvested directly, but things definitely become more interesting once you start creating secondary types of blocks from primary materials. You can store many items more efficiently (for example, by converting nine gold ingots into a single gold block), and climb more efficiently by crafting stairs instead of jumping up and down blocks on well-travelled routes. Building blocks are, without being too punny, the building blocks of creativity.

- **Decoration Blocks**—Decoration blocks are something of a catchall category. Generally, they are things you can use to make your constructions more interesting. Some of those are just visual, such as carpet, whereas others such as crafting tables, chests, and the bed that keeps you safe at night provide vital functions.

- **Redstone**—Redstone is an almost magical resource. You can use it to build powered circuits, quite complex ones, and then activate pistons to automatically harvest a farm plot, set up traps, open and close doors, and a huge amount more. The limits are set only by your imagination. Redstone is also used to craft powered rail tracks and a range of other useful items such as a compass and clock. See Chapter 9, "Redstone, Rails, and More," for more information.

- **Transportation**—Transportation is a small category, but one that's a lot of fun and very useful. It includes powered and unpowered rails, minecarts, a saddle, a boat, and anything else related to moving yourself and other items around. There are enough options there to enable you to build everything from massive transportation systems to incredible roller coasters.

- **Miscellaneous**—Miscellaneous contains a range of useful and obscure items. You'll find the buckets quite handy for setting up new water and lava sources, and you can use the eggs to spawn most of the mobs, populating a farm and more.

- **Foodstuffs**—Foodstuffs contains the full range of edibles, including the enchanted form of the golden apple, the rarest edible in the game. Take a few of these with you the next time you think you'll be in a tight spot, and you may just be able to make it through that moaning zombie horde.

- **Tools**—Tools can be wielded as weapons, but not very effectively. They are, however, great at digging, chopping, hoeing, and setting Nether Portals on fire with the flint and steel. You'll also find shears for stripping the wool from sheep, a fishing rod, and a few enchanted books that can add special powers to your tools.

- **Combat**—Combat provides your weapons and armor, as well as the remaining enchanted books that relate to combat items.

- **Brewing**—The Brewing tab contains all possible potions and a number of the rarer ingredients required that don't fit into other categories. Potions are incredibly handy. Caught outside at night? The Potion of Night Vision triples the brightness to almost daylight conditions. You can learn more about brewing in Chapter 10.

- **Materials**—Materials is the final catchall category, along with the miscellaneous and decoration blocks. It differs because it is composed of secondary items that are derived from another action. For example, killing a chicken can drop feathers, and you'll need those for the fletching on arrows unless you gather them from skeletons. Grow wheat to get bushels that can be used to tame horses, donkeys, and mules.

There are two other tabs on the Creative inventory. In the upper-right corner is a compass icon. This is the search bar. Just click on it and type in the item's name.

In the lower-right corner is a chest. This is your Survival mode inventory containing any items you were carrying when you switched to Creative mode. (This is empty if you started your world in Creative mode.) You can shift items between the Creative mode inventory and your Survival inventory. Any items you drag down to the access bar are common across both inventories. Remove items from your Survival inventory by dragging them down to the square filled with an X.

The Bottom Line

Congratulations! You've now learned everything you need to know to understand how your character is doing, improve your tools for better longevity, hopefully not get lost on your travels, and create your first mob-proof outdoor shelter.

These are the keys to Minecraft. Just remember to head back to your chest often to store the valuables you've gathered, or build other chests further afield.

You might also want to consider building a pillar and platform on top of your new shelter. It can help you survey your terrain and acts as an easy-to-see landmark when you're out and about. Put some torches on top because mobs can spawn on any platform, no matter how small, and you don't want to poke your head up through the platform only to discover a creeper on a short fuse.

The next chapter is all downhill—deep into your first mine.

Mining

In This Chapter

- Learn the essentials you need for your first mining expedition.
- Head down to the most profitable mining layers.
- Avoid a speedy death with essential tips.
- Build an express elevator straight down to the diamond layer.
- Discover the most efficient mining techniques.

Mining is a core part of the Minecraft experience. Sooner or later you're going to need to take a few pickaxes in hand, supplies to satiate hunger, and a bunch of torches and a sword or two and start plumbing the depths. There be resources down there—iron, gold, diamonds, redstone, and more. You'll find all the things you need to progress in the game. This chapter helps you find specific ores and develop efficient mining patterns that leave no stone unturned, and, as always, it gives you a few tips on how best to avoid an inadvertent respawn or at least recover with most of your hard-won resources and dignity intact.

Dig Deep, My Friend

Most of the desirable ores in Minecraft are located deep, close to the bedrock. Getting down there is a challenge in itself. There are a couple of different strategies you can take:

- Find an existing ravine, canyon, or cave complex. These can sometimes also lead to abandoned mine shafts. Some caves run on for hundreds of blocks, joining with the surface here and there, and occasionally running very deep. You'll usually see a range of exposed ores on their walls that make for easy pickings. The danger is that they are dark places, so in the larger caves you'll also run into a range of mobs. For now, even though they'll give you a head start, I'd suggest you leave these alone until you have armor, ranged weapons, and some sharp swords.

- The second strategy is to create your own mine. Keeping it well lit ensures there are no dark places for mobs to spawn, even over multiple nights, and you can go quietly about your busi-ness. For maximum convenience, you can even start this within your own shelter so there's no need to go outside. I'll focus on this strategy first. It is also likely you will break out into cave complexes as you mine, so we'll take a look at that second.

Before you begin, ensure you have the right equipment for the job. At a minimum, you need the following:

- At least 20 torches, but bring more if you plan to go down for an extended period of time.

- Wood blocks that can be turned into ladders, torches, tool handles, chests, and crafting tables. The only place you can find wood underground is in an abandoned mine shaft, so bring wood with you as often as you can. Fifteen or so blocks should do for now.

- At least three stone pickaxes to dig out iron ore, and a shovel for digging out dirt and gravel. Bring some swords as well, just in case.

- Food. Nourishment is absolutely vital because a full hunger bar helps you heal from any damage you incur. Bring at least cooked meat, and bread if you've had the chance to build a wheat farm. In Chapter 6, "Taming Mobs," and 8, "Creative Construction," you'll learn how to ensure a consistent supply of food.

This will get you started. When you have found enough iron ore, you'll also want to craft the following items:

- Two buckets: one for water and the other for lava. You can use the water bucket to create pathways across lava pools and even to create waterfalls that you can safely descend and ascend over otherwise lethal vertical distances. The bucket of lava makes a great source of energy for the furnace and for fighting off mobs in cave complexes. (It's not a great strategy because items the mobs drop can be burned up in the lava, but it's a good emergency measure.)

- An iron pickaxe for mining the more valuable ores such as gold, redstone, and diamonds.

NOTE

You'll Need Obsidian

You might not be lucky enough to find diamonds on this first expedition, but when you do you also need to create a diamond pickaxe for mining obsidian—the only type of pickaxe that can do so. Obsidian is needed to build the portal to access The Nether region described in Chapter 12, "Playing Through: The Nether and The End."

The Mining Layer Cake Guide

Before you start digging, let's take a brief look at the ore layers in Minecraft. The Overworld has seven types of ore, as well as bedrock, and there is one more called Nether Quartz that is found only in The Nether region. Figure 4.1 shows them all.

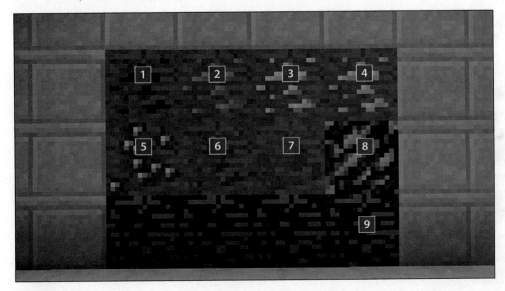

FIGURE 4.1   Each ore in the Minecraft world. Go get them all!

1. Coal
2. Iron
3. Gold
4. Diamond
5. Emerald

6. Redstone
7. Lapis Lazuli
8. Netherrack
9. Bedrock

World generation scatters various ores here and there in a statistical pattern that leads to a variety of striations. All the layers shown in Table 4.1 are counted from bedrock up. So layer 5, for example, is five layers above the lowest layer of bedrock, layer 0. (It might help if you think of layers as *altitude*.) Press **F3** to open the debug screen and check the value shown next to *y* to see your current height above Layer 0.

TABLE 4.1 Ore Layers

Appearance	Ore	Most Common Layers	Less Common Layers	Used For	Mined With
	Coal	5–52	Up to 128	Torches and a fuel source	Any pickaxe
	Iron	5–54	Up to 64	Tools, weapons, armor, and other	Stone, iron, or diamond pickaxe
	Gold	5–59	Up to 23	Tools, weapons, armor, and other	Stone, iron, or diamond pickaxe
	Diamond	5–12	Up to 29	Tools, weapons, armor, and other	Iron or diamond pickaxe
	Emerald	5–29	Up to 29	None	Iron or diamond pickaxe
	Redstone	5–12	Up to 12	Circuits and powered items, clock, and compass	Iron or diamond pickaxe
	Lapis Lazuli	14–16	Up to 23	Dye for decorative items	Stone, iron, or diamond pickaxe
	Nether Quartz	The Nether	The Nether	Crafting redstone comparators and daylight sensors	Any pickaxe
	Bedrock	0–4	4	None	None

The pattern of ore distribution in the table shows a few layers where every ore can be found: layers 5–12. Although you can hit lava just about anywhere, including on the surface, it pools primarily from layers 1–10. This makes layer 11 a good target for mining. On your way there, you will definitely see plenty of ore including coal and iron, and cart loads of dirt, gravel, and stone.

Getting there is a matter of luck and skill, and that can make for an exciting journey!

Lava Lakes and Other Pitfalls

Mining has its share of pitfalls, in both the figurative and the literal sense. Before you don your virtual miner's hat, check through the following list of do's and don'ts:

- **Don't dig straight down**—It's tempting, certainly. You could potentially dig all the way to bedrock using just one iron pickaxe. The problem with that approach is that you never know what lies beneath. You could break through the top of a cave's roof and face a fatal drop, fall into a nest of hostile mobs, or splash down in a lava lake and lose not only your life, but also all your possessions.

- **Don't dig straight up**—It's easy to get lulled into a false sense of security after tunneling for a while, but you have no idea what may be on top of the block just above your head. You may tap an underground lake and flood your mine. If you are mining higher levels, you could even tap straight into the bottom of the ocean. You could also tap into a lava flow, resulting in almost certain death. Or it could be a bunch of loose gravel or dirt waiting to suffocate you. Always mine up at least one block away from your current position so you have the chance to retreat and block off the tunnel if things go awry.

- **Keep some blocks in your quick access bar**—Always have cobblestone or dirt at the ready to block off your tunnel in case you break through into a danger zone. Water probably won't kill you, but it can wash you back quite quickly and put out your torches. Lava oozes along much more slowly but is far more deadly. Be ready to block off any unexpected breakthroughs.

- **Be careful, be prepared, and always know your way out**—It's easy to get lost down there, especially if you do break into a cave complex and decide to explore. Use torches, signs, cobblestone arranged into arrows, blocks attached to a wall with a torch facing the way out—they can all act like a trail of bread crumbs to help you find your way home.

- **Keep your mines well lit**—Any area you leave open and dark can spawn mobs that will come back for you eventually.

- **Block off any unlit areas**—These can include caves and fully explored tunnel branches. You can even knock your torches off the wall and collect them on your way out, as long as you remember to block off the entire branch when you get back to the main trunk so the mobs don't break through. If you do break into a cave, place a torch on the wall inside the cave, and block it off leaving no more than a one block gap. (Okay, if you must, explore, but remember, you're on a mission!) You'll be able to see the torch or at least the light from the torch on the other side as an indication that you can come back and explore it later. Then head in a different direction.

Mining is composed of two parts: getting down, and then cutting across to uncover as much valuable ore as possible. There are a few ways to do both.

Descending to Layer 11

Just the process of descending is also a process of discovery, and no two journeys will be the same. In all cases, follow any ore seams you find on the way down, and then return to the plan. Check in with your layer level now and then using F3, or just dig all the way to the lowest layer of bedrock you can find and then count 12 layers going back up.

The 2x1 Ladder Descent

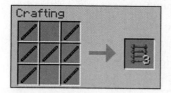

The fastest way to descend is in a 2×1 pattern placing ladders or vines as you go against one of the walls so you can climb your way out. Vines are plentiful in the jungle biome, but not elsewhere. Ladders are crafted from sticks in an H layout across the crafting grid, with each set of seven sticks making three ladder blocks. Their advantage over jumping up and down stairs, besides being a fast method of vertical movement, is that they don't use up any energy, so you won't see any drop in your hunger bar as you traverse.

TIP

Use the Shift Key to Pause on Ladders

Hold down the Shift key to pause whenever you are ascending or descending a ladder. While paused, you can place torches and do anything else required, including placing additional ladder segments and torches.

Dig out the block directly in front of you, as well as the one underneath. If all looks good, turn around and dig out the block you were standing on, the one underneath that, and you'll be down to a level pit. Place two ladder segments on the wall in front of you, and repeat. Attach torches to the other wall every 9 layers or so. You can also place blocks between the torches to break your fall. It shouldn't really be necessary because it's difficult to fall off a ladder, but staring down a 50-layer drop may induce feelings of virtual vertigo.

Figure 4.2 shows the view looking up to the sky from the bottom of a 53-layer pit.

FIGURE 4.2 Sunlight seems such a long way away when you're on layer 11, but ladders make for very fast ascents and it only takes about 20 seconds to reach the Overworld.

TIP

Defying the Laws of Physics

Falling down the side of the shaft without the ladder is deadly, but like the acrobat at the circus diving off the high board into a saucepan of water, you can easily break your fall. Just dig out a block in the nonladder side of the shaft, pour a bucket of water into it, and survive shorter falls of around 50 blocks every time, as shown in Figure 4.3. You can also use this as the world's fastest one-way express elevator to get down in a hurry. If you do take fall damage, try increasing the water's depth. A 250+ layer fall can splash down with zero damage in water just three blocks high.

FIGURE 4.3   Break an otherwise breakneck fall down a long vertical shaft with a single block of thud-absorbing water.

The Straight Staircase

The staircase is one of the most natural designs, and it's quick to move along. You'll need to break three blocks for each one down, so it's not quite as efficient as the ladder descent, but it's the simplest option available if you are short on wood for ladders and are lacking in vines.

Start by digging down one block in front of you. Hop in the hole, and then follow this pattern:

1 Dig out the block at eye level in front of you and the two underneath that.

2 Move into the hole in front of you, and repeat.

As you go, don't forget to place torches every 9 steps or so, and if you hit any problems, either take a 90-degree turn to the left or right and continue, or make a bit of space for a landing and do a 180-turn.

You can see a typical straight staircase in Figure 4.4.

FIGURE 4.4 The straight staircase descent is easy to go down and fast to move back up. You can improve it by crafting cobblestone stairs so that no jumping is required on the return journey.

The Spiral Staircase

A spiral staircase takes a little more care to build, and you might get a bit dizzy going up and down with all the frequent turns, but it has a couple of advantages over the other methods:

- The staircase descends vertically, which makes for more methodical exploration. It's also easy to build if you don't have the wood needed for a vertical access shaft.

- A staircase winds down around itself or a central core, exposing more surface area and therefore providing greater opportunity to discover seams of ore on the way down.

There are several different versions. The tightest staircase possible is the 2×2. You can build this following the same steps as for a straight staircase. However, each time you drop down one level, just turn to the right or left 90 degrees and start again. Keep turning in the same direction to ensure that you drop down vertically.

A 3×3 version of the same staircase involves going down two steps straight, turning, going down another two steps straight, and so on. This leaves a single-column central core that you can remove to create an open light well, gaining more illumination from each torch you place. It's also a bit easier to keep your bearings if you remove the central core as you go. Figure 4.5 shows the result.

FIGURE 4.5   A 3×3 spiral staircase provides a handy light-well down the middle single block core.

A 5×5 version is similar, but you go down four steps and then turn. This leaves a solid block of 3×3 in the middle. You can then dig out the central block in the pillar and place a ladder against the side when you're ready for faster ascents and descents. Open up blocks from the staircase into the core (except on the side reserved for a ladder) to bring light from the torches into the core. This style of staircase also exposes the maximum surface area, essentially mining out a block of 5×5 units all the way down. It is, however, a complicated method requiring that you keep careful count of the steps you dig on each side.

Layouts for Fast, Efficient Mining

There are numerous methods for mining, and some may lead to madness. You can wander around hacking at every rock in site, but this results in your missing a lot of ore deposits, and it's pretty easy to get lost in a maze of your own making. You can also go for grandeur, hollowing out halls as you go, dwarfing the Mines of Moria. Fortunately, Minecraft doesn't yet have a Balrog, although the ender dragon comes close.

A gigantic, modern, underground lair with powered rails allowing you to zip back and forth in minecarts also has its charm. (See Chapter 8.) There's nothing wrong with that, and it does make for a fantastic creative challenge, but for your first serious dig, with what is probably still a quite limited set of tools, your aim should be to collect as much ore as possible with the least amount of effort and using the fewest number of pickaxes possible. That mine is called a *branch mine*.

Branch mines generally cover a rectangular surface area. You can choose any size you like, but you may also be limited by the terrain. Breakouts at Layer 11 are quite common, and if you end up at a lava pool such as the one shown in Figure 4.6, you have little option but to treat it as the end of the trunk, or that particular branch. The good part is that lava pools provide a lot of light.

FIGURE 4.6   Lava lakes usually act as a natural barrier to further mining, at least in the beginning. Later you can use buckets of water to turn the lava into an obsidian bridge but in the meanwhile just work around them.

So what's the most efficient layout? The one I prefer is quite simple, easy to navigate, and effective. It relies on the fact that blocks of ore almost always appear in veins larger than a single block. Yes, even diamonds!

Branch mines use a horizontal central trunk, two blocks high by one block wide. Branches are then dug out perpendicular to the trunk, much like the branches of a tree, or at least a strangely geometrical one.

Because each block of ore can be identified from any of its six sides, a distance of two blocks per branch exposes at least one side of every block to the side, and also above and below you. In other words, move one space along a branch, and you expose a total of six blocks: two on each side, one below, one above, and the two in front of you.

This is the most thorough mining method available because it exposes every single block within the area the mine covers. But it's not the most efficient because ore veins almost always take up more than one block, generally in clumps of two to sixteen blocks. Think of the goal, therefore, as being to uncover veins of ore, not individual blocks. If you find one block in a vein, you expose the next, and you can then follow the vein to its end.

Spacing each branch every fourth block, with three blocks in between, works best. Take a look at Figure 4.7 for a top-down view.

FIGURE 4.7   Space your branches every three steps, off a primary central trunk, placing a base camp for convenient crafting and storage.

NOTE

Spacing Your Branches

If your mining target is the more common ores such as coal and iron that occur in larger veins, you could even space your branches with four or five blocks in between. You might miss some smaller deposits, but will intersect all the larger veins. This is a fast, efficient technique you can use in the higher levels.

When you've completed mining layer 12, head back up using the same spacing principal vertically that you did horizontally, leaving a gap of three blocks, or layers, between the roof of your first trunk and the floor of the next. As you work higher, you lose most of the chances for redstone, but other ores are plentiful. And you can head down to bedrock the same way, taking extra care because there's a lot more lava about.

Staying Safe While You Mine

Your first mining expedition will undoubtedly turn up a lot of valuable ore. Don't risk losing it all if you die. Chances are you won't be able to make it back down from your last spawn point to pick up your valuables. Here are some tips that will help:

- Use the Shift key so you can sneak around the edges of lava lakes and other hazards without risk of falling in.

- Build a small base to act as a staging point. It's easy enough to create a new crafting table and furnace, but if you've also been able to construct a bed and don't have wool for another, consider bringing your bed down with you from your Overland dwelling. You can break it up with any tool and pick up the floating icon so that it slots into your inventory. Set up your base somewhere central to your mine, and sleep in the bed at least once to set a new spawn point. Figure 4.8 shows a minimal layout where everything fits into a six-block space.

NOTE

The Mobs Might Not Let You Sleep

You might need to try several base locations before you can successfully sleep in a bed. Any mobs nearby, even if blocked by walls, will prevent this. Rather than searching for and clearing out caves, just pack everything up and find a new site somewhere else in your mine.

- Place chests in your base or anywhere that's convenient in your tunnel system. Regularly return to the chest to drop off any valuable items you've found so that you can pick them up again if you respawn.

FIGURE 4.8 A mining base makes it easier to recover after a respawn. See the redstone in the upper-left corner? There's plenty down here, so I left it as decoration.

The Bottom Line

Mining is the only way to gather many key resources, including the diamonds required to mine obsidian and get to The Nether region. Don't make the mistake of mining too high, because you'll miss most of the good stuff. Once you hit layer 12, you'll be amazed at just how quickly you amass a huge range of useful resources. Mine your way in layers back up, rather than starting at the top and working down, and you'll have a plentiful supply of iron for tools, coal for torches, and masses of cobblestone to expand your dwelling on the surface.

Minecraft places resources in 16×16 blocks that run all the way from bedrock to the sky. (These are known as *chunks*.) There are an average of just over 3 diamond blocks per chunk, and of course many times that of the more common ores. So if you don't find what you need, just dig across at least 16 blocks and try again. There's a wealth of material down there, and it won't be long before you can build an incredible powered rail system that can zoom you up and down from the surface as fast as a freight train, as well as carry resources for you.

You may have noticed one thing, though, while you were toiling away. Those caves you've no doubt uncovered look mighty tempting—all that exposed ore just waiting for you to collect. In the next chapter, you get battle-ready so you can head back down, take on the mobs, and take home the spoils.

Combat School

In This Chapter

- Mobs, meh! Learn their strange, wonderful ways and how to defeat 'em.
- Build snow and iron golems for additional defense.
- Wield a sword like a swashbuckler, dealing extra damage with critical hits.
- Don't bow down before them—use your bow instead for long-range attacks.
- Learn how to keep your quiver fully stocked. Arrows are everywhere, and they're easily crafted.
- Grow a thicker skin with all the information you need to craft the right armor, and even color it for the next Minecraft Mardi Gras.

It's perfectly possible to live a peaceful existence in Minecraft. Build a nice, safe mine, avoid cave exploring of any kind, create a self-sufficient farm that produces everything you need, protect your domain with mob-proof fences, keep it all well lit to prevent spawning inside, and retire at the end of each day with slippers on your soft, uncalloused feet in front of a warm fire, sipping a bowl of mushroom stew.

Ah, the serenity...but there's only one problem with that: you'll miss out on most of the fun! Sooner or later combat becomes a necessity. It's not full-scale war, but having the right equipment, some key tactics, and a few fighting skills will let you progress much faster and further in the game than you will if you take a purely passive path.

I've introduced a few of the hostile mobs previously, but now it's time to get into the specifics of tactics, weapons, armor, and defense.

Introducing the Menagerie

Minecraft mobs might be a pain in the derriere at times, but you'll never get to Valhalla without 'em. Let's take a closer look at each and the unique tactics you can use to defeat them.

Remember that, in most cases, hostile mobs switch to pursuit mode if they are within 16 blocks and have a line of sight to your location. As soon as they switch, they'll track you even if you move out of direct sight.

You can use this to your advantage, leading them to a location that's better suited for a counterattack or escape, or even maneuver them into a position where they can be pushed off a cliff or into a lava pool, but do ensure you keep your own footing while doing so.

Each hostile has specific strengths and weaknesses. While any tool can do damage, you'll be best sticking with a sword for short-ranged attacks and the bow for longer range. Mobs are also vulnerable to fire, so lighting the ground with a flint and steel can either weaken them enough that a final blow finishes them off, or actually do them in altogether.

In this chapter, I'll run through the mobs you are most likely to encounter in The Overworld. See Chapter 12 for complete details on those that inhabit The Nether and The End regions.

Zombies

The first mob you encounter in Minecraft will probably be the humble zombie (see Figure 5.1). The sound of one of them trying to beat down your door can set hairs on end, but their bark in single numbers is worse than their bite. Zombies are slow, and while a poorly handled encounter can definitely kill you, be the aggressor, and you'll stay on top.

FIGURE 5.1 Zombies are slow but have a habit of spawning in large numbers.

There are a few different ways to deal with Zombies. If you encounter them close to a cave entrance and it's sunny outside, just lead them outside as soon as they enter pursuit mode, and they'll burn up in the light. Keep your distance, though, because they can still attack while they're burning and cause you fire damage. Zombies can happily exist in daylight when it's shaded, overcast or raining, or when wearing helmets of pumpkins on their head—although they do look a little silly. (Then again, you can also wear a pumpkin on your head to prevent endermen from attacking, so let's not point fingers.)

For a more direct assault, keep your crosshairs on the zombies and hit first and hit often, clicking your left mouse button continuously. They'll only sometimes land a hit in return, and probably just the one before they're overcome.

If you encounter more than one zombie at once along with other mobs sprinkled in for good measure, hack through the zombies first and make your escape or retreat.

Now, there is just one problem: Zombies can call up their undead buddies as reinforcements and can cause additional zombies to spawn upon their death. The resulting zombie apocalypse can make it tricky if you're caught outside at night.

TIP

Watch Your Back

Consider placing a wooden door at the entrance to caves that connect back to your tunnel system. This will protect your base while you're exploring. The door also protects your retreat route if you need to make a hasty exit, and you can always knock it down for retrieval and permanently block off the cave once the mobs have wandered off.

Zombies drop rotten meat when they're defeated. The meat is poisonous but can still build up your hunger bar. The best strategy here is to save up a few pieces and eat them all at once, because you will still only get one hit of food poisoning. This is a great way to replenish your hunger bar from almost empty to full—your health will take a minimal hit from the poisoning and then start to replenish from the full hunger bar. Also, consider carrying a bucket of milk with you because this instantly cures all types of food poisoning. You can also use rotten meat to feed wolves to keep up their health.

CAUTION

The Dead Stick Together

Zombies are the most "mobbish" of Minecraft's mobs. If you attack one, others nearby—even outside of the usual hostile range—might come swarming to help out their undead brethren.

Zombies can also more rarely drop other items such as tools and armor.

Spiders

Minecraft has two types of spiders and a skeleton/spider hybrid.

You'll encounter the large spiders most often, shown in Figure 5.2. (See "Cave Spiders" and "Spider Jockeys" below for more information on the others.) The large spiders are jumpy, literally. They can leap two to three blocks in a single bound and can climb walls unless there is an overhang or a layer of a block type they can't climb, such as glass. They're fast, aggressive at night or in dark places, and a little bit tougher to defeat than your average zombie.

FIGURE 5.2   Spiders are fast and able to climb walls, but easy to defeat even with a wooden sword.

NOTE

Building Spider-Proof Walls

Spiders can crawl up almost any wall unless it contains transparent blocks. This isn't always practical. An overhang provides an alternative defense. Position a single block on the outside of the third level of any wall such that the block forms an upside-down ledge. Spiders can't get through single-block gaps, so these overhangs only have to be positioned every second space, somewhat like the battlements on a castle keep's walls. See Chapter 8, "Creative Construction," for examples of this and other defensive construction techniques.

Spiders are, however, also very useful. Spiders drop string, a vital ingredient for crafting a bow, and sometimes one of their eyes. Every four pieces of string can also make one block (or bale) of wool. Gather three of those, and it's enough for a bed, which can then be used to reset your spawn point. That's *very* handy if there are no sheep nearby!

Treat spider eyes as a sort of extreme food if you can handle the concept. They're poisonous along the same lines as rotten meat, but also make for a useful ingredient in some potions.

Spiders are just one block high and two blocks wide, so a 1×1 opening in a wall will keep you safe.

Their jumping ability gives them a slight edge in combat. The best strategy is similar to that of defeating zombies. Click fast and often to hit them as rapidly as possible, but also walk backward at the same time, so long as you know what's behind you. This can help keep you out of range of their jump attack.

CAUTION

I Always Feel Like Somebody's Watching Me

Ever had the feeling someone's watching you? In Minecraft, that someone is probably a spider with all eight eyes, bright points of red in the dark. Spiders don't require a line of sight to enter pursuit mode, so they'll be on your trail as soon as you get within 16 blocks, and they'll do almost anything to get closer. Lock yourself in your shelter for the night, but take care in the morning. If you hear the spider's hissing/slurping noise, it might still be waiting for you, hatred in every eye. Spiders have a habit of lurking in ambush on your roof, waiting for you to "tra la la" out the door the next morning without a care in the world—until you feel their fangs sink into your back! Fortunately, the large spiders aren't poisonous, so just make sure you have your sword in hand, ready to fight back, and you'll be fine.

Skeletons

The sound of skeletons' rattling bones usually gives these mobs away a few moments before their arrow pierces your breastbone. They're sharpshooters, so the best approach is to stay out of the direct line of fire, ducking out to attack only when they're close enough. Do it commando-style, moving sideways to avoid the feathered missiles that will undoubtedly be coming your way. It's not an arrow-proof strategy, but it can help. Figure 5.3 shows a skeleton with its ubiquitous bow.

FIGURE 5.3   Skeletons are sharpshooters, so keep your distance until you can strike, and don't let them sneak up behind you.

If you can get close enough, a sword can finish off skeletons quite quickly. For this reason, a good strategy is to try to wait somewhere protected, letting them get within reach. Skeletons also burn up in sunlight, unless they are protected by armor or are wearing a pumpkin head, so luring them out into the sun won't always provide deliverance.

Skeletons usually drop arrows, making them an easy way to resupply your stock if you are also using a bow. You'll also often find arrows that have missed their mark sticking out of blocks. Break the block to collect the arrows, but take care when doing that to one that's directly above your head, because the falling arrow causes you damage.

Also, keep in mind that skeletons will try to circle around you, approaching you from behind.

Cave Spiders

These invidious arachnids are found in abandoned mine shafts. They're fast, small, and poisonous, and they make large spiders look positively passive!

Cavers can slip through a gap one block wide and just half a block high, so a 1×1 block hole in the wall offers no protection at all. They're also easily spotted by their blue coloring (see Figure 5.4).

FIGURE 5.4   Inhabiting only abandoned mineshafts, cave spiders aren't common, but they are definitely among the top deadly mobs.

Cave spiders don't spawn naturally. They're spewed out of a spawning device, a small fiery cage that shows a miniature of themselves spinning around faster and faster until it seems they're flung out the side through centripetal force. It's a bit like a washing machine's spin cycle gone mad.

If you are lucky enough to find an abandoned mineshaft, consider it a huge bonus. These massive structures can hold well over one dozen chests with all kinds of goodies inside. The cave spider and other mobs that may inhabit it can be a bit of a challenge, but go ahead and claim that mineshaft for your own. It's now *your* mineshaft. Just take care as you go, ensuring you are well prepared.

Here's what you need to know:

■ A bite from a cave spider won't kill you. Like all poisonings, it can take you down to half a heart on Normal difficulty, but the damage from the bite itself, not the poison, can definitely do you in.

- Cavers are easy to kill but are smaller than other mobs, so you need to aim your crosshairs with a bit more care and click frenetically.

- Fighting while walking backward works as well as with the large spiders, but cavers are faster so will be able to launch more attacks.

- Cave spiders' habitat is filled with spider webs. These will slow you down, but cavers can slip through those webs at normal speed.

- Break the spawner. Kill the source, and you solve the supply. But keep your guard up, because there is often more than one spawner in close proximity.

- The good news: abandoned mineshafts are a treasure trove of resources waiting to be plundered. You'll find loads of chests and rails, and the mine braces provide the only source of wood available underground.

Spider Jockeys

Sit a skeleton on top of a spider, and you get a spider jockey. Spider jockeys jump like a spider, shoot arrows like a skeleton, and are best given a wide berth. Fortunately, they're rare. If you see one, smash the skeleton if you can and deal with the spider next. You may not survive, but isn't that why you keep your valuables in a chest next to your spawn point? Rhetorical question: of course, you do that!

Creepers

If Minecraft has an anti-hero, it's the creeper (see Figure 5.5). Think of creepers as walking improvised explosive devices (IEDs). I talked a little about creepers in Chapter 2, "First-Night Survival." Rather than repeating that, let's get into some of the specifics.

FIGURE 5.5 Creepers appear to be fairly docile until they get close and provide a taste of their truly explosive personality.

First, you can survive a creeper attack unless you are caught totally by surprise. If you turn a corner and there's one right in front of you, do your best to sprint away. Your attack on a creeper needs to be well timed, and you need space to sprint in, thwack it, and move back out again so that its fuse resets. The force of your blow should usually be enough to knock the creeper far enough that this happens with reasonable surety. A sword with a knockback enchantment (see the section "Spruce Up Your Weapons," in Chapter 10, page 204) also helps a lot against creepers but actually makes things worse when fighting skeletons.

Unfortunately, if you see a creeper swelling like a balloon (something it does just prior to exploding), it's probably already too late.

Try to ensure that you are not fighting the creeper near an important structure. Just about the worst situation occurs when stepping out the front door, straight into one. You'll end up with a crater where the front of your house used to stand. As one of the memes on the web reads, "I just undid in 2 seconds what you spent 5 hours building." You are generally safe if you can keep a distance of a few blocks, but they move quite fast.

Creepers do have an Achilles heel. If you find one swimming in water, you can easily deal with it by attacking from below. Creepers are also scared of ocelots, or their tamed version, the humble cat (see Chapter 7, "Farming and Taming Mobs").

As with most mobs in Minecraft, creepers can seem somewhat formidable at first, but with a little practice you'll find you can dispatch them fairly easily.

Creepers drop gunpowder, a key ingredient in crafting TNT blocks and making throwable "splash" potions described in Chapter 10.

Slimes

Slimes aren't too common because they generally spawn in swamps, and far less regularly in other underground areas. But because of this, slimes can ooze up far from a swamp biome and spawn in any light level.

If any mob needs frenetic clicking, it's a slime. That's because each large one splits into up to 4 smaller ones and up to 16 tiny ones (see Figure 5.6). The tiny ones don't do damage but can be annoying as they swarm you. Just click and click and click until you've finished them all, and switch to your fists to finish off the tiny ones. All it takes is one blow, and this will save durability on your sword.

FIGURE 5.6   Slimes split and split, seemingly ad infinitum.

Slimes drop slimeballs, a substance that makes ordinary pistons stickier than duct tape. Slimeballs are also used in creating magma cream, which is most useful in The Nether for swimming across lava lakes, and for crafting leads, which make passive mob management much, much easier.

Endermen

The Enderman is a curious, otherworldy creature surrounded by a purple haze (see Figure 5.7). The Endermen call The End region home, and you'll see them there in enormous numbers, but they also appear in The Overworld quite often, so I've also included them here.

FIGURE 5.7   Always look behind when the Enderman you're attacking teleports away.

Endermen tend to teleport when attacked and have a habit of popping up behind you, which can make them tricky to defeat. Your best bet is actually to do your best to ignore them. They're not hostile unless you put your crosshairs on them, and as mentioned previously, popping a pumpkin on your head, while not offering any protection or winning you any beauty contents, essentially hides your eyes so that Endermen don't turn hostile.

Endermen drop ender pearls, an essential crafting component for Eyes of Ender. These unusual items help find the strongholds that house the Ender Portals needed to access The End region. Although Eyes of Ender can be traded for with villagers, attacking and defeating Endermen provides a faster method. Attack the Endermen's legs to prevent them teleporting away.

Zombie Pigmen

Like Endermen, these inhabitants of The Nether region are neutral unless attacked. The main problem with doing that is that, just like wolves and zombies, attacking one causes them all to want to join in. If you do get zombie pigmen riled up, you may find it best to try to make your escape. They'll calm down eventually. Figure 5.8 shows their interesting visage—a mug shot if ever there was one.

FIGURE 5.8   With a pack mentality, zombie pigmen are best left to their own devices.

Defensive Mobs

Balancing out the host of hostile mobs are a couple of defensive ones that are unique because they are also the only player-created mobs. Neither of these mobs is created at a crafting table. Instead, you'll need to stack their blocks where you'd like them to spawn, always ensuring you leave the pumpkin block to last.

Snow Golems

Snow golems aren't the strongest line of defense because they don't cause damage to any of the Overworld mobs, but their furious rate of snowball throwing can be enough to keep zombies and other hostile mobs at a distance, making them useful around your home. Create your own snow golem with these simple steps:

1 Gather at least eight snowballs by right-clicking any snow lying on the ground with a shovel.

2 Craft two snow blocks using four snowballs for each.

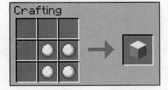

3 Create a stack of the snow blocks by placing one on top of the other.

4 Place a pumpkin on top of the stacked snow blocks to bring the snow golem to life, shown in Figure 5.9.

Unfortunately, Snow Golems have a tendency to wander, so place them behind a fence or walled area for best results, but ensure there's a roof over their head because they don't survive in rain.

FIGURE 5.9 Snow golems aren't particularly powerful, but who doesn't want a snowball-hurling automaton in their front yard all year round?

Iron Golems

Iron golems exist to protect villages and their inhabitants. They're incredibly powerful, and you really shouldn't attack them or any villagers either because the iron golem will rush to their defense.

They spawn naturally in villages of sufficient size (approximately 21 houses), but you can also build one in a similar fashion to a snow golem:

1 Build up a collection of 36 iron ingots. (These golems are incredibly expensive!)

2 Create four blocks of iron using nine ingots each.

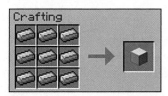

3 Place one block of iron on top of the other and then attach two more blocks to opposite sides of the upper block in the stack. You are, effectively, creating a stack of iron blocks in the shape of a T.

4 Place a pumpkin on top of the middle upper block where the head would go.

Iron golems, besides smashing the heck out of spiders, zombies, and most other hostile mobs, have the endearing habit of giving red roses to village children. Unfortunately, they don't really care too much about your own well-being, so unless your strategy is to help protect villages, iron golems are not really worth building due to the enormous amount of iron required.

FIGURE 5.10   Iron golems aren't directly on your side, but if you set up your house inside a village, you'll be within their circle of protection.

Weapons and Armor

Out in the wild? Getting stuck by skeletons? Zombies spawning everywhere? You can stand and fight, or you can decide to run. Either way, a decent set of weapons and a suit of armor will help you survive. Live by the sword, but don't die by it, too.

Minecraft has two primary offensive weapons: the sword and the bow. In a pinch, other tools will also do. None is as powerful as the sword, but if you do run out of swords in combat, switch, in order of effectiveness, to the axe, then a pickaxe and, if all else is lost, remember that you can also beat something over the head with a shovel.

TIP

Delivering the Winning Blow

Deliver a *critical hit* to cause up to 50% more damage. This works for every material (and tool) except the hoe. The trick is to make the hit as you are falling, and the easiest way to do that is to jump first, timing it right so that you have passed the apex of your leap by the time you strike. I'm not sure if it helps to yell "Hiiiiyaaa!!!" as you do so, but feel free to give it a try. You'll know you've succeeded when you see a little bloom of stars around the unfortunate recipient of your attack immediately after the hit.

Critical hits can be crucial for survival because they can kill some mobs in a single blow, saving your sword's durability. Put in a bit of practice when you can, and the timing of the hit, and the optional battle cry, will become second nature.

The same techniques that work in many other combat games also work in Minecraft. Keep on the move; don't just stand like a statue and flail. Float like a butterfly and sting like an infuriated wasp. Use the left-right keys to circle around the enemy and dodge direct blows, ranged attacks such as from skeletons, and melee attacks, which essentially are full-body broadsides by slimes and the like. Always use height to your advantage when out in the open. It will help both with avoiding attacks and in delivering critical hits.

Swordcraft

The sword will no doubt become your go-to weapon. In a pinch, it's easy to quickly craft a sword from a few raw materials, and its damage and durability increase quickly as you upgrade from the stone to iron and diamond. Table 5.1 lists the materials, damage inflicted, and durability of each material.

TABLE 5.1 Sword Materials

Material	Bare Fists	Wood	Gold	Stone	Iron	Diamond
Durability	Infinite	60	33	132	251	1562
Damage Points	1	4	4	5	6	7
Maximum Critical Hit Points	2	8	8	9	11	12

The damage points represent the minimum damage from a successful strike. Critical hits increase that by a random amount up to the totals shown in Table 5.1. Iron and diamond swords are obviously the most powerful, especially if you keep in mind that attack is actually the best defense. The quicker you can kill a mob, the less time it has to deliver blows in return. Dispatch them fast, and move on with your health mostly intact.

Sprinting while hitting also knocks back the target, a vital move for attacking creepers, but not so good against skeletons because it gives them time to line up another shot.

The sword is unique among all weapons because it also provides a blocking move. Right-click to block any attack, either direct or ranged, if you can spot that arrow or fireball heading your way in time. This provides an up to 50% damage reduction at the expense of dropping your speed to a crawl, so block at the last possible moment or in tight corners where there isn't enough room for the usual evasive maneuvers.

Bows and Arrows

A fully charged bow deals more damage than an unenchanted diamond sword, making them very powerful weapons. Bows and arrows also enable you to attack from a distance, giving skeletons a dose of their own medicine and keeping you well clear of creeper detonation range. Figure 5.11 shows the bow in action.

FIGURE 5.11 Archery target practice: Sorry, Porky.

Craft a bow from three sticks and three pieces of string and equip in any Quick Access inventory slot. There is one other part to the equation: arrows.

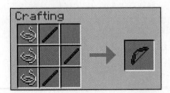

A piece of flint, a stick, and a feather will create a stack of four arrows.

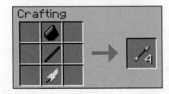

This isn't a lot, and you're going to need a lot of arrows to make a bow worthwhile—probably several dozen on any significant expedition.

A few techniques make this quite easy. The easiest is to go for a quick scout around in the morning when the sun comes up. Here's why:

- Skeletons often drop arrows when they burn up in the morning, so there's no crafting required there.

- Zombies sometimes drop feathers at the same time.

- Chickens can die during the night, a victim of wolves or cacti. You can also kill any random chickens you find during your travels to get both meat and often 1–2 feathers per chicken.

Sticks are almost always readily available, but what about flint?

Every gravel block mined with a shovel has a 1 in 10 chance of dropping a piece of flint instead of a block of gravel. It's completely random, meaning that every block of gravel, if mined, placed, and mined again will eventually yield the flint. That changes everything!

Gravel usually seems to be a bit of an annoyance in mines because it's so common, keeps falling down, and for best results usually requires that you change from a pickaxe to a shovel. But from now on consider it a benefit. Gather all the gravel you can because each and every one contains flint, just requiring a bit of gentle encouragement to give up its precious yield.

TIP

Superfast Flint Mining

The quickest way I've found to recycle gravel for flint is to create a room with a set of four eight-block long trenches that are two blocks deep with an additional step in the end so you can climb out. This creates a total of 64 gravel spaces—conveniently equal to a full stack of gravel in a Quick Access slot. Keep another full stack of gravel in a regular inventory slot. This is the replenishment stack. With the Quick Access gravel selected, jump into each trench, running up and down while holding down the right mouse button to place the gravel in a continuous stream. Switch to the shovel and do the same in reverse while holding down the left button to harvest the gravel and flint. Iron shovels provide the best durability without chewing up the much rarer diamond gems.

You'll get six to seven pieces of flint each time you clear the room, which is sufficient to make between 24 and 28 arrows. Now replenish and repeat: open your inventory window and hold down Shift while you left-click the spare stack of gravel. Just enough will be transferred from there to the Quick Access stack to bring that back up to 64 units.

Ready for some archery practice? Follow these steps to fling arrows of misfortune:

1 Make the bow the active item in your inventory. Arrows can stay hidden in a regular inventory slot and are depleted automatically.

2 Use the crosshairs to aim at your target. You'll need to learn to account for the arrow's arc through the sky and to lead your target's movement. Aim directly at nearby targets and increasingly above their head as they get further away. If your targets are heading clearly in one direction across your line of sight, just target slightly ahead of that move-ment to make up for the time it takes the arrow to reach them. There's no hard-and-fast rule here: practice does make perfect.

3 Right-click and hold to pull back on the bow. Hold longer for a stronger shot. When it's fully charged, the bow shakes slightly, showing that it's primed for a critical hit with a damage bonus.

4 Fire the arrow by releasing the right mouse button. Fully charged shots leave a trail of stars behind the arrow as it flies.

Arrows deliver substantial damage and are the safest way to deal with skeletons, creepers, and other mobs that also deliver ranged attacks or are just plan dangerous in close proximity.

Various enchantment effects can also greatly increase a bow's strength and versatility, and also provide an unlimited supply of arrows.

Armor-All

Armor is crafted from leather, iron ingots, gold ingots, and diamond gems. A fifth type of armor made from chain mail can't be crafted but is available as a tradable item in some vil-lages, if you are lucky enough to find it. (See Chapter 11, "Villages and Other Structures," page 217.)

A full suit of armor requires 24 units of source material, but they don't all have to be the same type. It's best to think of armor not as a complete suit but as its individual parts: a helmet, chest plate, leggings, and boots. Each can be made from a different material, depending on what you have on hand, and each adds to the damage protection value that protects your entire body, regardless of where you are hit. Your avatar is, to put it plainly, one giant hit box...like a punching bag that can also strike back.

I mentioned in Chapter 3, "Gathering Resources," that each armor icon represents an 8% reduction in the damage you'll take, so a 10/10 suit of armor will reduce the damage you take by 80%, whereas a 1/10 suit will absorb only 8%. Armor becomes less effective the more damage it absorbs, although the rate at which it deteriorates also depends on its material, leather being the weakest and diamond the strongest.

NOTE

Which Suit Suits You?

Finding 24 units of any of the materials that can be turned into a suit of armor isn't easy when you're starting out, but if you happen to have spawned near a few cattle, consider starting a farm as described in Chapter 7, and breed the cattle rather than trying to constantly find more out in the wild. Horses also sometimes drop two pieces of leather on death. If you haven't found any willing bovines (or horses, perish the thought—it just seems wrong), mining is the only reasonable option, but ensure you can build up enough of a stock of iron ingots for your tools before turning additional ones into armor.

Your HUD shows the total defense points for your current armor. As with the other bars, each unit represents two points, decreasing by half an icon as each point depletes.

Table 5.2 lists the maximum damage absorption provided by each armor material. Various enchantments can also improve the damage absorption of each type, with gold fairing the best, followed by leather, diamond, and iron.

TABLE 5.2 Maximum Armor Protection Values

Type	Icons Displayed	Percent Protection
Leather	3 ½	28%
Gold	5 ½	44%
Chain	6	48%
Iron	7.5	60%
Diamond	10	80%

Having said that, not all the armor components made from one material provide the same damage protection. The chest plate always provides the highest protection, followed by leggings, the helmet and, lastly, boots. The actual ratios differ somewhat between materials but, generally speaking, a chest plate is 3 to 3.5 times as effective as boots. This is also the recommended order for building armor.

The crafting recipes for the different armor pieces are quite simple. I'll show those for iron, and you can just substitute whatever materials you have on hand. The same material must be used for each piece, but as mentioned earlier, you don't need to wear every material from the same type. For example, if you have been able to collect a lot of leather but only a handful of pieces of iron, consider using the leather for a chest plate and the iron for a helmet because this will give you the maximum damage protection from the available resources:

- **Chest plate**—8 units of material

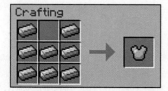

- **Leggings**—7 units of material

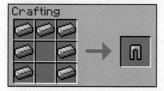

- **Helmet**—5 units of material

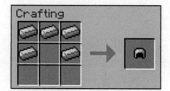

- **Boots**—4 units of material

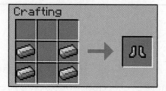

When you've crafted the armor, open your inventory window and Shift-click any piece to automatically shift it to the correct armor inventory slot.

Color Coordinate Your Leather

Leather armor is the only armor that can be dyed. Although this won't help one iota with damage protection, it's possible to step out in style by crafting up any of several hundred thousand different colors for the different armor pieces. Place the armor and different dyes in the crafting grid. Repeating the same dye more than once tends to weight the final color toward that dye. Figure 5.12 shows the result.

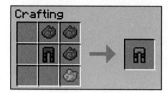

You may be asking the question: why bother? Well, that's true. It's fun to differentiate your character for multiplayer, but it makes no difference otherwise, and it's possible to change the entirety of your character's skin by logging into you account at http://minecraft.net and clicking the **Profile** link. See Chapter 13 for more information.

FIGURE 5.12   Ready for a spot of village trading in colored leather chestplate and leggings, and an iron helmet and boots.

The Bottom Line

Minecraft's hostile mobs are quite a piece of work. Literally. They're creatively constructed, have unique behaviors, drop vital ingredients that allow you to continue your journey, and present an interesting range of challenges. You can't live with them and won't succeed without them.

There comes a time, my friend, when loins must be girded, weapons honed, and armor polished to a mirrored gleam. Go forth and conquer!

Of course, don't do it blindly. Practice around your base first while sharpening your skills. Don't carry too much with you so you don't have to race back for it if you're killed in action. And keep the area around your base well lit to prevent too many hostiles spawning nearby. This will give you a nice stream of stragglers wandering by at night, but in most cases not too many at once.

You can also use a flint and steel to set grass on fire near a hostile, and spilling a bucket of lava can provide a last-ditch option, as long as it doesn't also spill on you.

One final tip: until you have an excellent perimeter defense set up, lead any creepers away from your base and practice your attack runs there. If you die, so be it; death happens, and may happen often. But you'll at least keep the side of your house from looking like it was hit by multiple RPGs.

In time, you will succeed, and picking off hostiles will seem like a walk in the park—maybe Central Park at 3 a.m., but a park nonetheless.

Crop Farming

In This Chapter

- Become self-sufficient with your first crops and optimize your farm.
- Learn the secrets of hydration—it doesn't take much to do a lot.
- Harvest your farm with one click of a button.
- Build a fully automated water harvester.

Farming is fun. There, I said it. I don't mean turning your Minecraft character into Farmer Joe, chomping on a stalk of wheat while slopping out a pigsty. I mean farming the Minecraft way.

Farming in Minecraft refers to any system that creates renewable resources. This concept goes well beyond a simple wheat field. It includes growing a host of different crops that all have a specific purpose and creating fully automated hands-off harvesting systems. In this chapter, I'll take you through the elements of a crop farm and how to transform harvesting from a multiclick chore to one push of a button or twitch of a lever.

Choosing a Crop

Given you can farm just about anything, you may be wondering where to start. Let's go for the basics first because you can easily branch out from there.

Wheat is the most useful to farm initially as three wheat sheaves crafted into bread forms a useful food staple, and wheat is also used for breeding cows and chickens, and taming horses. It's also easy to get started for two reasons:

- You can find the seeds just about anywhere by knocking down tall grass.
- Wheat will grow quite happily without water, although it does grow faster with hydration available.

First find your seeds. You don't need many. When harvested, all growable crops drop up to three times as many seeds as they take to plant. This means you can start with a small stock and quickly expand your plantation as the plants mature. Just harvest, replant, and repeat until the crop reaches your target size. Under optimal conditions, the crop will reach maturity in one day/night cycle.

Before you get started, here are some tips to keep in mind:

- All crops except cocoa beans grow faster when planted near water.

- All crops except cocoa and sugar need their soil prepared with a hoe, converting dirt or grass blocks into *farmland* blocks. The soil can revert to ordinary soil after it is walked on, unless you sneak. Planting a raised bed makes harvesting easier because you don't need to worry about stepping on the soil and can therefore run down the aisle quickly lopping off the produce.

- Use a perimeter fence at least one block high, or two of any other type of block to prevent mobs overrunning your farm and trampling your carefully grown product. This won't keep out spiders, but they don't trample crops.

- All crops grow better in light. Use torches at night to keep the area well lit to prevent mob spawning and to increase the speed at which your crop matures.

- Crops can also be grown underground using the same principals as in the preceding point.

- You don't need an enormous farm to become completely self-sufficient. Figure 6.1 shows one example with every possible crop planted, as well as pens for chickens, pigs, cows, and sheep. It's about as close as you'll get to having your own supermarket.

- Once a farm is established, it doesn't require constant tending. Matured crops don't rot or decay and can be harvested any time you need to top up your pantry.

FIGURE 6.1 The crop with the lot! A farm this size provides more than enough produce and has every component required for every Minecraft recipe.

Each Minecraft crop has some unique characteristics. Table 6.1 provides a full rundown on each.

TABLE 6.1 Crop Types

Crop	Obtain Seeds By	Growth Conditions	Used In
Carrot.	Directly replanting. Occasionally dropped by zombies, but more commonly found in village farms.	Plant on a farmland block with hydration.	Consume as is to restore four hunger points.
Cocoa beans.	Harvesting mature cocoa pods yields cocoa beans that are directly replanted.	Must be grown on jungle wood blocks. The blocks can be stacked with pods planted on each face.	Cookies, and also for creating a brown dye.
Melon.	Placing melon slices, obtained by harvesting melon, in a crafting slot.	Same space requirement as pumpkin.	Melon slices (each block provides 3–7 slices, with each slice restoring 1 hunger point). Also used to create glistering melon, an ingredient for brewing potions. Nine melon slices can be reformed into a single melon block and used for construction.
Potato.	Directly replanting. Occasionally dropped by zombies, but more commonly found in village farms.	Plant on a farmland block with hydration.	Consume as a baked potato by cooking in a furnace (restores six hunger points).
Pumpkin.	Placing a pumpkin block in a crafting slot.	Plant with clear space around each block to allow the pumpkin to grow.	Pumpkin pie (restores 8 hunger points) and to create a jack-o'-lantern.

Crop		Obtain Seeds By	Growth Conditions	Used In	
	Sugar cane.	Breaking the top blocks of sugar cane when harvesting and replanting. Leave the lowest block for regrowth.	Must be planted on sand, grass, or dirt that is directly adjacent to water.	Use to craft sugar and paper. Sugar is used in cake, pumpkin pie, and some potions. Paper is used to make books, bookshelves, enchantment tables, and firework rockets.	
	Wheat.	Left-clicking tall grass.	Best with hydrated soil, but any farmland will do.		Bread, and with other ingredients also used in cakes and cookies. Wheat is also an important tool for farming animals.

Establishing a Farm

The first step is to choose a suitable location. You'll probably want something fairly close to your house, and in a reasonably flat area, although you can also adjust the landscape as required by removing any stray blocks. Figure 6.2 shows the outer edge of the same farm from Figure 6.1. The entire rear quarter of the farm is essentially suspended on a floating platform.

FIGURE 6.2 In difficult terrain, farms can float using just a one-block-deep dirt platform.

CAUTION

Stay Close for Growth

As you've probably already noticed, Minecraft's world is enormous. If the game kept the entire lot in memory at once and kept all the different crops, mobs, and other blocks updating...well, let's just say you'd need a wicked fast computer—so tricked out you might find it getting co-opted by the Meteorological Bureau to run its weather simulations. Instead, Minecraft keeps just a small section of the world in memory at any one time—and that's the part that's around you to a distance of a few hundred blocks, although this does vary depending on your movement speed and the render distance selected under Video Settings in the Options menu. (In multiplayer, the default setting keeps a swathe of 441 blocks active around each player.)

This chunk updating therefore becomes quite important for farms. You could build a gigantic, fantastic grow-everything farm on a nice flat piece of land, but nothing will grow if you wander too far away, causing that area to be unloaded from memory. Keep your friends close and your farms closer.

To begin, mark out an area sufficient to fit. A single block of water can hydrate a square of 9×9 farmland blocks, assuming it is positioned in the middle (see Figure 6.3). This is a space 4 blocks in each direction from the water block, providing a total of 80 farmable blocks after discounting the one in the center occupied by the water. Each block will provide one bushel, or a total across the plantation of 26 loaves of bread each harvest. That's a lot of produce—more than is needed—so instead consider starting with something a little smaller. A smaller area will also be easier to fence.

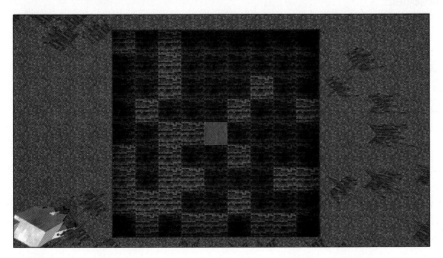

FIGURE 6.3 Hydration from a single water block extends out four blocks in each direction.

In Figure 6.4, I've laid out a smaller field of 35 farmland blocks. The lake provides hydration down one side, extending in a total of three rows from the fence bordering the lake. The single water block on the other side hydrates the rest. Placing a path up the middle isn't strictly necessary because there's no reason you can't trample up and down the field during the harvest, working your way in from the edges while holding down the left-Shift button to sneak across the fields, but I prefer touches like that for aesthetic reasons. Also, particular blocks will mature earlier than others, so the path ensures access to matured blocks in the middle of the field that would otherwise require walking over planted ground to reach.

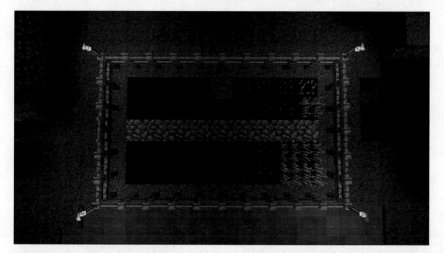

FIGURE 6.4   The seeds that come from harvesting crops allow almost any sized plantation to quickly multiply. There's no need to plant every block when you're starting your first field.

The first harvest provided a total of 16 bushels of wheat and 27 seeds. The bushels produce 5 loaves of bread with one bushel left over. The 27 seeds are almost sufficient now to plant the entire field with just 8 blocks still vacant. They'll be planted with the seeds from the next harvest shown in Figure 6.5.

The steps for creating your own field are therefore quite easy:

1 Find a suitable area using terraforming if necessary.

2 If a water source isn't available nearby, craft a bucket from three iron ingots, place in a quick access slot, and then fill it from a source. You'll need to right-click the bucket on a water source block to successfully fill it. Water source blocks are present anywhere there is water, but water can also flow seven blocks from the source, so you may need to try clicking several times to get to the actual source block. You also need to be playing in Survival mode because buckets don't fill in Creative mode.

TIP

Creating a Permanent Watering Hole

Give yourself a constant source of water by digging out a 2x2 hole and filling the two diagonally opposite corners with water. The water source becomes self-sustaining, replenishing indefinitely no matter how many times you fill your bucket. This same trick does not work for lava.

---

3 Use a hoe to till any grassy or dirt blocks into farmland.

4 Put up a fence or erect any other barrier two blocks high to keep out mobs. Fences are created from sticks, with each set of six making two fence panels.

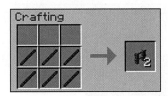

5 Fences are actually **1.5** blocks high, so they can't be jumped. Add a gate for easy access.

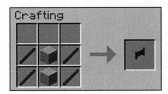

6 Add some torches to the perimeter to ensure mobs don't spawn inside the field and to keep the crops growing through the night.

7 Plant the seeds you collected previously by right-clicking on the tilled blocks.

Give the crop a little time to grow. It can take a few day/night cycles depending on light conditions, although it might take just one if lighting and hydration are optimal. Wheat bushels are only produced on mature wheat crops that have reached their final stage of growth. When the tops of the crop turn brown, they're ready.

TIP

Grind 'Dem Bones

Bone meal, crafted from regular old skeleton bones (assuming they're not using them to shoot arrows at you!), gives almost every crop a boost. The growth spurt won't take a crop instantly from seedling to fully grown plant, but it does push the crop forward one or more stages. Although bone meal can help melon and pumpkin plants grow to maturity, it won't speed up their crop formation. However, one dose of bone meal on a grass block will also encourage tall grass to grow in a 10x10 space. This is a great way to collect all the seeds you need to start a wheat field! A little bit of fertilizer can go a long way.

You can use any tool to harvest the wheat, because harvesting does not impact durability. Just left-click each crop block and pick up the results.

Figure 6.5 shows the second crop ready to harvest, producing 27 bushels and 43 seeds.

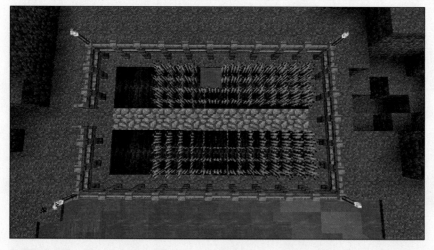

FIGURE 6.5 The wheat field now produces enough seeds to be self-sustaining, allowing the complete field to be planted and leaving plenty left over for bread and other uses.

It won't take long until you are producing more than enough wheat and seeds. Keep them handy. You can use wheat to lure and breed cows, and seeds do the same for chickens. See Chapter 7, "Taming Mobs," for more information.

Figure 6.6 shows an alternate farm layout with two raised beds to make harvesting easier. You can just run up and down the aisle with the left mouse button held down, quickly collecting the wheat. When planting, do the same with the right mouse button held down. The central water troughs collect any harvested bushels and seeds that fall into them and sweep them to the end of the rows making for easier collection, although you'll need to run around to pick up any strays that didn't get knocked in. Arranging this system correctly is quite important. Follow these steps:

1 Make two raised beds 17 dirt blocks long, leaving a single row in between. I generally make the beds two blocks wide.

2 Place two blocks on top of each other directly in the middle—that's nine blocks from the end—and attach a torch to each side of the top block that faces water. Leave the other sides free so that you can plant crops on the two adjacent farmland blocks. The additional light will help your crops grow. In Figure 6.6, I've also placed a jack-o'-lantern on the center block because lanterns throw out a bit more light than torches, and if you squint hard, they look a tiny bit like a scarecrow's head.

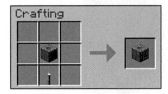

3 Place a water source on either side of this block. Each water source creates a river that runs down the central channel ending after exactly eight blocks, directly aligned with the end of each row.

TIP

Leveling Up Your Hydration Skills

Water can hydrate one level down but never up, so always ensure your water flows either on the same level as your crops or just above them. In both cases, it will still hydrate up to four horizontal blocks away, even with a gap in the middle.

3 It isn't absolutely necessary to build a nice cobblestone path all the way around, as is shown in Figure 6.6, but it's nicer that way.

4 Fence the area off any way you think will work best and then hoe and plant the blocks. You'll find it easiest to work on the inner section of each bed, first running along the edge holding down your left mouse button to till the blocks, and then with seeds selected using your right mouse button to quickly plant them.

5 When harvest time comes, just use any tool to quickly knock out the wheat and seeds. Most that are flung away from you will wind up in the water and wash down toward each end of the beds. Because the beds are hydrated, you can also run up and down them to pick up any seeds or wheat left behind without too much worry about reverting the beds to dirt blocks. Dry beds revert much faster!

6 Knock the mud out of your shoes (just kidding), and go bake some bread!

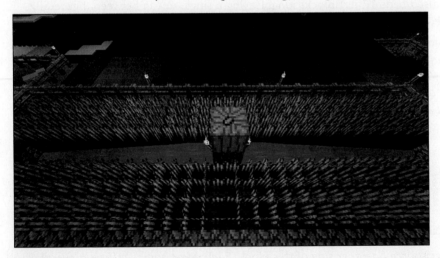

FIGURE 6.6 Raised beds make it easier to plant and harvest, and the central water supply never dries up and conveniently washes harvest crops down to collection points at either end.

Automated Farms

Automated farms can save a lot of the tedium involved in harvesting crops, even if they don't help with the planting. There are an essentially endless numbers of ways to build these, with some variations according to the crop, but each primarily relies on one of three methods:

- Pistons cut across the top of crop, sweeping the harvest into a channel of water that carries them to a convenient central collection point.
- Pistons move the block on which the crop stands, shaking the harvest loose.
- A torrent of water floods the entire crop, carrying the harvest down to a single location. The water can be controlled using sticky pistons or a water dispenser.

NOTE

Want to Be Moved? Use a Piston

Pistons are one of the most useful features of Minecraft's redstone system. I'll show you how to use them here for farming, but you'll also find a lot more detail on these and all the other juicy redstone equipment in Chapter 9, "Redstone, Rails, And More."

Figure 6.7 shows a piston farm that uses the first two methods mentioned earlier: using a piston to cut the top of the crop, and shaking the farmland itself to break loose the harvest.

The principles used in Figure 6.7 are fairly simple. Pulling the lever with a right-click of the mouse causes the sticky pistons to extend (see Figure 6.8). This pushes the raised farmland across the top of the lower rows, harvesting those crops by scraping them into the central water channel. At the same time, the movement of the raised farmland causes its crops to shake loose. Return the lever to its off position, and the pistons retreat. Because they are *sticky*, they also pull the attached farmland block back into its original position.

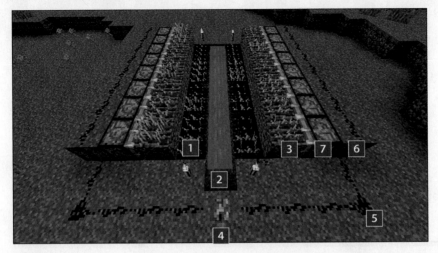

FIGURE 6.7 This wheat farm uses two types of piston farming to automate the harvest.

1. A row of standard farmland block, hydrated by the water flowing from a water source block positioned up the far end of the central channel

2. Collection point for the harvest

3. The raised row of farmland blocks

4. The lever provides an on/off switch and power to the pistons

5. Redstone dust placed on the ground to deliver power to the pistons

6. Pistons placed on their side must be powered by a raised block behind them that carries the redstone current the rest of the way

7. A row of sticky pistons

FIGURE 6.8 The happy harvest. It's still a bit messy, but it completes the harvest more or less instantly.

The only problem with this method is that a lot of the harvest falls outside the collection channel. Also, as you can see from Figure 6.9, once the pistons return to their original position, the entire lower section has to be hoed once more, and the upper farmland blocks revert quite quickly because they're not hydrated. That's a fairly easy fix, though, with some strategically positioned water blocks at each end of the upper rows, shown in Figure 6.10.

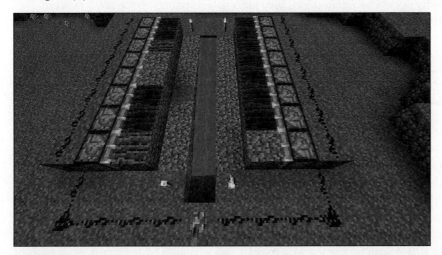

FIGURE 6.9 After harvesting, a lot of the farmland reverts to dirt or grass blocks. The water harvesting method described later solves this issue.

FIGURE 6.10 The corner water blocks help hydrate the upper farmland rows. Actually, in this layout, water in one corner is able to hydrate the nearest raised blocks on the other side because they are still just four blocks away. The gap in the middle is ignored. This can help greatly with creative and efficient farm designs.

NOTE

Semi and Fully Automated Farms

Automated farming doesn't mean quite the same thing for every crop. Melons, pumpkins, and sugarcane can be farmed in a fully automated manner because the stem of the plant stays behind. With a timer-delayed circuit, you can just set it all up and walk away. It will operate indefinitely. All the other automated farms (those for wheat, carrots, potatoes, and cocoa pods) really only handle the harvesting for you. You'll still need to replant seeds for the next crop and break out the hoe to repair any farmland that has reverted to a standard grass or dirt block after harvesting.

Setting up an automated farm can be quite resource intensive. The basic piston used for cutting a crop requires three wood plank blocks, four pieces of cobblestone, an iron ingot, and one redstone. If you've mined extensively and knocked out enough wood, you'll probably already have plenty of these, but it may get trickier when building the sticky piston used for pushing farmland and controlling the flow of water. These are built from a standard piston and a block of slime. If you haven't come across any slime mobs during your travels, you may need to find a way to get to a swamp biome where slimes are much more prevalent or head into a cave structure where you may be lucky enough (if fighting a giant blob of slime can be considered such) to find a few oozing their way across the floor.

However, an automated farm can also be a great way to learn about some of Minecraft's more advanced features. It may all seem a bit confusing at first, but once you have down the basic moves, the rest are really just repetitions of those building blocks, and it won't take you long to start developing some quite amazing layouts. Let's take a look at the different methods step by step

TIP

Getting Creative with Farming

Practice makes perfect, right? Automated constructions can definitely take some time to build and understand. If you're low on resources but really want to try building some of the examples shown in this chapter, consider starting a new world in creative mode and run riot with the unlimited resources. You can then switch back to your current world and continue in "Survivor or Bust!"

Creating a Piston Harvester

The simplest piston harvester is quite easy to build. Figure 6.11 shows a push-button-operated harvesting piston. Levers and redstone provide a way to connect multiple systems so they all operate together, but let's take a look at this first design.

FIGURE 6.11 Automated farming can be quite simple, schematically speaking. No need to get up to your ears in an electrical engineering degree.

1. Water hydration and collector
2. Farmland with crop
3. Piston facing the crop
4. Cobblestone block, although almost any block will work
5. A wooden push-button crafted from a wood plank block

Building this is easy and is a great way to get a basic understanding of how all this automated stuff works. Just follow these steps:

1 Dig a hole for your water supply and fill it from a water bucket.

2 Hoe the grass or dirt block to turn it into farmland and plant some seeds.

3 Create a standard piston. Minecraft always places pistons so that the face of the piston points toward you, snapping toward the closest of the six possible degrees of orientation, so place this one by standing on the block next to the water supply facing the farmland block. Right-click to place the piston on the far side of that block.

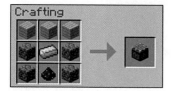

4 Place a dirt, wood, cobblestone, or other kind of solid block behind the piston.

5 Craft a wooden button from wood planks, and right-click to place it on the side of the block behind the piston.

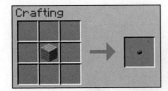

Position yourself close to the button and right-click it to operate the piston. The piston powers up, sweeping the crop off its farmland block. The results may spring directly into your inventory depending on how close you are standing or float around waiting for you to collect them. The piston automatically retracts after a brief delay because buttons send just a brief pulse of power.

Well done! That's all there is to creating a simple piston harvester.

One piston an automated farm does not make, but it's remarkably easy to extend this design into one that is much more effective. Follow these steps:

1 Just replicate the same pattern side by side, minus the button on the side of the back-piston block because there's no room for it.

2 Then run a little trail of redstone dust (right-click on the top of each block with redstone selected in your quick access bar), and you'll create a circuit that links each from the first to the last. Figure 6.12 shows the final picture.

3 Click the button again to push each piston out in unison.

4 For extra props, create the sticky piston harvester and add an extra block of harvesting to each piston every click of that button.

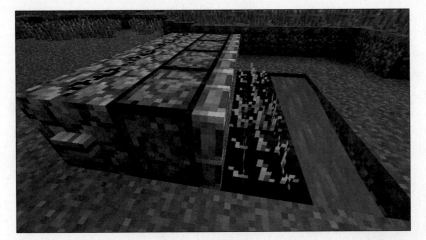

FIGURE 6.12 Set up a row of pistons with a line of redstone dust to create a synchronized one-click harvesting row.

Sticky Piston Harvesting

Sticky piston harvesters work on the same principle as the simple piston harvester with one key advantage: the harvesting power of the piston is doubled because it can also push and pull back a farmland block shaking its harvest loose (see Figure 6.13).

Start by crafting a sticky piston using a standard piston and a slimeball (the sticky part). Then follow the same routine as for a simple piston harvester, but place an additional dirt block directly in front of the piston, hoe it to turn it into farmland, and plant seeds on it and the farmland block in front.

FIGURE 6.13 Sticky pistons stick like glue to the block in front, keeping it attached as the piston moves back and forth. This handy property also makes them an easy way to construct sliding doors and windows and all kinds of other fascinating machines. More on that in Chapter 9.

There's just one problem with using the button system. It's fine for a single row of crops, but what if you wanted to create a system where the entire farm's harvesting is automated with a single click?

Running redstone along the ground provides a central control panel and a coordinated system across multiple crop rows. It has many benefits and only takes a few more steps.

Just decide on a central point, put the button on a block, and run a redstone trail back to the pistons from either side of that block. A redstone current runs for only 15 blocks, so if your trail is longer than that, insert a redstone repeater to boost the current.

Creating a Water Harvester

Using water to harvest wheat has a major advantage over the regular piston harvester: the water washes away the crops but doesn't revert the farmland to a regular dirt block.

There are two basic methods:

■ Use a sticky piston to drop water from a raised water source so that it flows out over the farmland.

■ Use a dispenser containing a filled water bucket to send out a stream of water.

Figure 6.14 shows a farm built using the first method.

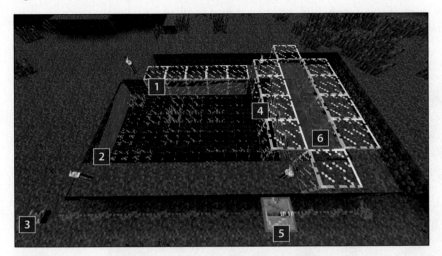

FIGURE 6.14 A water-harvested wheat farm: the glass blocks are just for illustrative purposes and can be replaced with dirt, cobblestone, or any other type of block.

1. Hydration source
2. Collection stream
3. Lever set to "On" because this type of harvesting only drops water when the power goes off
4. Row of sticky pistons in their extended position holding back the water
5. Redstone repeater required to amplify the power due to the length of the circuit
6. Water source used for harvesting, suspended by the extended pistons

The layout of the piston system is a little difficult to detect in a completed working farm, so Figure 6.15 shows a simplified view. The water source is held in place by the surrounding blocks. In Minecraft's geometry, the extended piston beneath also prevents it from flowing down. However, as soon as that piston is retracted, the pathway through the block under the water opens, allowing the water to flow out over the crops.

Levers work better than buttons on this type of layout because you want the water to keep flowing until the crop has been washed away. Make one with a block of cobblestone and a stick.

FIGURE 6.15   Close-up of the piston and water source block.

When creating this type of farm, make sure you build up all the surrounding components including the pistons, powered and therefore extended, before you place the water sources in the upper reservoir. Otherwise, you end up wading through a constant flow of water, fighting the current, as you build the rest of the farm. You also can't place redstone dust in water, and that can make the wiring something of a challenge if any water has escaped to places it shouldn't.

The other method described relies on a dispenser block. Figure 6.16 shows, again, a simplified view that you can easily extrapolate into a complete farm.

The dispenser layout is easier to build than the water-drop used previously but also more resource-intensive because dispensers require redstone, an undamaged bow, cobblestone, and, in this case, a bucket filled with water.

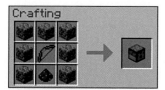

Place the dispenser with its outlet facing the crops. Then right-click the dispenser to open its own inventory window. Place a full water bucket in one of the slots. Your dispenser is locked and loaded! By the way, dispensers are a lot of fun. You can load them with all kinds of items, shooting out arrows at mobs, pumping out lava, bone meal, shooting fire. They're great for traps because they can operate with trip wires and pressure plates—a popular feature in jungle temples where they're pretty good at transforming anyone in mere moments from intrepid explorer to something more akin to a skewered kebab!

Finally, rather than using a lever, I've used a wooden button attached to the side. Just right-click the button to start the flow of water, and right-click again to stop it. Connect a number of dispensers in sequence by running redstone dust along the top of each block. That single button still controls them all.

FIGURE 6.16 Simplified layout for a water dispenser harvester.

Harvesting Other Crops

Sugar cane, pumpkin, melons, and cocoa pods all work best using a slightly different and nondestructive method of farming.

Sugar cane can be harvested using a standard piston raised above ground level (see Figure 6.17). This piston is operated from a lever made from cobblestone and a stick.

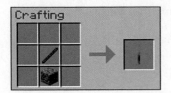

The piston shears off the sugar cane, leaving the original stalk still implanted so that it can grow again.

You can harvest all the other crops by placing pistons beside the main stem's growth blocks. As with sugarcane, the piston shears off the crop, leaving the original plant untouched.

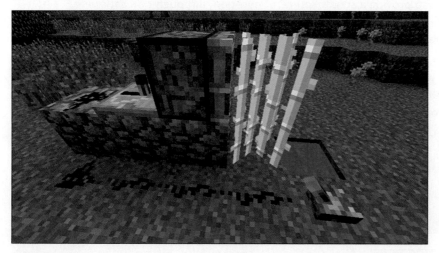

FIGURE 6.17 This cane-shearing piston is operated by a lever.

UNDERGROUND FARMING

If you've found that you prefer to spend most of your time building a mine, you may also like to go full time with an underground farm. The principles are the same as for any farm. Just hollow out a large enough space and place plenty of torches to keep things well lit and to prevent mobs from spawning. Underground farms have the advantage that they can be properly secured from hostile mobs so that you can tend the crops anytime of the day or night without fear of being sniped by a skeleton over the fence or straying too close to a lurking creeper.

The Bottom Line

Crop farming is an important part of Minecraft because the results play a huge role in crafting, brewing potions, and satisfying hunger. And, as you know, a full hunger bar restores health, so you absolutely shouldn't contemplate venturing out for extended periods without also carrying a good supply of food. Without potions, it's the only way you can quickly restore health.

You can start with very simple layouts, choosing the crops according to whatever you can gather from nearby biomes. If there's no tall grass for wheat seeds, look for a nearby village. You can probably pinch some potatoes and carrots while you're there. Avoid food poisoning by baking your potatoes in a furnace before consuming—unless you are in desperate straits. Melons also provide a steady source of nutrition, although only satisfying 1.2 hunger points per slice. Cocoa beans, pumpkins, and sugar cane all require at least wheat to become food grade, so it's best not to start with them.

Of course, cows, pigs, and chickens are all good sources of food, and there is one other natural harvest worth mentioning: the fungi. Find some red and brown mushrooms, and you can make a hearty mushroom stew that also provides a huge 7.2 points of saturation. First create a wooden bowl from three wood plank blocks (bonus: you'll get four bowls from this!), and then arrange the mushrooms and bowl on the crafting table. Yum!

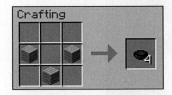

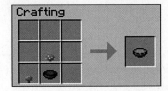

Taming Mobs

In This Chapter

- Create a passive mob farm for a constant supply of eggs, meat, and more.
- Tame ocelots to scare off creepers and use wolves for self-defense.
- Gallop across the world by taming and riding horses and use donkeys and mules to cart supplies and resources.
- Fancy a spot of fishing? Hop on a boat and tap one of Minecraft's unlimited food resources.

Crops are nice and easy to grow, and there is very little hassle involved. If you wanted to live a vegan life, crops could provide everything you need, but you'd also miss out on some key resources that will help get you to the end game.

Minecraft's passive and neutral mobs (those that don't actively seek to kill you) can provide food, ingredients for crafting, decorative items, transport, and, very handily, defense and attack assists.

In this chapter I'll show you how to make the most of Minecraft's animal kingdom.

Farming and Working with Friendly Mobs

Mob farms create replaceable resources through breeding. Each animal is a little different, so I've compiled the list of characteristics in Table 7.1.

The most useful are all shown in Figure 7.1, a working farm with sheep, chickens, cows, and pigs. Fortunately, all the animals are self-sufficient and never starve to death. All you need to do to keep the numbers up is breed one pair for every other one that goes to the friendly mob farm in the sky when you need some of their rather handy resources.

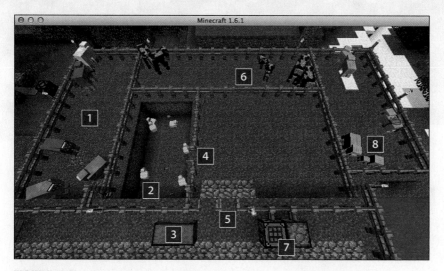

FIGURE 7.1   A passive mob farm.

1. Sheep pen, with sheep dyed a couple of different colors
2. Chicken yard dug down two blocks to prevent them flying out
3. Chest for storing harvested items
4. Gate to chicken yard—access gained from a ladder against the wall just below the gate (chickens haven't yet learned to climb ladders)
5. Double gate provides access to the corralling yard
6. Cattle pen
7. Crafting bench and furnace for working on the spot
8. Pig pen—can you see the one with the saddle?

Farming involves a few basic steps that I'll take you through in more detail as this chapter progresses:

1 Do like Noah, and collect at least two of each creature.

2 Lure them back to your farm, either with food or, even easier, dragging them on the end of a lead.

3 Ensure their enclosure is secure with a one-block high fence or a two-block high dirt or other type of wall. (Chickens need a two-block high fence or a three-block high wall.)

4 Get the animals in the mood for breeding using the specific food for that species (no need for candlelit dinners for two).

5 Wait 5 minutes and they'll be ready to breed again, so repeat step 4

6 Wait 20 minutes (24 Minecraft hours), and the newborn will have matured and can also start breeding.

In just a few day/night cycles, you'll have the farm fully established.

By the way, there's no need to go all Texan and build a giant cattle-yard. If this is just for your needs and not a cooperative multiplayer game, two breeding pairs of each type will provide plenty of resources.

TABLE 7.1 Passive Mob Leading and Breeding Guide

Animal	Lead or Tame With	Breed Using	Provides
Cows	Wheat	Wheat	Leather, raw beef when killed, and milk
Sheep	Wheat	Wheat	Wool; can be dyed to create different colors of sheep
Mooshrooms	Wheat		Mooshroom stew (by milking) and red mushrooms from shearing
Pigs	Carrots (or wheat on Xbox)	Carrots (or wheat on Xbox)	Pork chops; pigs can also be ridden with the help of a saddle and a carrot on a stick
Chickens	Seeds	Seeds	Chicken, feathers, and eggs
Horses	Right-click with an empty hand to tame; wait until thrown off, and then repeat	Golden apple or golden carrot	Ride to gain super-fast transport
Donkeys	Right-click with an empty hand to tame; wait until thrown off, and then repeat	Golden apple or golden carrot	Ride and equip with a chest for transportable storage
Mules	Right-click with an empty hand to tame; wait until thrown off, and then repeat	The only way to get a mule is by breeding a horse and donkey	Ride and equip with a chest for transportable storage
Wolves	Tame by feeding them bones	Porkchops, raw beef, steak, chicken, and rotten flesh	Tamed wolves will follow you (unless told to sit) and attack any mob that attacks you or any that you attack
Cats (Ocelots)	Approach carefully with a raw fish in hand without sudden movements of the crosshairs; when the ocelot approaches, you right-click to give it the fish	Raw fish	Tamed ocelots turn into cats and in both cases scare the creeps out of creepers

Farms take a little bit of planning; otherwise, they turn into an exercise in herding cats. Ensure that all animals have to go through a corralling yard to actually escape. This is a double-gate system, with the same purpose as an air lock and can be shared by all pens. It can be quite tricky to get out and close a fence gate with the herd wandering around at random. Herds have a habit (or perhaps a secret strategy) of preventing you from closing the gate before one or two have slipped through. The second yard will stop those that do make a run for it from escaping the entire farm. You can try to lead them back by enticing them with food, but that just attracts the rest of the group, making for double-trouble. A lead makes it easier (see below), or you can just treat any escapees as volunteers for the chopping block.

Farm animals don't need to be fed, but wolves do. Their tail acts as a health indicator. If a tamed wolf's tail sticks straight out, it's in full health, gradually dropping down as its health decreases. Any sort of meat will do, cooked or not, including the rotten flesh that zombies drop.

NOTE

Your Farm Is (Mostly) Safe from Hostiles

None of the hostile mobs intentionally attack farm animals, although collateral damage from creepers exploding near you is a possibility, and if you are caught off guard by a skeleton firing arrows over the fence you could—but I'm not saying you should—use a cow for cover.

Using Leads

Although friendly mobs can be enticed to follow you with the items listed in Table 7.1, a surer method is to craft a lead from four pieces of string and a slimeball. Right-click to attach the lead to the mob and, if possible, it will follow you as shown in Figure 7.2. You can also right-click to tie a lead to a fence or post—handy to help prevent them wandering off during the night if you haven't had the chance yet to fence them in. Leads can stretch a maximum of 10 blocks before breaking.

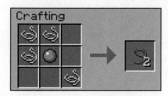

FIGURE 7.2 A wild horse on a lead. It, admittedly, doesn't look very wild. In fact, it waits indefinitely hitched to a fence post while you go looking for that elusive saddle. By the way, horses don't like water too much but can stand on ice.

TIP

When Pigs Fly

In Creative mode, any mob you have attached to a lead can also fly with you. It looks a little like a fire-fighting helicopter carrying a water hopper, but it can be done. Just ascend gently so the leash doesn't break. The mobs sustain damage if dropped heavily onto land, and it is quite difficult to do this gently because they tend to bounce up and down at the end of the lead like yo-yos. It's easier to drop a mob down into a body of water instead of onto a hard block so they don't sustain any damage.

Breeding Animals

Breed animals by right-clicking on them while holding their favorite snack. You'll know you're on the right track when you see the floating love hearts appear above them (see Figure 7.3). To create offspring, feed two of the same species that are standing close together. Minecraft doesn't have any sex determination, so any two will do. They'll quickly find each other and, well, I'm not sure how to describe it, but it looks like kissing. A short while later, an infant will appear, taking 20 minutes of real time to reach maturity.

FIGURE 7.3   Love is in the air for this Miss (or Mister) Piggy.

Breeding two sheep whose wool is dyed results in an offspring of the same color. (If the parents are different colors, the offspring's color is randomly chosen as one of the parent's coloring, although some combinations produce a new color.) Dyed wool is used to make colored carpet, so use sheep breeding to generate as much as you need without having to source more dye. It's also possible to dye leather armor and hardened clay, a useful blast-resistant building material made from clay blocks.

NOTE

Dying for Dye?

Minecraft has 16 dye colors made from a combination of original materials and crafting. For example, place a rose on the crafting table to get rose red dye. A dandelion produces yellow dye. The Lapis Lazuli ore produces a deep blue dye, and cocoa beans produce brown dye. Combine Lapis Luzuli dye with bone meal to create a light blue dye. While wool and stained clay are limited to the 16 dyes available, armor can be stained using any combination of dyes. An internal formula mixes them up to produce a new color.

Taming and Riding Horses, Donkeys, and More

The equine contingent in Minecraft provides the fastest transport available, besides flying in Creative mode. Horses are first past the post in the flying hooves race, and with a speed potion can be even faster. Donkeys and mules are pack animals, so they plod along a little slower but are still quite speedy. Even better, you can do anything you would normally do on any of these beasts, including fighting mobs, mining, and collecting dropped items. And their additional length means you can fly over single block holes in the ground without fear of falling, and even jump over much longer gaps.

There is just one associated challenge: you need a saddle to stay on any of the animals for any useful amount of time, and saddles are not too easy to come by. They can't be crafted, so instead try looking in the chests located inside dungeons, desert temples, and Nether fortresses. You may also be able to find a saddle by trading with a villager.

When you're properly equipped, follow these steps to acquire your own equine transport system. (These steps are identical for donkeys and mules, all shown in Figure 7.4.)

1 Find a horse in the wild. This might take some time, so if you do, assume you've been smiled on by the mob-spawning gods. Approach a horse with an empty quick access slot selected in your inventory bar—in other words, empty hands.

2 Right-click the horse to mount it. You'll more than likely be thrown off, but persevere. It may take four or five tries, perhaps even more, but getting thrown off won't bruise you, and you can sweeten the deal for the horse by feeding it wheat, sugar, apples, bread, or a hay bale between attempts.

3 The horse will display the love-heart animation when it's finally tamed.

4 While still mounted, open the inventory window and transfer the saddle to the horse's own saddle slot in the top left of the inventory window.

Now you have a fully steerable mount. Use the standard movement keys to ride and press left-Shift to dismount.

Donkeys and mules aren't as fast as horses, but they can carry items by right-clicking them while dismounted to hang a chest on their side. Each chest holds 15 items, making them the first mob that can help you bring home your haul from the mine.

FIGURE 7.4 From left to right: Horse in iron armor, a mule with chest panniers and saddle, and a camera-shy donkey with the same.

The HUD display changes when riding any equine, as shown in Figure 7.5. The experience bar is replaced by the jump bar, and the animal's health replaces the hunger bar and oxygen bar.

Jumping is easy but, as they say, timing is everything. As you run forward on the horse, you need to hold down the spacebar, charging the jump bar until it peaks all the way to the right. Actually, Figure 7.5 shows a near maximum charge. It may take some practice, and quite honestly you may want to build a little equestrian park if you are determined to perfect this.

Horses, donkeys, and mules vary somewhat randomly, so not all can jump as high or as far as others. Horses are the strongest, and the best seem to be able to clear a wall four blocks high, which is actually pretty amazing given every other mob except spiders can clear only a single block. Horses can also clear up to 12 blocks (or so) when running at full speed, although a slower mount won't make a leap quite so far.

Although riding a horse at full speed can be quite exhilarating, stay away from deeply wooded areas, where it's easy to become entangled in low-lying branches. These can take some time to hack your way out.

FIGURE 7.5 A jump bar almost fully charged. I find it easiest to release the spacebar when it reaches the end of the blue section. Usually, due to my reaction time, it then hits the fully charged point.

Armoring Your Horse

Horses differ from donkeys and mules because they can also wear armor, as shown in Figure 7.6. Armor can't be crafted and can only be found in the same places as saddles. Equip the horse with armor by mounting it and opening the inventory window. Then transfer the armor to the slot just below the saddle.

FIGURE 7.6   A horse in full iron armor. There are three types of armor, in increasing damage resistance: iron, gold, and diamond.

Loading Up the Pack

Attach a chest to a donkey or mule to access additional inventory slots. You need to dismount to do this, right-clicking with the chest in hand.

As a pack animal, donkeys or mules can't be beat, transporting everything you need from one location to another. Figure 7.7 shows an example.

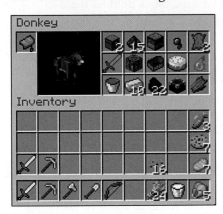

FIGURE 7.7   A donkey loaded with all the essentials for an expedition, including crafting table, chests, a furnace, and a boat.

Riding Pigs

Pigs can't fly in Survival mode, but they can be ridden; they were for a long time the only rideable entity in Minecraft. They also don't need taming first. Just place a saddle on a pig's back and right-click it with an empty inventory slot selected. The pig will move randomly to begin with, but if you craft and hold a carrot on a stick, you can steer the pig normally.

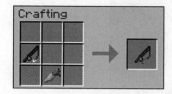

Now that the larger beasts are available, there's not a lot of use for rideable pigs, except for one small trick. Place one in a mine cart, jump on its back, and the pig powers the mine cart, actually moving faster than powered rails. It's another fast way to get around, especially if you don't have the gold available for the powered rails. (See Chapter 9, "Redstone, Rails, and More," for more on railed transport.)

Fishing

Fishing is a great way to ensure a steady supply of food, and it gives you the raw fish required to tame ocelots, turning them into rather cute house cats.

First build a fishing rod from three sticks and two pieces of string.

Any body of water will do, but casting in a way that hits a solid block doubles the decrease in your rod's durability, so always try to cast into deep water. You can do this standing on land, in water, or even sitting in a boat.

Watch the bobber carefully. As soon as it dips below the surface, right-click to reel in the line, and a fish will come flying toward you.

It's generally better to fish in the rain. You'll catch an average of four fish per minute. Otherwise, expect to catch around two per minute. Each rod can catch 65 fish before it breaks, and because it's possible for fish to fly back over your head, losing the catch, it's usually best to fish with your back against a tall wall.

A safer way to fish is actually from a boat, as shown in Figure 7.8. The key advantage is that boats provide protection from land-based mobs. Craft a boat with five wood plank blocks. Place it in a body of water and right-click to jump in. Use the **W** key to move forward and steer by pointing the crosshairs in the direction you want to go. (The left/right keys aren't effective in this mode of transport.) Avoid lily pads and solid blocks while you travel, because they cause damage to your boat. Break up the boat with any hand tool when you've finished fishing to pull it back into your inventory.

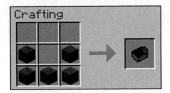

FIGURE 7.8 After a hard day's mining, why not relax in a boat doing a spot of fishing? Boats are also a very fast method of transport—great if you're near an ocean biome.

The Bottom Line

Friendly mobs are more than just field-dressing—they're an important part of Minecraft's gameplay.

Friendly mobs can, however, be tricky to find. If you're lucky enough to spawn in a place with more than a few, go out, hack and slash for some fast food, and then work on pulling in the rest. If you're choices are more limited, try to resist giving the sword-arm a work-out. Friendly mobs don't respawn, so the numbers won't increase, and they can be quickly thinned out. Work on bringing some in and setting up a farm.

You'll find sheep and cows heading toward well-lit, grassy areas. Horses do much the same. Ocelots prefer jungle biomes, and chickens seem to be, well, just about everywhere. Oh, and perhaps the oddest friendly mob in Minecraft, the mooshroom, can be found hanging around their namesake: the relatively rare mushroom biome.

There is one other friendly mob: the squid. It can't be bred, so farming is out of the question, but if you kill one you'll find its ink sacs do make for a mean black dye.

Creative Construction

In This Chapter

- Time for a block party! Build your first aboveground base.
- Decorate your pad with chairs, tables, and paintings.
- Chill out Zen-style with flowing water, pools, and fountains.
- Warm things up with a fireplace or two, not forgetting the BBQ.
- Follow step by step while building an underwater abode
- Protect your perimeter and take pot-shots at mobs with a water trap

This chapter is packed chock-a-block with construction ideas, from a few starting tips on finding sources of inspiration to a detailed list of all the things you can add that go beyond the basic functional elements.

Construction is easy—put one block on top of another. But take heed: once you start, it's hard to stop. Every step is like opening another door, and you'll soon find your imagination running riot.

Even if you have no particular architectural talent (and I must confess that I am absolutely astonished by the incredible feats some have achieved with soaring gothic cathedrals and entire cities that are nothing short of a wonderland), construction starts with a single click.

Leaving the Cave

If you've been busy mining, farming, and doing all the other Minecrafty things that get you established, you probably haven't had the time to build a glorious aboveground structure or to decorate your home with a few nonfunctional items. Well, now's as good a time as any to take a bit of a break. Unleash Minecraft's bevy of building blocks and unlock your creative potential.

Some of the incredible creations players have already created include

- Highly accurate models of famous real-world locations and buildings including cathedrals, towers, castles, palaces, and cultural landmarks. Think the Reichstag, Taj Mahal, Louvre, Westminster Abbey, Sydney Opera House, Empire State Building, and so much more.

- Fictional locations either as faithful replicas or as near as can be achieved, including Tolkien's Middle Earth, Caribbean pirate towns, and in the ultimate homage, levels and locations from other video games, movies, and TV series including, of course, the U.S.S. Enterprise from *Star Trek*. Trekkies are everywhere! See Figure 8.1.

FIGURE 8.1   King's Landing from Game Of Thrones built in Minecraft with incredible attention to detail. (Image courtesy of WesterosCraft)

- Giant pixel art depicting almost anything at all: statues and sculpted creations that are nothing but a glorious exploration of the maker's creative capabilities.

The list can go on and on, but I'll curtail it here. Suffice to say that anything is possible.

NOTE

Get a Whole New Look with Resource Packs

In a standard installation, Minecraft has an organic, pixelated appearance, but it's possible to completely change the look of every block. Resource packs (they used to be called texture packs) make this easy and can change the way your creation looks from the default to rustic, realistic, modern, hi-tech, or even cartoon-like. Hundreds of resource packs are available. More on this and some handy download links in Chapter 13, "Mods and Multiplayer," page 251. If you can't wait see how these look, click over to http://www.minecrafttexturepacks.com to get a feel for them now.

Each Minecraft block is one cubic meter, so many replicas are built to a 1:1 scale—even the entire center of historic Beijing from the ancient city walls torn down by Mao all the way back toward the Forbidden City, with, it seems, almost every *hutong* in place.

Many of these creations are too much for one person, so they have sprung up on multi-player servers. Others, though, represent thousands of hours of effort by dedicated individuals who will often then share the map as a free download.

So, having set the scene, what's the easiest way for you to get started without necessarily budgeting the next six months to a building project?

You can take several approaches:

- **Extend your current shelter**—Keep all the basics in place while building out and up a little at a time.

- **Start from scratch above ground**—Pick a location close to your current spawn point, or strike out to a better location with your bed in hand to reset your spawn. Figure 8.2 shows an example.

FIGURE 8.2 Home, sweet home, perched far above the madding crowd.

- **Head to the nearest village**—A village is a handy location to set up home if you don't mind the villagers' constant creaky grumbling that makes them sound like they need a quick squirt of WD-40. Once established you can harvest their farms without them getting upset, and there's often at least one villager happy to swap wheat for emeralds, which you can then use to trade for other items. Just don't forget to replant their fields for the next time because the villagers, a lazy bunch, don't do that themselves.

- **Dive**—Not all shelters need to be aboveground or deep in a cave. I've included a tutorial on building underwater later in this chapter.

TIP

Floating Blocks

Minecraft ignores basic physics on almost all the standard blocks except for sand and gravel. This enables the creation of gravity-defying structures. Stack them as high as you like, build out to a platform, and then remove their lowest layer to create a floating structure in the sky. Imagine a fortress connected to the ground with just a single block. It's perfectly possible.

There are as many approaches to building aboveground as there are different worlds in Minecraft. The easy way is to go for a box design. It doesn't take much effort and is something of a natural starting point. But you could also go for a walk around your actual neighborhood grabbing photos with your phone or camera. If you'd prefer not to have a run-in with Neighborhood Watch, check out some online real estate sites. They often have multiple photos and architectural plans. YouTube also hosts numerous videos that players have created to show off their amazing creations.

NOTE

Multiplayer Construction Rules

Multiplayer servers implement different sets of rules around construction with blocks often locked down to prevent *griefing*, aka wanton vandalism by random visitors. Knock a block out, and it immediately pops back. Trusted, or *whitelisted*, players typically gain greater access to allow for co-operative builds, or to build on their own lots. Gaining this trust can be as simple as registering your email address, or as complicated as submitting the equivalent of a resume to prove that you have the necessary construction credentials before you're set loose.

Unleashing Your Interior Decorator

Not everything in Minecraft has to be functional. Figure 8.3 shows there are all kinds of components that can be put together in different ways to create a homey ambience, both indoors and out.

FIGURE 8.3   The living room with wide-screen TV, modular lounge with coffee table, sun bed, dining table, and fireplace. There's also a kitchen tucked in the back-right corner.

I've put together a collection of different ideas for you, but this is also one of those things where your own creativity and experimentation comes into play. Try out some of these in a world set to Creative, and let the juices flow:

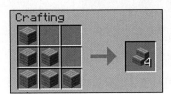 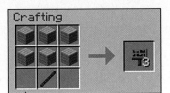

■ **Chairs**—Chairs are made from staircase blocks. Craft a staircase from six wood blank blocks. The chairs can be as long or as short as you want, from single seats to a modular lounge. Placing signs or trapdoors (in their open position—right-click to toggle them) on the sides creates armrests. Extending the base of the chair with a slab creates a deck-chair effect that's perfect around a pool or on a sun deck. Figure 8.3 shows a view of chairs around a dining table (see the next bullet).

NOTE

Placing Signs

Signs placed against a block attach to the side of that block. Signs placed on top of a block become freestanding with their orientation fixed so that they face you at the time they're placed.

- **Dining table**—Create a table by placing a single fence block, which becomes the stand. Then place a pressure plate on top of the post to form the table's surface. Pressure plates don't create a seamless surface, so for larger tables consider using squares of carpet instead. Surround the table with a few chairs to complete the picture. If you make a giant dining table, use regular blocks and then place pressure plates or carpet as placemats. Remove some squares of the table's surface, and pop some cake down in their place to finish the picture, as shown in Figure 8.4.

FIGURE 8.4 A dining table with Antoinette-approved centerpiece. Let them eat cake.

- **Beds**—Think of the standard Minecraft bed as just the starting point. Put two side by side for a double, or make a king size bed out of three and some blocks behind for a headboard. Then place some slabs at the foot to get the proportions right.

- **Bedside table**—Use a standard construction or wood block or a bookcase—anything that matches your color scheme. Then put a torch on top in the middle of the block. The torch will burn permanently, but if you put a redstone torch in the middle and then a lever on the side of the block, you'll have a light you can switch on and off. Replace the redstone torch with a redstone lamp for much brighter lighting.

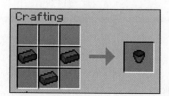

- **Indoor plants**—Choose a plant such as a flower, sapling, cacti, or leaf block cut from a regular tree with shears or a tool enchanted with silk touch. Pick a base block such as grass, dirt, or sand; plant it, and attach signs or trapdoors to its sides to give it a nice boxed look, as shown in Figure 8.5, or create a flower pot from three bricks. Smelt clay to make bricks, arrange them into pots, and plant flowers, saplings, ferns, and mushrooms (see Figure 8.6).

- **Hedges**—Leaf blocks also work well in decorative construction. Use them to build hedges lining a path or parkway. You can even use them for the walls of a tree house. The blocks won't decay, unlike regular leaf blocks that are no longer attached to their trunk.

FIGURE 8.5 Planter boxes and hedges add a leafy touch to rooms and balconies. Saplings are also safe to plant indoors because they won't grow without empty blocks above.

FIGURE 8.6 Flower pots are a decorative planter. Place them on almost any surface.

- **Fantasy trees**—Use wood and leaf blocks to create unique trees dotted around your estate. You can even place them inside a giant atrium, creating your own Crystal Palace.

- **Item frames**—Crafted from eight sticks and one piece of leather, item frames serve a decorative and practical purpose as single item storage. Place the frame on any wall and then take the object you'd like to store in hand and right-click the frame to place it inside. Store that enchanted diamond sword you plan to save for later combat, or maybe a diamond pick for when you need to retrieve more obsidian. Left-click the frame to retrieve both it and the object at a later date. Use an item frame and a clock to create a wall clock, or place a map in the frame for permanent reference. The map updates to show the locations of all other item frames containing maps, making it the only way to actually place a "pin."

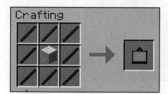

- **Paintings**—These are purely decorative. They have the same recipe as an item frame, but with the leather swapped for any piece of wool. Placing paintings is a little bit random because Minecraft tries to scale it up to suit the flat space available, with some limits. There's a built-in inventory of 26 pieces of art in different shapes and sizes. One way to try to force a correctly sized painting is to first surround the target area with other blocks and then click in the lower-left corner of the target space and remove the additional blocks. It doesn't always work, but this is a little less random than other methods.

- **Fountains**—Build fountains as simple or complex as you like. Place a water source on top of any other structure. Glass blocks work quite well for this, but any block will do. Create a hollow fountain by removing the blocks after you've placed the water. Also, don't forget to put a surround around the base so the cascade doesn't turn into a flood. Figure 8.7 shows one example.

- **Ponds and pools**—As long as water drops one level every seven blocks, it can flow on forever from a single source. Use this to create water features that flow down and through your house into a pond. Add a few floating lily pads to complete the effect.

Pools are a nice touch that can look good surrounded by almost any smooth blocks, especially with the addition of deck chairs mentioned above.

FIGURE 8.7 This small indoor fountain feeds the swimming pool located on the recreation level of the house.

- **Netting and wisps**—Cobwebs gathered with shears or silk touch can stand in as netting between two posts. Tennis, anyone? Use redstone to draw lines on the court. Cobwebs can also suggest smoke billowing from a chimney, or for the lashings and cargo nets on ships.

- **Bookshelves**—Although bookshelves have an official use for enhancing enchantments (see Chapter 10, "Enchanting, Anvils, and Brewing," for the full details and crafting recipes), they're also an excellent decorative item. Stack them up where needed to build a library or add some interesting ambience to any living room. Slabs also work well and are easier to make than the bookshelf item. Stack them up to create multiple shelves and dress the sides with regular blocks, or just run them straight to the wall to make them appear as built-in shelves.

- **Raised and lowered floors**—Slabs are half a block high, making them ideal for creative flooring and embedded fixtures. Although items placed on a slab seem to float, two sets of slabs can lead down to a sunken lounge or indoor pool. And if your design extends to the bathroom, create a slab floor leaving a one-piece hole against the wall. Place a cauldron in it and fill it with water to make a recessed sink. Slabs are also a useful way to hide redstone wiring. They'll float one block up with the redstone running underneath out of sight, saving an additional layer of trench digging. More on this in Chapter 9, "Redstone, Rails, and More."

- **Fireplaces**—You need to know just two things about fireplaces. Netherrack (a block from The Nether) burns forever. Set it on fire with a flint and steel and bask in the glow. The other thing, perhaps slightly more important, is that fire is catching. Don't surround your fireplace with wood blocks. As a matter of fact, don't have anything flammable within at least two blocks, or more just to be sure. Use nonflammable materials such as cobblestone and bricks. Fireplaces look great with a glass pane in front of them (see Figure 8.8). They also make a pretty decent BBQ (see Figure 8.9) or fire pit outdoors. S'mores, anyone?

FIGURE 8.8   A modern fireplace set inside a wall with a pane in front. The fire provides a dynamic animation, making a room feel warm and alive.

FIGURE 8.9   This BBQ is made from a mix of brick blocks and staircases. Note that the trapdoor, like a door, doesn't burn, so it is safe to position above the fire.

Construction is one of the indulgent pleasures in Minecraft. In Creative mode, you'll have access to the full range of available materials, but there is also something to be said for building an amazing structure in Survival mode. Having to find the materials first really adds to the experience.

Building Underwater

There's not a lot of justification for undertaking the effort to build an underwater house—except that you can! It's a fun challenge. An underwater house provides great visibility, is immune to hostile mobs including the creeper, and, well, it's just pretty darn cool. This type of house can take a little bit of extra work, but it's fairly easy, and you can let your imagination take you anywhere you want to go, from the equivalent of a reversed aquarium, with you as the soul internee, to a full remake of Bioshock's Rapture. Figure 8.10 shows a small underwater base.

FIGURE 8.10 Make like a dolphin and head underwater to build your aquatic base.

Building underwater is a methodical process. The trick is to consider it the inverse of mining. Instead of removing material, you actually want to fill in the entire shape of your structure to displace the water, place the final shell of the building around that (for example, glass blocks), and then remove the internal material to create the living area. There's no method of pumps or pipes to suck water out or pump air in, so this displacement system is the only viable method.

There are a few ways to go about it.

In Creative mode, it's just a matter of taking the time and a bit of care. You can stay underwater as long as you need.

Survival mode adds a twist because running out of air is a constant risk. It becomes vitally important to keep a close eye on the oxygen bar and your health bar. Swimming up from the bottom of a lake *always* takes longer than expected, causing hits on your health, so the real trick is to find a way to create an air supply down below.

At a minimum, ensure your kit includes these items:

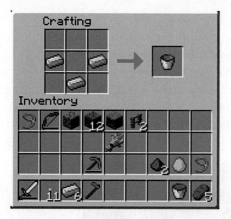

- **One bucket**—Crafting a bucket takes just three iron ingots and provides you with the equivalent of a limitless tank of air.

- **Doors, ladders, and signs**—These blocks displace water but leave space for you to stand and grab a breather. You can make do with just one of any type, but it's best to pack a few.

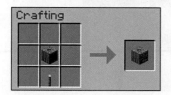

- **Light sources**—Torches go out in a soggy fizz as soon as they hit water. Jack-o'-lanterns work best and can be smashed up and repositioned as required. Glowstone from The Nether also works well. See the sidebar "Light Up Your (Underwater) Life" for another option.

- **Construction equipment**—Bring the usual suspects—a couple of shovels for digging sand, dirt, and gravel, and some pickaxes for the harder stuff. An axe also makes it easier to reposition other equipment such as doors.

- **Soft blocks**—You need several full stacks of dirt, wood, sand, or gravel as temporary filler material to remove the water from your construction. By the way, I'll use the term "soft blocks" to refer to the temporary blocks you'll use during construction—those you can remove quickly with a shovel while underwater.

- **Construction materials**—You need lots of glass blocks for the outer shell, as well as any other material you want to use.

■ **Food**—It's important to keep a full hunger bar underwater so that your health recovers quickly if you run out of air.

TIP

Survive with an Island Spawn Point

Underwater construction can be a hazardous business, so place a bed nearby and take a nap before you begin. If your spawn point is nearby, you can get back down quickly enough to pick up any dropped items should you suffer a watery demise. If you are building too far offshore, use a boat to return quickly, or build an island platform on the surface, perched on top of a single block tower. It just needs to be big enough for a bed and a torch to prevent mob spawns at night.

There are plenty of methods for getting started, including tunneling in from the side of a lake, but these aren't always practical. The most comfortable I've found is to just jump right in. Here's how:

1 First find a location. At a minimum, the water should be four blocks deep. This gives you two blocks of standing room, a glass roof (because it looks awesome!), and one block of water over the top, but you may also want to go deeper. There are no practical limits; the only concerns are having sufficient air and light, but keep the structure on the conservative side initially. Figure 8.11 shows the exterior view of the structure shown in Figure 8.10.

FIGURE 8.11 Keeping your initial structure to a conservative size helps you get used to building underwater while providing plenty of room to breathe. This one is 9×9 and three blocks high.

2 Keep the bucket in your Quick Access slot, along with a door or, if you are using ladders or signs, have some soft blocks and one of those at the ready.

3 Head to the bottom, and keep a close eye on the oxygen bar. It depletes in 16 seconds. As it drops, take a practice breath. Just right-click with the bucket selected to create a brief pocket of air. If it doesn't work on the first go, click again. Once you start the cycle, it takes one click to empty the bucket and one more to refill it, so as soon as you get used to the double-click, you shouldn't have any problems grabbing a quick gasp to fully reset the oxygen bar in a split second.

4 Place the door as soon as you reach the seabed (see Figure 8.12). If you are using ladders or signs, create a stack of two blocks and then put the ladder or sign on the top block. Any of these actions creates a permanent air pocket you can step into and breathe. Incidentally, jumping into a lake with any of these items at the ready is also a good way to escape hostile mobs at night, and you can poke at the bottom-side of any curious creepers swimming by. What's not to like?

FIGURE 8.12 Doors create a two-block-high breathing space. The jack-o'-lantern provides a waterproof source of light.

TIP

Light Up Your (Underwater) Life

Things get gloomy in the deep. Anything over seven blocks down comes close to pitch black, even during the day, and torches need a full block of clear air to stay lit. How can you light up the murky mire? Jack-o'-lanterns and glowstone both work well. Another option: change your screen settings. Press Esc to open the Options menu. Select **Video Settings**, and shift the **Brightness** slider all the way to the right.

Light tunnels also work well. Place blocks and ladders above your first air-pocket block until you reach the surface. The light flows down the tunnel brightening up the sea floor and provides a convenient access shaft for your submerged traversals.

Now that you have a survivable location on the seabed, it's time to get started on the structure.

Building underwater takes a few steps and a lot of care:

1 Plan out the perimeter. I find it easiest to create an air tunnel around the perimeter using dirt blocks and ladders at eye height, filling in the interior as I go. Figure 8.13 shows an example. All the ladders are recoverable later, and I generally put them on the interior wall so that I can work on the exterior without worrying about removing a ladder and getting swamped by an inrush of water.

FIGURE 8.13 A one-block wide tunnel and ladders keep the water at bay. I've removed all the stray water sources in the lower half of the tunnel by swamping them with sand blocks dug out earlier.

2 As you fill in the interior, also start building up the external shell on the outer side of the tunnel. Use your final construction materials such as glass blocks because this will form the permanent structure. Keep some soft blocks at the ready to plug up any water breakthroughs. The wall only needs to be two blocks high. Given that you're on the bottom of the sea, you can always dig down later to create more height. Place some torches as you go to create additional light, although they won't attach to glass.

NOTE

Flooded In? Head to the Source

It's quite usual to find your tunnels still half flooded even after all the walls are done and every ladder is in place. The damp ankles are caused by water source blocks that still exist on the floor of your perimeter tunnel. To remove them, place any kind of soft block wherever you can see anything that looks like the head of the water spring. This kills the water source, and you can then quickly shovel out the soft block. Rinse and repeat until all the source blocks have been extinguished and your tunnel has dried.

3 With the interior full and the external wall done, it's time to attach the ceiling. This is easy. All you need to do is jump out of the tunnel into the water and run backward across the interior fill, placing blocks as you go. Unless you've planned an enormous structure, it's easy to do a row or two without having to stop for air, but keep your bucket handy just in case. Fill in any gaps you spot in the interior as you go.

4 You're almost there! Just dig out the internal material to fully open the space. Breaking up the soft blocks dislodges the ladders so they can be scooped up into your inventory and perhaps used to create a laddered pillar all the way to the surface.

5 Finally, make an access point. You can place a door or just use a pillar and a ladder outside the wall (see Figure 8.14). Add any finishing touches to the interior, and you're done!

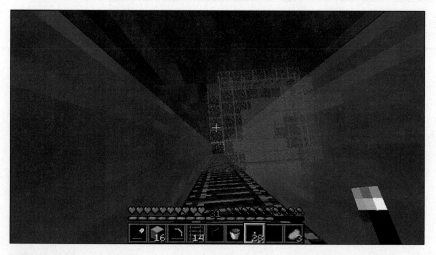

FIGURE 8.14 Looking down a long access ladder from the sea's surface to the undersea dwelling.

Once you've built one room, the rest is even easier. Place a bed down in the first and sleep in it to reset your spawn to the ocean floor, and take it bit by bit. You should have just about all the materials you need, except maybe wood. And you are on the ocean floor, so there's plenty of sand for glass, and there's nothing stopping you digging straight down and mining up other materials as required.

NOTE

Underwater Enchantments

Two enchantments help underwater work. The first is *respiration*, which applies to helmets and increases the length of time you can breathe underwater while also reducing suffocation damage; in addition, it improves your underwater vision. The second is water affinity, a speed boost for tools when they're mining underwater.

One of the key advantages of underwater dwellings is that they don't require protection, at least not until the squids launch their revolution. But those overland do. In the final part of this chapter, I take you through some key strategies for protecting your other perimeters.

Protecting Your Perimeter

There's nothing worse than stepping outside your front door only to hear the quick hiss of a creeper's fuse running down, and to find two seconds later a massive crater that's taken out half your house. (Creepers can take out a block of dirt that measures 5×5×5.) If the explosion doesn't kill you, the next influx of hostile mobs probably will. In any case, rebuilding will be a painful experience, especially if you've gone all out with a delicately aesthetic blend of textures and materials. (A cobblestone wall—okay, that's not so bad, but that's the Building 101 course.)

There is an easy way to step out in the morning and enjoy a breath of fresh air without a pang of fear interrupting the ritual. It's the perimeter—your stake in the world. Varmints be gone!

Become a Ditch Witch

Ditches provide protection without interrupting the view. They were even a feature of English country gardens, known as the *invisible fence*, designed to keep the sheep from trampling the peonies without the fence line blotting the landscape.

In Minecraft, no mobs except spiders can cross a ditch that is two blocks deep and just one block wide, but creepers can still detonate if you're nearby. Build three blocks deep, and they won't trouble you unless you fall in. Or dig two blocks deep and put a fence around the inside edge of the ditch. You won't need to worry about an inadvertent stumble, and creepers will stay nicely defused.

So what about spiders? I don't worry about them too much. They're easy to kill and provide string for bows, fishing rods, and, with sufficient numbers, enough string to make the wool for a bed—handy if sheep aren't around.

TIP

Mobs Go with the Flow

Place water sources in strategic locations in the ditch to wash the mobs downstream away from critical areas. This can help you build a smaller perimeter because you can force them to bunch at the far end of your property (see Figure 8.15).

If spiders still give you the shivers and you want to keep your AAA insurance rating, build a ditch for all other mobs and then a wall behind it with an overhang. Or if you want to get a little fancier, make the third layer of the wall iron bars or a glass pane, and put a final layer on top. Spiders can't get a grip on bars or glass, so you'll still be able to look out on the marauding hordes.

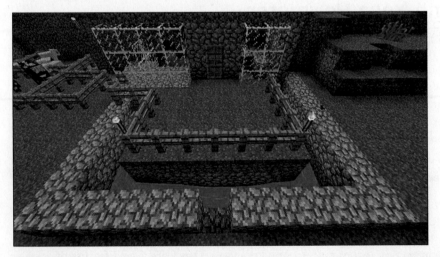

FIGURE 8.15 A ditch with water flowing to a central point (the middle-front here) sweeps any mobs away from the entrance so they can exit through the gap in the front.

CAUTION

Knobble Their Knees

The ditch gathers all kinds of mobs. Some such as zombies and skeletons burn up during the day, but others such as creepers stay. Leave an easy egress of steps out of the ditch to the exterior if you want your ditch to self-clear and aren't using a mob pit and water clearing method described later in the "Mob Pitfalls" section. Or cut in a tunnel under the wall at eye level for you and knee level for the mobs so that you can hack at their feet to collect their drops while being safe from attack. This works best if the tunnel is two steps back from the edge of the ditch so that creepers don't detonate. Your sword can still reach them just fine.

Alternatively, put your house in an unassailable position atop a small stone tower. Enter through a door in the base, build a stairway or ladder going up at least three blocks (or many more if there's a good view!), and create as large a platform as you like. The overhang from the platform keeps spiders at bay. Use other perimeter fences to provide protection for farmland if you don't want to build them all in the air.

CAUTION

Don't Forget the Torches

It's easy to forget, while focusing on the defensive perimeter around the house, that an unlit roof also provides a mob spawning platform at night. If you're wondering how that spider surprised you in the bedroom, it could be because it simply dropped from the sky and climbed in through that opening you left leading out onto a sunny morning verandah. (Been there, done that!) Always place a few torches on your roof to keep things clear. Torches can also help you spot home when you're out and about exploring the Overworld.

Mob Pitfalls

Mobs may be a nuisance, but they're also a boon because they carry all sorts of useful items from enchanted weapons to food. Why not reap the benefits of their fall?

Here's how to do it:

1 Dig a ditch two blocks deep and nine blocks long around your perimeter.

2 Create a vertical pit in the ninth block. The most effective height is a drop of 22 blocks because this leaves spiders, skeletons, and creepers with just 1 point of health—enough to dispatch them with a single punch and gather the resultant experience points that

help with enchanting and anvil repairs. However, if you don't mind using weapons instead, the pit can even be just two blocks lower than the water flow.

3 Place a water source at the other end. It flows for 8 blocks, pushing mobs toward the pit. You can also place a second water source coming in from the other direction, providing a total of 19 blocks of coverage around your perimeter, and the water can flow around corners if required.

4 Choose a safe location inside your perimeter or even inside your house, and tunnel down and toward the bottom of the pit so that your eye height ends up at the same level as the lowest part of the pit. Any mobs that stray into the ditch gradually wash down toward the pit, fall in, and gather at the bottom. Head down the access tunnel to safely finish them off and collect the spoils. Figure 8.16 shows a trapped creeper.

FIGURE 8.16   Creeper knobbled: the water keeps it in place while attacked, and the water washes its drops (gunpowder in this case) toward you.

TIP

Ding! Your Zombies Are Ready

For extra points and convenience, add a pressure plate to the bottom of your pit, connected to a redstone lamp sitting somewhere in normal sight. When a mob hits the bottom of the pit, the pressure plate sends a signal to the lamp, lighting it up. Note: Use normal wooden or iron pressure plates. Weighted pressure plates only react to items, not mobs.

If you have no particular interest in collecting mob drops, fill the pit with lava. Keeping a mob's feet to flame will see the mob off quite quickly, but it also burns up any items. You can also use cacti in the ninth hole of the ditch for the same purpose, serving up death by a thousand cuts. Just place a cacti block instead of digging the pit, but keep in mind that the cacti can also destroy any dropped items.

Thick as a Brick

The defenses previously mentioned are designed to keep mobs at a distance, but the final line in the sand, or cobblestone, will be your own building's walls. This is also an aesthetic choice. Design your castle's keep, so to speak, more than one block thick. A direct creeper hit can take out a couple of layers of cobblestone and up to five layers of other materials. If you really do want that log cabin look, consider creating a sandwich of wood outside, an internal cobblestone section, and then a wood interior. Switch these around to suit your own needs. A couple of layers of external cobblestone with a wood interior is much safer than a single layer of wood. Sandstone has little blast resistance, so definitely create a 3-ply if you like the sandstone look.

Keeping with the concept of a castle's keep, attack is also part of any defensive strategy. Knock out a 1×1 block in a wall and then fill with a slab, leaving just a half block gap. Fire arrows at targets through the slit. You'll have an excellent field of fire, and skeletons will have a much more difficult time getting a clear shot at you.

Finally, obsidian is the toughest minable in Minecraft. It's a little difficult to collect, but you'll find a guide that makes it easy in Chapter 10.

The Bottom Line

It takes a little bit of time to build a beautiful home, but it does provide a pleasant interlude between mining, farming, and fighting mobs. Enjoy the time. As you master the different techniques, you'll no doubt develop your own and create soaring, graceful masterpieces in the sky.

This chapter has been about letting your imagination take flight. In the next, you explore a completely different side to Minecraft: redstone and transport. It may be enough to make you think about all construction from a different perspective.

Redstone, Rails, and More

In This Chapter

- Create automated contraptions with redstone power sources and components.
- Build cool circuits with redstone wiring.
- Understand different types of power to avoid wiring problems.
- Create a perimeter warning system, piston-powered doors, repeater loops, and more.
- Learn to use AND, OR, and NOT gates.
- Use redstone to build powered rails for a minecart transport system.
- Hop into hoppers to automatically load and unload items from containers and carts.

Redstone and rails create an entirely new Minecraft experience.

- **Redstone** is one of the ores you will probably have seen in mines. When dug out and placed on the ground it provides a way to transmit power between different devices, like a strand of electrical wire, and is used for operating pistons, controlling doors, and doing all sorts of other neat tricks.
- **Rails** are tracks on which minecarts run, and when those rails are powered by redstone, they provide a system like an electric train track that can transport goods between different areas, and also give you, sitting in a minecart, quite a thrill ride.

It's a brilliant, almost magical system that draws on some real-life parallels with electrical circuits but is different enough to be absolutely confusing, even baffling, at the same time. It will challenge you to rethink everything you already know. Is it worth it? Absolutely.

The trick to understanding redstone is to try your very best not to bring any real-world assumptions with you. It's a different type of energy than electricity. For example, it runs on a single strand so doesn't have positive and negative wires, and it can be created by many types of devices, even a lever stuck in the ground, or a wooden button attached to the wall. Redstone has its own rules, its own behavior, and its own results. Some of those are almost beyond imagination. I'm betting when

Mojang started thinking about adding a few logic circuits to redstone, they didn't think someone would spend possibly months of his life building a simulacrum of a computer complete with a 1,000-pixel graphical display, the entire system filling hundreds of acres and using tens of thousands of components.

In the same way that the building blocks of Minecraft deliver an architecturally infinite construction playground, redstone adds a whole new dimension. In some ways, it harks back to the genesis of the electronics industry, simulating the breadboarding of electronics with wires and vacuum tubes. Very retro.

This chapter is an introduction to redstone and transport. It teaches you the essentials, and you won't need an engineering degree to succeed. Even if you're not switched on by some of the more complex aspects of this extraordinary system, it is definitely worth coming to grips with a few core techniques. They go well beyond the water harvester from Chapter 6, "Crop Farming," and you'll have fun exploring this creative new world.

Seeing Red: A Beginner's Guide

Certain aspects of Minecraft are completely intuitive and can be understood in the usual process of discovery. Redstone is different, but it's not so hard. The complete redstone system is made up of just a few core concepts: power sources, wire, modifiers, and output devices.

TIP

Use Creative Mode

I recommend that you test and explore this chapter in a world set to Creative mode. It's just so much easier as a learning exercise to place and wire up components this way, including the more exotic ones.

Once you get a grip on redstone essentials and start to figure out how to put these building blocks together into more interesting systems, you will never think of Minecraft the same way again.

Power Sources

The power sources provide the energy to power devices or to signal that an event has occurred, such as a mob (or someone in multiplayer) stumbling over a tripwire. Figure 9.1 shows the complete set.

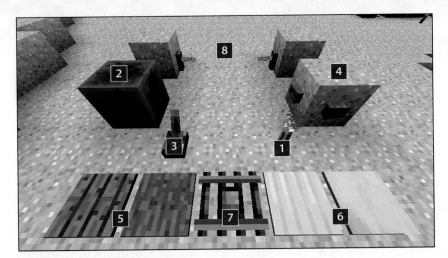

FIGURE 9.1   Redstone power and signal sources.

1. Redstone torch

2. Redstone block

3. Lever

4. Wooden and stone buttons

5. Wooden and stone pressure plates

6. Iron and gold-weighted pressure plates

7. Detector rail

8. Tripwire with hooks shown on either side

Signals and power sources provide the same redstone energy and are somewhat inter-changeable as terms, but consider signals to be intermittent providing that energy when an event occurs, such as someone or thing stepping on a pressure plate. Power sources provide a continuous flow of power like a signal switched on permanently. Here's the most essential information on each type of signal or power source.

Redstone Torch—The torch is Minecraft's electric utility. Clean, green energy, even if it's red. It provides a continuous source of power but also has a few handy tricks up its sleeve. Feed a power source into a torch and it will turn off, making it a useful switching mechanism for almost every circuit. You'll see many examples of this later. Craft a torch from a stick and a chunk of redstone.

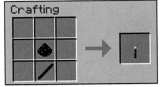

Redstone Block—Redstone blocks are crafted from nine pieces of harvested redstone. They act as a continuous power source to any nearby wiring, modifiers, and devices. They are also the only power source that can be moved by pistons, turning them into a handy mechanical junction box.

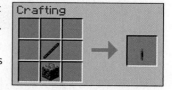

Lever—Minecraft levers act like an on/off switch, but spruced up with their own built-in power generation. Like buttons, they're also safe from being flipped by any of the nonplayer mobs. Wire up a set of levers as described under "Redstone Wiring" to create a secure keypad entry.

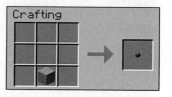

Button —There are two types of buttons. The Stone button provides a 1-second pulse of power, whereas the wooden button delivers a pulse for 1.5 seconds and, if you've a sharp enough eye, can be activated being shot with an arrow. For an extra challenge, try doing that while galloping by on horseback! Craft a button from one wood plank block or a block of stone obtained by mining stone with a pickaxe charmed with silk touch, or by smelting cobblestone back into a stone block.

Pressure Plate—Similar to buttons, pressure plates come in wood or stone variants, both delivering continuous power while activated. Stone plates react to mobs, a low-level fly-by in Creative, and by a minecart containing a mob. Dropped items, all minecarts regardless of contents, the lure on the end of a fishing rod, and arrows also trigger wooden plates.

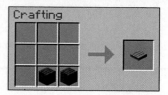

Weighted Pressure Plate—Although similar to the standard plate, these plates emit a signal of strength 1 to 15 according to the number of items on the plate. There are two versions. The gold plate, made from two gold ingots, is more sensitive, stepping the signal one level for every four items placed. The iron plate made from two iron ingots jumps the signal output every 42 items. The plates can count dropped items, but the items must be loose and risk despawning unless they're sucked back up into a hopper. They also can work for creating a lock where placing a particular weight of items unlocks a door, or even for creating a payment system in an adventure map. A sign placed nearby might say, "Place eight gold bars on the plate to move to the next stage."

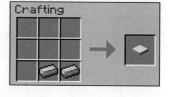

CAUTION

Don't Run Off the Rails

Pressure plates disrupt a contiguous minecart rail, so they are most reliably used at the end of the line. Detector rails and tripwire provide better alternatives.

 Tripwire Hook—Use string and two tripwire hooks to create a devious detection system with two tripwire hooks placed up to 40 blocks apart in a straight line. Join them by placing string between. The string creates a tiny, difficult-to-see texture between both hooks, making it a favorite trap creator. It's also an efficient way to "string up" a perimeter alarm. The hooks generate power while any mob is standing on or in the same block occupied by the string. Elevate a tripwire to one block above a minecart track, and it can detect a minecart carrying a mob, including yourself, making it an easy way to separate minecarts by load and switch tracks, shunting items in one direction and players in another.

TIP

Trapped Chests In Multiplayer Worlds

Place a tripwire hook and a standard chest on a crafting table to create a trapped chest. This sends a signal when opened and is great for multiplayer. You can use the signal for almost anything from kind intent to evil intention. Play a happy note from a note block, or slide open the floor under the player's feet to boil him in a lake of lava. You can be as nice or as diabolical as you like.

Trapped chests have a small red square surrounding the latch that may send a warning to an alert player. Place a sign on the front to hide the texture. (You'll need to *sneak place* by holding down the Shift key while right-clicking). The text is up to you, but saying "FREE TOOLS; HELP YOURSELF" or "DIAMOND STORE" can be quite effective. A small amount of the red texture remains visible but probably won't be seen by a ravaging player intent on stealing your horde. You can also hide the texture entirely by digging a hole and sinking the chest into the ground. Oh what fun!

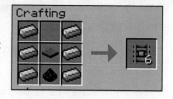

Detector Rail—Detector rails send off a signal as a minecart rolls over the top. This can be used to switch tracks, turn off other powered rails to prevent collisions, open doors, fill and empty hoppers, and so on. Connect a comparator to a detector rail to trigger a signal that can shunt full minecarts in one direction and empty ones in another. This is useful for dropping empty minecarts into a dispenser ready for reuse while sending a full one (one that you might be riding) to another destination such as a train station, but there are many other uses.

All other containers (the chest, hopper, furnace, dropper, dispenser, jukebox, and brewing stand) also emit a signal that varies in strength according to their contents. Tap this signal with a redstone comparator, described later in the chapter, to turn it into an output that you can use elsewhere.

Redstone Wiring

Redstone is harvested from redstone ore with an iron, gold, or diamond pickaxe. When placed on the ground, the redstone transforms into a trail, also called *redstone wire*, that carries power or signals between components.

Redstone wire has some interesting properties (see Figure 9.2):

■ Laying a trail is quite easy because the wire automatically connects adjacent nodes. Just click on blocks where you'd like to place the wire, and it bends around corners, goes up and down solid block ramps, and creates three- and four-way junction points as required. It's sticky stuff, so prevent separate circuits from connecting by keeping them separated by at least one block or they'll connect themselves together to form a lattice. If space is tight and you must run two separate strands side by side, use a parallel run of repeaters instead.

■ Water and electricity don't mix. The water just washes away the redstone wire turning it back into collectable redstone. Be prepared to climb over or tunnel under any water blocks.

■ Powered wire sparkles with a red glow that gradually diminishes until the current runs out in 15 blocks. You'll need repeaters or torches to boost the power for longer circuits as described below.

■ The current runs in the space above the block on which the trail appears but provides power (see below) to the block underneath and the block directly in front of the end of the wire.

■ Redstone powers the blocks on which the wire is drawn but conducts the power through the block above that. Think of the wire as actually occupying the space above its depicted location. That space must be contiguous with the exception of slabs or transparent blocks such as glass, ice, leaves, and glowstone. Figure 9.3 shows a blocked current.

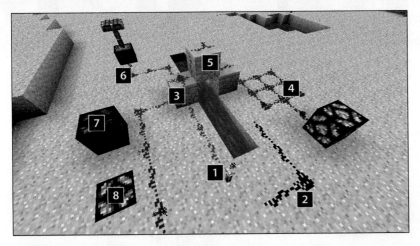

FIGURE 9.2 Redstone properties.

1. Powered wire emits a glow and sparkles

2. Unpowered wire has a dull red color

3. Wire transforms automatically into junctions as you place nearby nodes

4. Connecting nearby blocks creates a lattice but continues to transmit power without short circuits

5. Wire can also climb up and down blocks arranged in a stair-step pattern

6. Devices can activate at the end of a wire at the same level...

7. ...but don't activate when placed next to an adjacent wire

8. Wire does power the block below, lighting up this adjacent glowstone lamp that is sunk into the ground one block

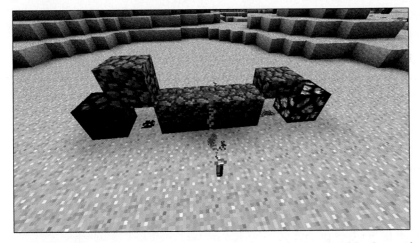

FIGURE 9.3 Blocks can't break a wire's current: the block on the left prevents the current from flowing down and to the glowstone lamp, while the slab on the right (taking up just half an actual block space) allows the power to flow through it and down to the ground, lighting up the lamp. Replace the interfering block with a slab if keeping a similar texture is important, or a transparent block.

Powered Blocks

Redstone power propagates from the source as *strong* power. Strong power can light up redstone wire and activate devices. Feed strong power into a normal opaque block such as dirt, cobblestone, or wood, and that block will propagate *weak* power, which can only activate devices. Basically, it's not strong enough to reconnect with a redstone wire and continue acting like a partial insulator. Figure 9.4 illustrates this concept.

FIGURE 9.4   Strong and weak power.

1. The cobblestone emits weak power, sufficient to activate the lamp and other devices, but not enough to power the wire leading to the second lamp
2. Running wire over a block continues the current through the space above the block
3. The lever provides strong power to the block, firing up the wire

It's also worthwhile mentioning that a direct connection between a power source and a device isn't always necessary. Most of Minecraft's blocks—the opaque ones—can also be powered directly by a source. This enables the creation of very small circuits. I included one example of this in Chapter 6, where the piston was powered by a button placed on a block. I'll show you some other examples later in this chapter.

Most redstone sources are attached to a block of some kind. For example, buttons are placed on the vertical surface of a block such as a wall, a lever to any surface, or even the ceiling. Generally speaking, the source powers the block to which it is attached (the *anchor* block), and this can then activate any devices adjacent to it. This is why a button placed on a block beside a door opens that door. It's not the button acting directly on the door through some hidden link. Rather, pushing the button powers the block to which it is attached, and that block being adjacent to the door triggers it to open.

NOTE

Torches Power the Block Above

Of course, there is an exception to this rule. The redstone torch powers the block above it rather than the block it is attached to.

Now, here's the important part. All sources except the redstone block also strongly power the space they occupy, not just the anchor. (Redstone blocks are anchored on themselves, so they only provide strong power to the space they occupy.) This provides a choice of two blocks to which you can attach components: do so either at the anchor block or at the block occupied by the power source item. Figure 9.5 shows how this works.

FIGURE 9.5 Sources provide strong power to two blocks each.

1. This wire is powered by the space occupied by the lever
2. This wire gets its power from the block the lever is anchored to
3. Redstone torches power the block above, so this wire gets its power from the cobblestone block above the torch
4. The torch also powers the space it occupies, firing up this redstone wire

Keeping the two-block rule in mind gives you many more options for linking components and running circuits. In other words, more power to you!

Modifiers

Modifiers change the current in useful ways. There are two types: repeaters and comparators.

Repeaters

Redstone repeaters can amplify a strong or weak current and add a 1- to 4-tick delay that is useful for adding timing to circuits. The repeater also acts like a diode, ensuring current only flows in one direction.

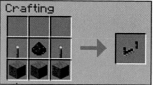

The power boosting function allows current to flow through solid blocks such as walls without finding a way to go over or under them. This in itself can solve some otherwise difficult design problems. Figure 9.6 shows two examples.

FIGURE 9.6 The repeater on the right picks up the weak current reaching the block and amplifies it back to strong. Without this, the block just emits a weak current insufficient to light the wire on the far left. The repeater on the right turns the block into a strong emitter, lighting up both redstone trails.

A repeater's current always flows in the direction of the single fixed light on the repeater. You may be able to make out a faint triangular texture on top of the repeater that shows this direction. Place the repeater facing in the direction you want the current to flow and it will align correctly.

Right-click the repeater to add a delay to the circuit. The default is 0.1 seconds, increasing to 0.4 seconds with each right-click until the light has slid fully back to the base of its channel.

Repeaters are also useful for running current in tight spaces because they can be placed next to each other without forming the lattice effect that placed wire develops. Place them in series, as shown in Figure 9.7.

FIGURE 9.7 Two sets of repeaters keep current separate. Terminate the sets with blocks and use the sides of the blocks to run the separate strands to their destination.

Repeaters have one other useful feature: T-bone one repeater's output into the side of another, and any power applied to the first locks the second's output. This creates a latch, and quite literally something that can be used to provide a masterlock for a door or even to create a 1-bit memory cell.

FIGURE 9.8 The back repeater has latched the front repeater in a power-off state (shown by the block across the top that replaces the sliding torch), even though power reaching the repeater would normally flow through and light the lamp.

Comparators

The redstone comparator increases or decreases an output signal according to the strength of the input signal. Comparators can check the contents of a chest, hopper, furnace, dropper, dispenser, juke box, and brewing stand or compare the relative storage of each and then trigger another function such as making a railcart with the hopper move to another location for unloading. See Figure 9.9. I'll show a few more useful scenarios in the examples that follow. The comparator requires nether quartz, which is only available in The Nether region.

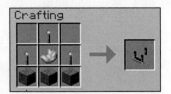

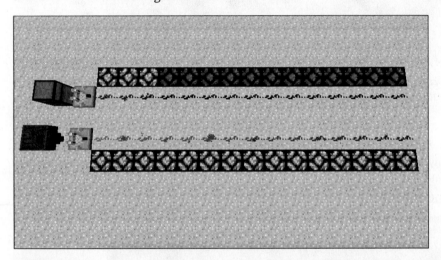

FIGURE 9.9 Comparators report inventory contents by emitting signal strength equal to the number of slots available in that item divided by the number of full slots available, converted to a percentage out of 15. The hopper and the chest each have 5 full slots. Because the hopper also only has 5 slots available in total, the comparator issues a 15-strength signal, or 100%. The chest has 27 slots in all and is approximately 18% full, which rounds to the emitted signal strength of 3.

Comparators always output the same strength signal as their input unless they also receive a side signal, which can be delivered by any input source. In this case, they operate in two modes:

- **Compare mode**—If the side signal is greater than the input, the output is zero. In all other cases, the input equals the output.

- **Subtract mode**—If the side signal is lower than the input, the output is the input minus the side signal. In all other cases, output is zero.

This is a lot to take in, understandably. Some examples later will help.

Output Devices

All those power sources, wiring, and modifiers are a bit useless without the circuit actually doing something. Minecraft provides a large number of devices, activators, gadgets, and more. Figure 9.10 shows the full set, described in the following list.

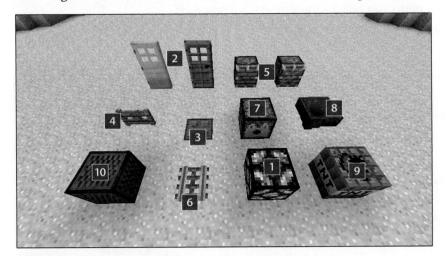

FIGURE 9.10 All of Minecraft's output devices

1. Redstone lamp
2. Iron and wooden doors
3. Trapdoor
4. Fencegate
5. Regular and sticky pistons
6. Powered rail
7. Dispenser
8. Hopper
9. TNT block
10. Note block

 ■ **Redstone lamp**—The lamp, as you've seen from many of the figures in this chapter, is a handy way to check the output of circuits. It also happens to make a pretty good light source, although crafting one requires glowstone from The Nether. Glowstone is plentiful, but obviously you'll have to venture into The Nether first.

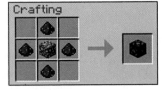

■ **Doors**—The *de rigeur* entryway. Doors come in iron and wood variants and switch between a fully open or closed state instantaneously, meaning one can't hit you in the rear on the way out. Iron doors can only be opened with some sort of power input. They also keep zombies out when playing on Hard difficulty.

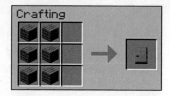

■ **Trapdoors**—Although a little obvious for use in a trap, a pressure plate in front of a trapdoor will save you from fumbling for a right-mouse click.

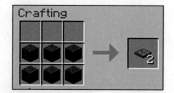

■ **Pistons**—Both the regular and the sticky variants are incredibly useful. You'll see some examples soon.

■ **Powered rails**—Sure, you can power a minecart by jumping on board while riding a pig, but is that any way to get around? You'll be a laughing stock. Powered rails provide a more stylish way to move you and your minecarts from A to B.

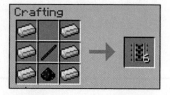

■ **Fence gates**—They open, they shut, and they're good for keeping the livestock in place.

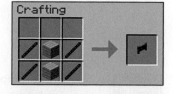

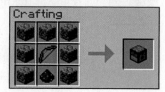

■ **Dispensers**—The dispenser pumps out almost anything that's been put inside. Typically used for firing arrows, supplying a flood of water, and, well, an enormous range of things, they're an indispensable (sorry) part of any automated system.

- **Hoppers**—Hoppers move items between other objects. Although hoppers don't rely on power, they'll stop transferring contents out or in when they receive a signal from the side.

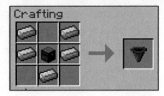

- **TNT**—TNT is the most destructive force in Minecraft, except for a creeper that's been hit by lightning, and that's incredibly rare. Set it off with a power pulse or use a minecart crafted with TNT to create a rolling disaster zone that's set off by an activator rail. Craft TNT with gunpowder collected from slain creepers (that's easier to say than to do) and regular sand.

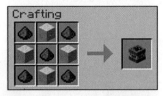

- **Note blocks**—Note blocks add a nice aesthetic to the game and are an easy way to create audible notifications or warnings of certain events. Right-click them to change the tone that plays when they receive power. You can even create your own doorbell with a string of blocks hooked up using repeaters to create delays. Bring out your inner composer.

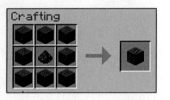

The output devices make quite a collection. You'll use them in various ways later.

You can make advanced circuits and mechanisms by combining all the components in different ways. The redstone system can do a lot more than connect a button to a light or a lever to a water dispenser.

Automatic Doors

Let's start with something simple and useful. You've probably already experimented with powered doors. Place a wooden or stone button on the wall next to any single door and it will spring open. You can do the same with two doors placed side by side, but a single button placed on one side won't open them both. Wouldn't it be nice if you could link that button to both doors so they both swing open the way you'd expect?

All you need is a little redstone dust. Follow these steps and refer to Figure 9.11:

1 Position the doors. The order you place them is important. Place the left door first, and then the right. This causes the right-hand door to flip around, becoming a mirror image of the left.

2 Place blocks to surround the doors as shown, a stack of two on each side.

3 Position the button on the top-left block. Wooden buttons provide a 1.5-second pulse of power, whereas stone buttons provide a 1-second pulse.

4 Run a trail of redstone dust from the base of one door pillar to the other in a U-shaped bend until it drives directly into the base of the other. The redstone receives its current from the space the button block occupies, transmitting the current to the opposite base block, powering that and triggering the opposite door to open.

The only obvious problem with this? It isn't attractive. You can't throw a welcome mat over it to hide the wire, but there are other ways to improve that.

FIGURE 9.11   A simple circuit to link two doors.

Let's remove the wiring and start again. Take a look at Figure 9.12. It's still the same concept, but the wiring now runs from the side of the button's anchor block, down a few blocks to where it can be hidden by ground cover, and back up the other side in a mirror image. Follow these steps:

1 Dig out the blocks shown to re-create, although you can leave the forwardmost row in place—I just removed those to better show the circuit.

2 Add the two single side blocks on either side of the door jambs and run redstone along the top of the blocks and down into the trench.

3 When you reach the middle, stop and place a redstone repeater to amplify the current because it needs to run a touch longer than 15 steps. Place it facing in the direction the current should run (in this example facing toward the right) and then continue the redstone wiring out the other side and up the steps on the other side.

4 Time to test! Click the button, and both doors should spring open. The left one first, followed by the right after a tiny tenth of a second delay caused by the current as it runs through the repeater

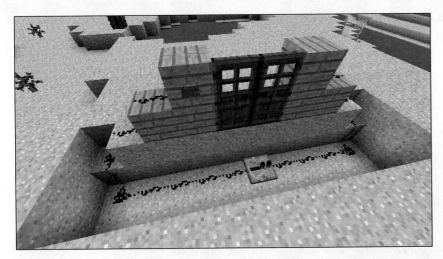

FIGURE 9.12 It only takes a few minutes to rerun the wiring so that it can be hidden from sight. Going two blocks deep leaves room for a layer of flooring above flush with the ground.

5 Now let's cover this back up. Start by filling in the main trench using any material you prefer, even glass blocks if you want to see the current fire up each time you enter, but leave the two blocks at the far end empty for now.

6 Figure 9.13 shows the blocks at the end of the trench. One is one block deep, and the other is two blocks deep. Place a slab instead of a full block over the space that is two blocks deep. This allows a surface flush with the ground while also letting the current run underneath.

FIGURE 9.13 Cover the space on the right with a slab to allow the current to run down and into the trench.

7 Build up other blocks around and on top of the wiring until you've achieved the desired result. Figure 9.14 shows an example that turns the entry into something a little grander while also hiding all the wiring.

FIGURE 9.14 A completed portico. I've used fence posts and wooden slabs to create the roof.

8 Position a couple of pressure plates behind the door for an easy exit. The plates aren't quite perfect. Each one opens just the door in front of it. For extra props, dig a trench two blocks deep under the plates and lay some redstone under both plates that connects somewhere with the other wire originating from the button. This ensures that no matter which plate is jumped on, the original double-opening circuit will receive the hit and swing both doors open.

TIP

Forgot to Shut the Door on Your Way Out?

Place a wooden pressure plate inside every door leading outside even if you don't do any other wiring. You won't need to click the door to get out, and the door will automatically close behind you every time.

This is just one example for connecting doors and running wiring; there are many ways to slice this. The wiring could run over the top of the door. It could also be made shorter on the delivery side by placing a redstone torch two blocks under the door and powering it through an inverter, but the repeater significantly simplifies the design. And, of course, the entire thing could be flipped so that the wiring runs behind the doors.

Let's get a touch more sophisticated. Swinging doors are great, but if you have in mind something more high tech, perhaps a modern fortress decked out with everything that opens and shuts (literally), you might consider leveling up to doors that glide open before you. They're not whisper quiet and they don't even give that swoosh sound of the doors in every sci-fi show. However, they do look great, and you can make them from any material, including glass blocks, so they'll add a certain something to any construction.

Sliding doors add an extra circuit to the loop. The pistons have to stay powered and therefore extended for the door to stay closed. But pressing the button delivers power rather than cutting it off, and flipping a lever will just keep the doors in one state or the other. What this circuit needs is a method of keeping the pistons powered constantly, but a way of interrupting that only when the button supplies its own current. This setup is known as an *inverter*, or a *NOT* gate, and is provided by a redstone torch attached to the button block.

Figure 9.15 shows the basic layout, with all components identified. The image shows the pistons powered. They'll be retracted at first, but you can place the actual door blocks either in the middle or up against the pistons, and they'll work just fine as soon as the pistons are extended for the first time.

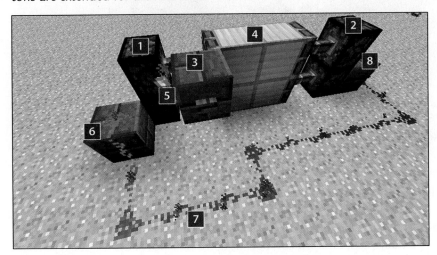

FIGURE 9.15   Place these components to create the mechanics of a sliding door.

1. A double-stack of sticky pistons
2. The second stack of sticky pistons required for the opposite slider
3. Block with button attached
4. Blocks for the door—I've used iron for that fortress look
5. Redstone torch attached to button block forming an inverter
6. Start of redstone wiring
7. The wiring must step around the block beneath the button's own space so it isn't fired when the button is pressed
8. Place the trail up and onto the block behind the second piston stack

I've shown the wiring at ground level for simplicity, but bury it the same way as for the wooden doors example, and then build up the rest of the entry way to hide everything. Figure 9.16 shows one example, but feel free to achieve any look you like. Piston doors provide quite an entrance into a fortress buried into the side of a hill, where you can place natural terrain to hide the inner workings. You can also flip the workings 90 degrees and make doors open vertically, or add some vertical doors and pistons on top of the horizontal ones to create a three-way iris.

FIGURE 9.16 One approach to hiding piston door wiring.

Try the same design with an added latch circuit: run wire from pressure plates through the latch, feeding the power into the side repeater from a lever inside. Use the pressure plates to get in and out quickly, and then use the lever to lock the doors closed at night.

One final example of piston-controlled devices: Figure 9.17 shows a set of three automatic iron block storm shutters hidden within a wall cavity. (I've opened up the inner wooden wall and floor so you can see the workings.) A system like this controlled by a lever provides more blast resistance than glass, and you can open it up to take pot shots at mobs. Wire this up to a lever and bury the wiring under your floor.

Vertical Currents

Although redstone wiring can easily climb and descend steps, there are times you'll want to send it vertically instead. The easiest way to do this is to use an alternating series of redstone torches, ensuring the final one is in sync (not inverting) with the current at the base of the tower. See Figure 9.18 for an example.

FIGURE 9.17 Sliding windows created with sticky pistons. The repeaters keep the current feeding directly into the base block under the pistons. Without them, the wiring would revert to a lattice and stop working.

FIGURE 9.18 Redstone torches power the block above, so they are an easy way to create a vertically ascending current.

TIP

1×1 Vertical Ascending Alternative

Current (or really the current's signal) will ascend in a 1×1 pattern by placing redstone torches on top rather than on the side of each block. This requires a temporary tower behind the planned ascent that you can remove when you're done, but it's also ideal if you can just place the ascent against a wall. Attach blocks to the tower or wall every second space. Fix redstone torches to the top of each block, and they'll pass their signal to the block above until you can draw power from a final torch placed into the side of the uppermost block.

The only way to descend a current is through a 2×2 staircase (see Chapter 4, "Mining," page 69). You may want to use this in Survival mode as well as for ascending currents because it provides an easy way to get up and down the circuit.

Advanced Circuits

The creators of Minecraft did something interesting when they designed the redstone system: they made it possible to mimic the binary logic system that is also at the heart of every integrated circuit that runs your electronics. It's nowhere near as crazily complicated as today's CPUs, and it's more like a breadboard of wires studded with vacuum tubes, but the basics are there. Let's take a look at some prototypical logic gates and how they're used to do actual useful things.

NOT Gates, aka Inverters

NOT gates take an input value and flip the output value. For example, if the incoming current is on, the output of the NOT gate is off. If the current is off, the output is on. Redstone torches act like this. By default, they supply a current, but if the block they are attached to is powered by another source, the torch flips off. NOT gates are also known as inverters because they invert the current.

We've already used an inverter to flip the current from the torch with a button in the sliding doors example. They have many other uses, though. For example, two inverters in a row act as an amplifier, just like a repeater (see Figure 9.19).

Inverters can also turn a daylight sensor into a night-light, as shown in Figure 9.20. The daylight sensor emits a signal according to the amount of light it's receiving. Feeding this into an inverter turns the lamp on when the sensor is off, and vice versa.

FIGURE 9.19 Inverters as amplifiers: the foremost inverter pair is a more compressed version of the furthest set (two inverters in sequence).

FIGURE 9.20 Need a night-light? That's easy to arrange, and you can add further lamps and noteblocks to create a full lighting system with an audible sound as night hits.

OR Gates, or Any Input Will Do

OR gates provide a positive output if any of the inputs is also true. This is a natural function of redstone wiring. Just connect two or more wires to a T-junction, and the single output will always be on if any input is on, or off if all inputs are off. Figure 9.21 shows an OR gate with three types of input, any of which can light the lamp.

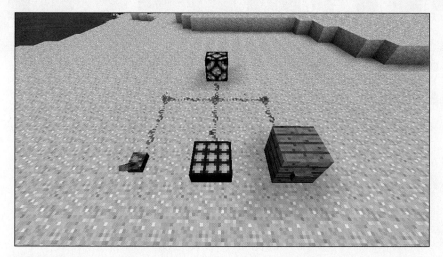

FIGURE 9.21 The OR gate is represented by the junction point of the wiring. In this case, the daylight sensor is providing the power that lights up all the wires. Use repeaters or inverters on each strand if it's important the current always flows in just one direction.

OR gates have many uses primarily because they allow multiple inputs to feed into the one circuit. For example, a row of pressure plates or strands of tripwire around the perimeter can hook up to a single wire that runs into your house, creating a perimeter alarm system. You can also add a timed circuit to a note block to create an audible beeping alarm.

I'm sure you'll find many other uses.

NOTE

If it's Not OR, It's NOR

NOR gates operate as OR gates but with the output signal inverted. Think of it as NOT+OR. In these gates, the output signal is TRUE only if both inputs are FALSE. Just place an inverter on the single-wire output from the OR gate to create a NOR.

AND Gates, Two True

AND gates output current (or a value of TRUE) only if both inputs are also TRUE. In real life, this is often used in security systems where two keys must be inserted to open a vault. You can do something similar to create a secure room, and this can be especially useful in Multiplayer. Place a lever close to the door (although not so close it can directly activate it) and hide a lever in another part of the structure. String them together and feed the output to the door. Now the obviously placed button won't work unless the hidden lever is also flipped on.

The AND gate is a more complex construction using three inverters for two inputs and one output. Figure 9.22 shows the gate with both inputs on, and Figure 9.23 shows the same with one input off.

FIGURE 9.22 AND gate with both levers switched on. This cuts both torches above the levers, ensuring no current flows to the inverter on the side of the block. That inverter therefore sends power to the output wire lighting the lamp.

FIGURE 9.23 With one lever turned off, current flows from its torch to the output inverter, cutting its own current.

Repeater Loops

Loops set up a pulsing circuit. They're possible with just some redstone torches, but redstone repeaters make them more compact with adjustable timing by changing the repeater delays with a right-click.

Figure 9.24 shows a prototypical design with a single repeater adjusted back to provide a 0.4-second delay. The torch adds one more tick to that, making this a 0.5-second loop. You can extend the circuit, adding more repeaters, to increase the delay. Replace the lever with wire connected to any other power source or signal to hook the repeater up to other circuits.

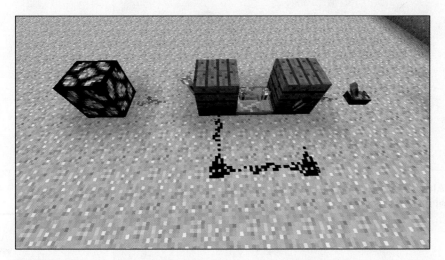

FIGURE 9.24 *The repeater loop works off any type of input.*

For an extra challenge, turn the repeater into a trip circuit. That is, the loop is to run permanently on the input of any signal until it's reset, like an alarm system. An easy way to do this is to use a redstone block sliding between two regular (not sticky) pistons. Figure 9.25 shows this approach. Note that an inverter has been added before the lamp so that its usual condition is off. The additional repeater is just there to extend the circuit.

FIGURE 9.25   A repeater circuit with a trip system. The push button on the right triggers the repeater loop by pushing the block away from the circuit, allowing the repeater loop to fire. The loop will keep running until the push button on the left pushes the redstone block back to its original position.

Rail Transport

Minecraft's rail transport system, as with much else therein, can be as simple or crazily complex as you like. It is definitely part of the charm and the challenge. It can operate in a simplistic way, but the tendrils of redstone work their way deep into the rail system. Powered and detector rails provide key hooks that integrate rail and redstone into a homogenous whole.

In earlier versions of Minecraft, before the Horse Update that came with the release of v1.6.2 and introduced a slew of equine-related features, rail travel was the fastest way to get from A to Z, via B to Y if you prefer a scenic route. The carts travel at an average speed of 8 meters (or blocks) per second and can climb hills, traverse valleys and, depending on how you design the track, offer something of a rollercoaster thrill ride in between. You won't break any land-speed records, and it's not as fast as a fast horse, but it's definitely better than walking. Now that horses are here, there are faster ways to get around, but rail is still a great system for moving items, resources, and yourself.

The system is limited by your imagination. In this section, I introduce you to the basic components, track-laying strategies, and some more advanced hints and tricks—enough to get you more than chugging along.

Have Minecart, Will Travel

A rail without rolling stock is about as useful as a car jacked on bricks. (I'm waiting for a maglev mod—maybe TrainCraft will float one in. See Chapter 13, "Mods and Multiplayer.")

There are several versions of the standard carriage shown in Figure 9.26. It would be wonderful if these were glorious celebrations of the gilded age of the iron horse; they aren't, not even steam-punk, but they do the job. Let's take a look in the stable:

- **Minecart**—This is the bare-bones version of the rolling chariot. Hop aboard by right-clicking the empty cart and get taken for a ride. Use the forward key (W) to move in the direction you're facing. To back up, just flip yourself around to look in the other direction and press W again. Press the left Shift key to exit the minecart. Self-propelling is effective but slow. Slopes (if you have the inclination), a powered minecart, or powered rails will speed things up. Other mobs can also ride in this minecart.

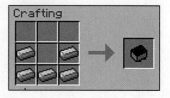

FIGURE 9.26 Minecarts

1. Standard minecart
2. Powered minecart
3. Storage minecart

4. Hopper minecart
5. TNT minecart

- **Minecart with Furnace**—This is also known as a powered minecart. Burn, baby, burn! The furnace cart is powered by coal or charcoal and can push other carts in front. It's bidirectional: just click on one with the fuel in hand facing in the direction you want it to go. You can also change its direction at any time with another click. The engine runs for 3 minutes on each piece of fuel (enough to travel about 600 blocks), and you can fuel it for a long haul by clicking with fuel multiple times. A single powered cart can push numerous others, although some glitches may occur, leaving carts jammed or stranded.

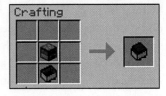

- **Minecart with Chest (storage minecart)**—Add a chest to a standard minecart to gain another 15 inventory fully stackable slots. This minecart rolls with the same momentum as an occupied minecart, irrespective of the contents of the chest. Place a hopper underneath the track to automatically unload the chest, and a chest under the hopper to create an automated unloading and storage system.

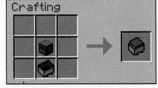

- **Minecart with Hopper (hopper minecart)**—Craft a minecart with a hopper to create a hopper minecart. These minecarts automatically scoop up loose items lying on the track and can fill with the contents of a container such as a chest or another hopper placed in the space above the track.

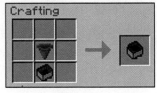

- **Minecart with TNT (aka the TNT minecart)**—Exploding minecarts? Why not. Actually, they're a little special because the TNT will destroy nearby blocks but doesn't destroy the rail tracks or their directly underlying blocks. This is a little hit and miss, though, and you may find some unintended collateral damage. TNT carts are a fun addition to Minecraft, but they aren't the most feasible method for mining. Use a powered activator rail to set them off. They can also be set off through collisions with other blocks or carts, by falling more than three blocks, and by fire, lava, or another explosion.

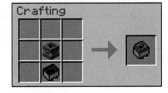

If you plan to build a bunch of minecarts and treat them like a train, keep in mind that they don't latch together, but instead can be used to push each other along. This works best with a powered cart doing the pushing. But even if you're just propelling yourself in a standard minecart, you'll find that you can push a practically unlimited string of storage carts ahead of you simply by bumping into them—shunting them along, as it were—as long as you stay on the flat. A powered minecart can push about four carts up a hill, but this doesn't always work out well in practice because the minecarts sometimes get stuck as the chain works its way around corners and over slope transitions.

NOTE

Destroying and Reusing Minecarts

By the way, you can destroy minecarts with a few hits from any tool and place them back in your inventory for reuse. You can also load them into a dispenser placed at the start of your track, for easy one-click deployment.

TIP

Build Now, Rail Later

Real-life cities tend to be a mess of transportation compromises. Roads and rail fight for space with buildings, sidewalks, parks, and utilities, not to mention utility infrastructure. Take a leaf from their book: tunnel. Put your rails underground rather than demolishing your hard-built structures, and pop aboveground with access points when you can. The ability to run rails on a 45-degree slope makes your life much easier than that of a town planner, and subways with underground concourses add their own ambience to a vibrant landscape.

Rolling on Rails

Minecraft has four types of rail. Some are more resource expensive than others, but fortunately they don't need to be used all the time. Here's a quick guide:

- **Normal rail**—Six iron ingots and a stick of wood will create 16 rail track segments. Place them with a right-click, and the system will take care of bending them around corners or up and down terrain. You can use normal rail exclusively if you like, trundling along in a minecart, but your speed will be somewhat limited. Only normal rails can bend into curves or a T-junction.

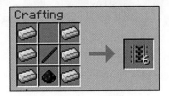

■ **Powered rail**—The powered rail is expensive: for six gold ingots, a stick, and a lump of redstone, you'll get just six segments. Use wisely! Fortunately, you don't need a lot because a single rail can boost an occupied minecart or storage minecart for 80 blocks on level ground. (Unoccupied minecarts lose steam after just eight blocks.) The rail is itself powered by any redstone source, but some work better than others, and I'll use them in the examples that follow. These rails light up when powered and so are easy to recognize. When this type of rail is unpowered, it will slow you down, making it a good option for placing at the start and end of a track for a soft landing. Just one block can stop a minecart, even trundling down a slope. Powered rails provide a boost in the direction the minecart is moving, or if stopped on a slope, the minecart will always head down the slope when the rail becomes powered. If the minecart is stationery and at the end of a track with a block in front, the rail will instead give the minecart a kick in the direction it can travel. This is really the key to making a station where you can board a cart without trying to jump on one trundling past. Powered rail segments chain together up to eight segments from any powered source. Generally speaking, one powered rail is needed for every four steps up a slope, although you can work this as two rails in every eight to make it a bit easier to manage the power supply. On the flat, you should place one powered rail every 37 blocks to keep an occupied minecart zipping along at a moderate pace, or two powered rails to stay at high speed.

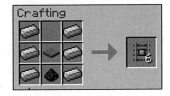

■ **Detector rail**—These rails are like a standard rail combined with a pressure plate, emitting a redstone current when a minecart rolls over the top. You can use this current or signal for anything really, including controlling hoppers, opening doors to a tunnel, setting off a note block, switching tracks at a T-junction, and so on.

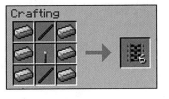

■ **Activator rail**—These rails have just two purposes: to enable or disable a hopper minecart passing over the top, and to set off a minecart with TNT. The size of the explosion is proportional to the speed of the TNT minecart, and the rail needs to be powered before it becomes operational. When unpowered, it acts like any other rail track.

Making Tracks and Stations

It's easy to lay tracks: just right-click where you want to place them. If you make a mistake, you can easily dig up the tracks and reuse them. This allows for some trial and error, especially when working out the minimum placements required for the expensive powered rails.

TIP

Zig-Zag to Speed Up

Whereas a cart travels on level ground at a maximum of 8 blocks per second, a slight sideways dodge boosts this to 11 blocks. Lay diagonal tracks in a continuous zig-zag pattern to get this free speed boost. They'll look a little off on the ground, but the minecart will travel over them smoothly. Lay the tracks on diagonally adjoining blocks, and they'll connect with a series of corner tracks, creating the zig-zag pattern for you.

TIP

Efficient Powered Rails

The cheapest way to permanently power a rail is with a lever rather than a redstone torch. You just need a piece of cobblestone and a stick to craft the lever. Then place it by the track and flick it on. If you prefer to leave your power sources hidden, place a redstone torch under one of the blocks holding a powered rail, and the rail will transmit the power to any adjoining powered rails.

As you lay tracks, you need to consider inserting powered rails. The first place to start is really at the beginning of the track. Create a small launch station using Figure 9.27 as a guide. The station works like this:

1 The single powered track at the end acts as the launcher, gaining its power from the button attached to the wood block.

2 Place a cart at the end, hop aboard, and push the button.

3 You'll accelerate out of the dip and then get a speed boost from the track powered by the lever.

4 When returning, that same powered track gives your cart a speed boost sufficient to nestle it back against the block at the end of the line, ready for the next launch.

FIGURE 9.27 A simple minecart station that returns carts to their ideal starting position.

T-Junctions

The T-Junction allows a train track to branch off in two directions, with the direction controlled either via detector plates or some other power source. Create this track by placing your rails into a T-section. Minecraft takes care of converting the head of the T into a working junction. Generally speaking, the most useful way to switch the tracks is to place a lever at the top of the T, as shown in Figure 9.28, but you can also run redstone to achieve the same result perhaps all the way back to a destination switching board at the station. The power needs to terminate at the block underneath the track, making it possible to hide any wiring from view.

FIGURE 9.28 Switch the lever to choose a different track branch.

Halfway Stations

One final note before I leave you to your own track-laying devices. So far, you've seen stations at the end of a track, but what about those along the way? Creating a midpoint station provides a convenient stop 'n' go system. They use the same principle as the end stations, with powered rails in an unpowered state to slow you down. Create them by digging a trench one block deep and two blocks long, and place the track in it so it forms a V-shape, as shown in Figure 9.29. The minecart will stop on a downward-facing track in the direction of travel, and a quick click of the button on the side will get you moving again. The lever provides an override that permanently powers the tracks in case you decide you don't always need to stop here. If you do have to bail out as you go flying by, you can be thankful that empty minecarts stop after 8 blocks or so, rather than 80! It's easy to collect again and be on your way.

FIGURE 9.29 Switch the lever to choose a different track branch.

CAUTION

Protecting Tracks from Mobs

In Survival mode, you are as vulnerable riding in a minecart as you are at any other time. Carts don't, unfortunately, run over hostile mobs, turning them into mincemeal. They just stop or bounce off them. Either way, it's a problem. If you are serious about using minecarts to get around, consider building them underground in well-lit, protected corridors, or put up fences when they have to run aboveground.

A Word About Hoppers

 Before I close this rather lengthy chapter, there's one final, brief topic: hoppers. The humble hopper is really like an automatic item feeding system. It connects containers such as chests to other things like a furnace or a dispenser. Essentially, it moves items between containers while also offering five inventory slots of its own. Hoppers can also, as mentioned earlier, be placed on wheels by combining them with a minecart and will unload a minecart with a chest when placed underneath the track. (You'll need to place the hopper first and then hold down the left Shift key while right-clicking to "sneak" place the rail on top of the hopper.)

Figure 9.30 shows a fairly extreme example, just to demonstrate how wildly complicated a hopper system can become, although even this layout can be extended more or less indefinitely. Once you've fed in enough raw materials, the entire thing automatically drops raw materials into the top of the furnace, fuel into the side, and the end result into the chest at ground level. It's set and forget.

Hoppers configure themselves automatically according to their attachment point (you will need to sneak place them onto chests and other containers that react to a right-click), and they can be connected to each other to create a sort of endless conveyor belt feeding items to the side and down.

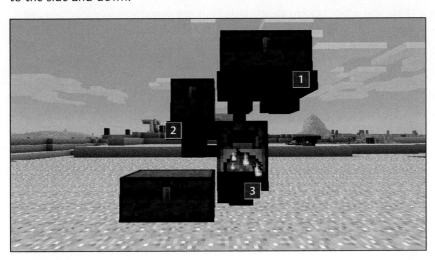

FIGURE 9.30 A sample hopper setup.

1. Two hoppers side by side can support a large chest—in this case feeding raw material into the top of the furnace

2. The side hopper supplies fuel, even buckets of lava providing an incredible amount of smelting power from a single chest

3. The hopper under the furnace collects its output and sends it to the large chest next door

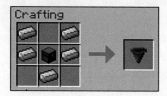

Craft a hopper from five iron ingots and a chest. The hopper has five inventory slots of its own but acts to transfer items stored above it to anything below it at a rate of 2.5 items per second unless the transfer is stopped with a redstone signal. Place a redstone comparator next to a hopper to receive a signal when it contains items.

The Bottom Line

As you've seen, redstone offers many interesting possibilities. Like so much in Minecraft, redstone is limited only by your imagination. Although redstone differs enough from electricity to give an engineer conniptions, it's a lot easier to work with, and you're not going to die from an electric shock if you cross wires. You'll just get a nice little wire lattice forming instead.

Redstone also plays nicely with the rail transport system, providing fast transport and an easy way to move items and other resources around. Rails are quite resource intensive, so in most survival worlds you'll probably start with something simple and efficient. In pure Creative mode, however, there really are no limits at all.

Enchanting, Anvils, and Brewing

In This Chapter

- Learn Minecraft's enchanting ways.
- Safely store your hard-earned experience levels.
- Spruce up your weapons, enhance your armor, and improve your tools.
- Hammer something out on the anvil for better repairs.
- Mix up some magic in the brewing stand.

By now you may well have made it all the way to a diamond sword, your base is nothing short of a warlord's fortress, and you're so armored up you can take on a corps of creepers without breaking a sweat on your squared-off brow.

All's good in the Overworld...but it could always be better.

This chapter walks you through a few extra skills involving a special crafting table, a very large block of iron, and a few wee drams of potion.

Enchanting Wiles

Experience points (XPs) accrue through the normal course of the game, providing small green nudges to the experience bar shown in your HUD. (Those colored orbs flying toward you after you bravely slay a mob or patiently smelt a batch of iron all devolve into experience points.) When the bar fills, it delivers an XP level, a type of currency, and promptly resets. Spend that XP wisely through enchantments, and you can power up your weapons, armor, and tools.

Enchantments improve an object's core abilities. Among other things, they can help a pickaxe mine with more efficiency, make a sword cause more damage and become unbreakable, make your armor practically (although not completely) impregnable, and build up a lot of other vital improvements that will help you in The Nether and End regions.

Enchantments also add capabilities that are a little more mystical: the respiration enchantment can dramatically increase your underwater survivability, a bow with infinity enchantment will never run out of arrows (at least not until the bow breaks), and your enchanted boots will let you leap off tall cliffs with nary a thought for a distinct lack of feathers. Enchantments also have a practical use: they can help your tools gather more resources from every mined block, or even pull out whole blocks in their original form instead of just digging out dropped components.

So how do you start enchanting? It's actually pretty easy, and there are several ways to go about it:

- Use an enchantment table to apply a random enchantment to an item, at the cost of XP.

- Pay a villager priest with emeralds in return for a specific enchantment on an item you must already have in your inventory. This also works like a free repair by swapping damaged items for their undamaged, enchanted equivalent.

- Combine an enchanted book with an item at an anvil. This will cost some XP but at a discounted rate to creating the original enchanted book. This is a bargain if you've been fortunate to find an enchanted book in some of the chests scattered around the world in villages, dungeons, and so on. Villager librarians will also trade them for other items.

- Combine an item with an enchanted item of the same type at an anvil. If you combine two items with different but compatible enchantments, the final item gains both enchantments. You can also use anvils to repair and rename items in a process not dissimilar to using them to enchant items.

Let's start with the simplest method: an enchantment table as shown in Figure 10.1. We'll get to the bookshelves surrounding it shortly.

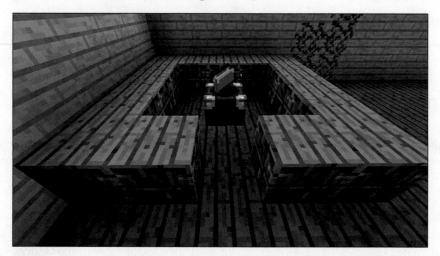

FIGURE 10.1 An enchantment table surrounded with 15 power-boosting bookshelves.

Enchantment tables take up one block, just like a crafting table, but creating them is a little more difficult because they require two diamond gems, a book, and four obsidian blocks.

Of all the ingredients, you might find obsidian the most difficult to obtain. It lurks in some village chests, but otherwise you need to discover it in a natural setting or create it yourself with a steamy combination of water and lava.

Creating and Mining Obsidian

Obsidian is naturally formed when *flowing* water meets *still* (not flowing) lava. This is a key condition because any other variation of water and lava flowing or not, in either order, just results in cobblestone, and that's not going to put a spell on anything.

Obsidian is practically indestructible, making it a great construction material, but it's a little risky to mine given its close proximity to lava and the latter's proclivity for turning your character into an instant Korean BBQ.

But enchantment tables don't require very much obsidian, and I'll show you a sure-fire technique for getting there. Just follow these steps:

1 Fill some buckets with water. You might only need one, but take some backups just in case.

2 Now find a lava pool. If you're lucky, you've spotted these on the surface, but your surest bet is to head down to the lowest levels of your mine where you've probably already stumbled on several. Lava is most common below layer 11, counting up from the unbroken bedrock that exists at layer 0. If you're still looking, head back down your mine and dig some additional branch lines until you do. It shouldn't take long.

3 If you find a lava pool with water that has already flowed over some part of it (Figure 10.2 shows an example), you can try to block the water source, fencing it off with cobblestone or any other handy blocks to dry up the flow and then mine the obsidian exposed underneath. Figure 10.3 shows the result. A further border of cobblestone dropped into the lava lake along the obsidian border allows you to mine the obsidian without fear of getting swamped by the molten magma. Don't forget to use the left Shift key to sneak around the lava so you don't fall in.

FIGURE 10.2 A natural lava pool and waterflow. The obsidian already formed by the water creates a thin black line under the front edge of the waterflow.

1. Flowing water that has already covered some of this lava pool
2. A still (not flowing) lava pool

FIGURE 10.3 Fencing or blocking off the water flow with a cobblestone barrier exposes the obsidian.

1. The flowing water has been blocked off from the still lava pool with cobblestone

4 If there's no water nearby, stand back a little and pour water from one of your buckets so that it spills down onto a bordering block and then flows over the lava. The best way to do this is to stand at least one block up. (Place a block and jump on it if a block isn't

there already, or there's no nearby ledge.) This ensures you don't get washed toward the lava, or backward into another danger zone.

TIP

Is The Lava the Only Source of Light?

Place some torches around before you extinguish the lava so you're not left standing in the dark as the lava's extinguished.

---

5 Let the water flow as far as it can, converting the lava lake to an expanse of obsidian, and then fill your bucket from the water source block to remove the water and expose the obsidian, as shown in Figure 10.4. If you can't pick up the water source block, place other blocks around, and you'll eventually dry it up.

FIGURE 10.4 Water poured from a bucket has converted the entire lava pool to obsidian.

1. Obsidian

6 Take your diamond pickaxe in hand and start mining obsidian! Obsidian takes a while to break, so be patient. There's also a good chance you'll expose more lava under the obsidian as you go. Pour some more water on top of that lava to convert any surrounding blocks to obsidian, and then scoop the water back up into your bucket to use again. Mine more obsidian than just the four blocks you need for the enchantment table. Try to gather at least 14 blocks in all, as you'll use the remaining 10 to create a Nether portal in Chapter 12, "Playing Through: The Nether and The End," and you'll need to visit that before creating a brewing stand later in this chapter.

Crafting Books

Books have several uses: they're used for crafting the enchantment table, for boosting its powers with bookshelves, and for storing enchantments. (They can also help you play Minecraft!)

Books require three pieces of paper and one piece of leather, although on Xbox and Pocket Editions you can leave out the leather—those editions must only contain paperbacks.

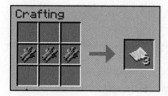 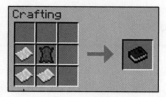

Start by crafting paper from three pieces of sugarcane. Then bind the paper with leather to make a book. Go ahead and make as many as possible because you'll need up to 45 books to create a full set of bookshelves to surround the enchanting table. (Don't drop everything to do this, though: you can build up to it, starting with just a few.)

Casting Enchantments

Now that you have the raw ingredients it becomes much easier. Follow these steps:

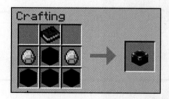

1 Create and place an enchantment table. Leave a clear perimeter of two clear spaces between the table and any walls for future bookshelves, as shown in Figure 10.1. As you approach the table, the book flips through a few pages in a rather nice animation.

2 Right-click the table to view the enchantment interface.

3 Place the item you want to enchant (a weapon, a tool, armor, or a book) in the empty slot beneath the book. You'll see a list of three possible enchantments appear to the right, as shown in Figure 10.5.

4 The actual enchantments listed are unreadable and randomly generated. The only information provided is the bright green numbering that shows the number of enchantment levels that will be expended for each enchantment. The enchantment you get is, essentially, up to a roll of the dice. An enchantment can run up 30 XP in cost, but the higher the level, the better the chance you have for gaining a more powerful enchantment. Any enchantments for which you don't have sufficient XP are grayed out, and an enchant table without nearby bookshelves can only offer enchantments up to level 8.

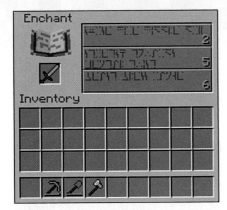

FIGURE 10.5   Enchanting a diamond sword.

5 Select an enchantment from the list. Stay at the lower levels for now, saving your experience for additional enchantments. You can also use the anvil to repair an item, but bear in mind that the number of times an item has been repaired attracts an XP penalty that impacts its potential enchantment level.

6 Drag the enchanted item back to your inventory. Hover your mouse over the item to see the actual enchantments applied.

TIP

Chancy Enchantment Tables

The formulas used by Minecraft for generating the list of enchantments aren't exactly obvious. Too many random factors are involved to provide a generic table of probabilities. A few sites online use the actual program code to generate a guide. To gain some more insight, visit www.minecraftenchantmentcalculator.com/, select the material, tool, and enchantment level, and this neat utility will roll the die 10,000 times, collate the results, and give you a list of possible enchantments along with their likelihood.

CAUTION

Crafting Table Repairs Remove Enchantments

Repairing an enchanted item by combining it with another on the crafting table destroys any attached enchantments. Use the anvil for the repair if you want to retain and combine the enchantments.

Improving Enchantment Chances with Bookshelves

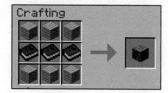

Bookshelves open up higher levels of enchantment. Craft them from three books and six wood plank blocks—any wood will do.

The level-up from bookshelves works the following way:

■ Each bookshelf unit boosts the level by 1 to 2 points, with 15 bookshelves delivering the highest enchantment level possible.

■ The shelves must be placed two spaces from the table with nothing in the intervening space. Torches, snow cover, and anything else will block the boost from the shelf.

■ Even with a full set of bookshelves, you'll continue to see enchantments at the lower power. There's a random distribution of levels from the lowest to the highest possible between the three enchantment slots.

■ The bookshelves must be on the same level as the table or one block higher. A single layer of 15 shelves looks like Figure 10.1, but you can also stack the shelves two blocks high against the walls (see Figure 10.6) to achieve the same power boost and leave the other two sides clear.

■ Stacking objects such as chests and torches directly on top of the bookshelves won't block their usefulness. You can also place another bookshelf on the two-wall layout to make the shelves symmetrical, even though it won't improve the actual enchanting.

TIP

Choosing and Storing Enchantments with Books

Books provide an opportunity to be more selective with the enchantments that are applied to an item. Enchant the book at the table in the usual way. The result is still random until it's complete, but it carries an identifiable enchantment as soon as you drag it back into your inventory. Combine the one you want with an item at the anvil for a small additional cost in XP. Store any others in a chest so they stay safe.

FIGURE 10.6 A slightly different bookshelf layout that still provides the maximum power boost to the table. Objects placed on top don't reduce a bookshelf's effectiveness.

Earning and Managing Experience

Experience points (XP) are earned through different actions and then "spent" through enchanting or using the anvil. What's the quickest way to gain XP fast, and how can you maximize your return on XP? Read on:

- Killing mobs, mining, smelting, cooking, fishing, and breeding friendly mobs will gain you XP. And if you cook the food, it becomes more nutritional. A quick way to gain lots of XP is therefore to breed animals, increasing the population as quickly as possible, and then kill any extras, picking up their dropped meat and cooking that in your furnace. Breeding chickens is easy because the seed is available anywhere there is tall grass, but cows are more useful because you can also use their leather to create books in the PC Edition (that is, the edition installed on Windows, OS X, and Linux computers). However, you'll gain more XP killing hostile mobs than friendly ones.

- Try to stay long enough to collect the colored experience orbs that gradually float your way after an XP earning event.

- Enchant gold weapons and armor. Gold benefits the most from enchanting and has a better chance of getting a higher-level enchantment than iron or diamonds.

- A priest villager enchants items at no cost to XP in exchange for payment with emeralds.

- Start with low-level enchantments first, in the 1 to 10 range on the enchantment table. There's little difference in the enchantments that can be had at the cost of 1 XP to 10 XP, so stay low and grow.

- The first 16 XP levels are the easiest. At 17 and above, it becomes gradually more difficult to climb each level, so if you want to enchant a lot of items quickly, keep your XP below 17, spend it, and then build it up again.

- All XP levels disappear on death, and while some experience orbs may drop for collection after your respawn, at best they'll only be sufficient to build you back up to level 5. If you have spare XP (say, anything above level 17) but don't have anything to enchant, use those spare XP levels to enchant books. Store them in a chest so they survive your death and you can apply them to new items when you come back from the afterlife.

TIP

Adding XP Levels with a Cheat

If you're playing around, have cheats enabled, and want to add some XP fast, use the cheat command **/XP <amount>L** to quickly gain any number of XP levels. For example, **/XP 30L** adds 30 levels of experience to your character. A negative amount subtracts it instead. This also works in Survival mode if you enabled cheats.

Spruce Up Your Weapons

Show your foes the thin edge of the wedge with a range of powerful weapon enhancements. You'll be amazed at how quickly you can dispatch a zombie with a sharper blade, or how far you can fling a creeper with the knockback enchantment. Table 10.1 shows the full list.

TABLE 10.1 Combat Enchantments

Enchantment	Maximum Level Attainable	Table Items	Anvil Items	Description
Sharpness, Smite, and Bane of Arthropods	V	Sword	Axe	Increases inflicted damage. Sharpness works on all mobs, smite on the undead, and bane of arthropods on spiders, cave spiders, and silverfish. An anvil is required to gain Level V on diamond weapons. Note that you can apply only one of these enchantments at a time.
Knockback	II	Sword	None	Knocks back an entity farther than a sprinting attack. Combine with sprinting for even greater efficacy.

Enchantment	Maximum Level Attainable	Table Items	Anvil Items	Description
Fire Aspect	II	Sword	None	Sets the target of your attack on fire for 3 to 7 ticks according to the level, but it has no effect on mobs from The Nether.
Looting	III	Sword	None	Improves the number of items killed and the number of mobs dropped, and improves the chance of zombies and zombie pigmen dropping additional items such as iron or gold ingots.
Power	V	Bow	None	Increases arrow damage from 50% to 150% according to the level. Level V available only through using an anvil.
Punch	II	Bow	None	Increases the knockback that a mob experiences from a hit with an arrow.
Flame	I	Bow	None	Sets the arrow on fire, causing fire damage to any mob hit except for those from The Nether.
Infinity	I	Bow	None	Provides an infinite supply of arrows until the bow breaks, but those arrows can't be collected in Survival mode for reuse.

Enhance Your Armor

Iron Man is a trademark, so I won't run that gauntlet, but armor enchantments do give you the Armor-All of defense, allowing blows to slide off your polished pauldrons like so much Teflon.

All of the "protection" enchantments combine to an upper limit set by the item's material. Table 10.2 shows the full list, keeping in mind that the upper limit for enchantments runs from lowest to highest as follows: iron, diamond, chain, leather, and gold.

TABLE 10.2 Defensive Enchantments

Enchantment	Maximum Level Attainable	Table Items	Anvil Items	Description
Protection, Fire Protection, Blast Protection, and Projectile Protection	IV	Helmet, chestplate, leggings, and boots	None	"Protection" reduces the damage passed on for that piece up to a total for all pieces, varying according to the material. The other enchantments help more specifically against fire, explosions, and ranged weapons. These enchantments are mutually exclusive.
Feather Falling	IV	Boots	None	Reduces damage experienced from falling farther than three blocks.
Respiration	III	Helmet	None	Increases the time you can breathe underwater by 15 seconds per level while also delaying suffocation damage by 1 second per level. Also improves underwater vision by reducing the opaque blue haze.
Aqua Affinity	I	Helmet	None	Removes the speed penalty associated with underwater mining.
Thorns	III	Chestplate	Helmet, legging, and boots	Provides the chance of the armor causing damage to an attacker, at the cost of the armor's durability. The effect is noncumulative, so the highest scoring armor piece wins.

Improve Your Tools

Of all your activities in Minecraft, resource collection is one of the most important. The enchantments below provide ways to gather new types of resources, ways to improve their speed and efficiency, and help them last longer.

TABLE 10.3 Tool Enchantments

Enchantment	Maximum Level Attainable	Table Items	Anvil Items	Description
Efficiency	V	Pickaxe, shovel, and axe	Shears	Increases mining speed from 0.3 times faster to almost 4 times according to the level.
Silk Touch	I	Pickaxe, shovel, and axe	Shears	Allows certain blocks to drop as themselves instead of their usual derivatives. Applies to grass blocks, coal ore, diamond ore, cobwebs, ice, and nether quartz ore, among others. Cannot be used at the same time as Fortune.
Fortune	III	Pickaxe, shovel, and axe	None	Provides a better chance that a breakable block will drop more items, and increases the rate of flint production from gravel.
Unbreaking	III	Pickaxe, shovel, and axe	All weapons, other tools, fishing rods, flint, and steel	Improves the tool's durability by reducing the chance of wear from normal use.

Enchantments are incredibly useful, but they usually only last for the durability of the item and are lost in their entirety when repaired at the crafting table. What if you could repair that item without losing the enchantment and even add an additional enchantment? Enter the anvil.

Hammer It Out with the Anvil

The anvil has many talents. It can repair and rename items, apply enchantments from books, combine two enchanted similar items, and combine the enchantments in two enchanted books, as long as the enchantments are compatible.

Anvils do, however, require a lot of iron: 31 ingots in all.

 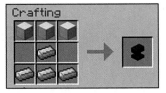

Start by crafting 3 blocks from 27 ingots. Then combine the blocks with another 4 ingots to create the anvil.

Place the anvil somewhere handy (see Figure 10.7), and nowhere it's likely to drop on your head. Falling anvils do cause damage and, for reasons Wile E. Coyote could well attest, prove quite popular in multiplayer traps.

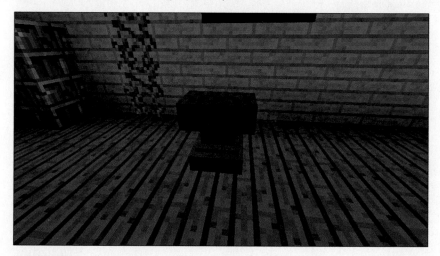

FIGURE 10.7 The anvil is the largest chunk of iron in the game. Fortunately, there's no damage from stubbing one's toe.

The anvil provides a single interface for all its different actions. Right-click it to open the Repair & Name window shown in Figure 10.8.

FIGURE 10.8 Repair, combine, or enchant items at the anvil, at a cost.

1. First item slot
2. Second item slot
3. Renaming box
4. Output slot
5. XP level cost to complete

Here's how you use the anvil:

- **Repairing an item**—Place the item to be repaired in the first item slot and the raw material in the second item slot. The item can be any item with a durability value. Figure 10.8 shows an iron pickaxe being repaired courtesy of three iron blocks at a cost of three XP levels. (You may need to place more than one of the raw material in the slot to bring the item back to full or close to full durability.) In the example, the pick was so worn out it required three iron ingots to bring back to almost full durability. Hover over the proposed repaired item to see its resultant durability value. (You may need to press **F3+H** from the normal view to turn this on.) Don't over-repair items because you'll receive no bonus for using additional repairs above the item's maximum durability level.

- **Combining two**—Place the items to be combined in the first and second item slots. The items must be compatible and the total XP cost less than 40 to be successful. This applies to weapons, tools, and armor as well as enchanted books.

- **Enchanting items**—Place the item to be enchanted in the first slot and the enchanted book in the second slot. The enchantment from the book transfers to the item.

- **Combining enchantments**—Place the enchanted weapons, tool, armor, or books in each slot and pick up the item with the combined enchantments from the output slot.

- **Renaming items**—Use the renaming box to name an item while carrying out any of the other anvil operations, or as a singular operation on its own. There are two reasons to rename an item. First, each repair on an item accumulates a 2 XP level penalty, and this eats into the total 40 XP that can be expended during any anvil operation. However, renamed items remain at a maximum 2 level penalty no matter how often they are repaired, so a renamed item gets an XP price-freeze. Second, a renamed sword with particular enchantments is easier to find while rummaging in a chest among a collection of enchanted swords whose icons are otherwise identical. You can also use the rename facility to assign names to nametags found in dungeons and Nether fortresses. Attach them to friendly mobs to get yourself a Fido, Killer, Daisy, or whatever you fancy. The mob's name is visible up to seven blocks away.

Brewing Potions

Let's brew up some trouble. Potions give you an offensive and defensive advantage that will keep limb attached to limb in the Overworld, but more importantly help you complete the other regions. Although potions don't require an eye of newt or toe of frog, they do, like a hell-broth, require a trip to The Nether for some core ingredients.

The first essential ingredient is *Nether wart*, the starting point for almost all the potions. It only grows in pits dug around the bases of staircases in Nether fortresses (see Figure 10.9). Those planting grounds and the Nether itself also contain the *soul sand* you'll need to start a

Nether wart farm back home. Fortunately, soul sand is quite plentiful, growing in dull gray tracts around many of the lava lakes you'll find.

FIGURE 10.9 Nether wart growing in soul sand at the foot of a Nether fortress's staircase.

The other elusive component is the blaze rod, required for creating the brewing apparatus. Obtain this by defeating a blaze, one of the hostiles that inhabit nether fortresses. This, admittedly, is something of a challenge. You won't do it in five minutes. I've written Chapter 12 to help you prepare for that journey, handle the hostiles, and get you home in at least one piece. Treat this first venture into The Nether as a quick snatch and grab. You don't want to spend too much time down there until you're truly prepared. You will, however, want to get a range of protection enchantments (fire protection is vital), as well as feather falling on your boots. An unbreaking enchantment on tools will save you some trips back to the Overworld until you've had time to create a well-stocked Nether-base.

Head over to Chapter 12 now, and come back when you have a blaze rod, Nether wart, and soul sand. You'll also need some glass blocks (smelted from sand) and a supply of water, although even a single block of water will fill an endless number of bottles. Figure 10.10 shows my own brewing chamber.

NOTE

Nether Not Yet?

Try some of the potion recipes that follow in a different world set to Creative to learn how they work and test the results. Sprint around with a 40% speed boost (it's quite an exhilaration after the normal plod/sprint), and try some combat at Normal and Hard difficulty. Minecraft is all about exploration, and you can do this one in advance.

FIGURE 10.10 The "Home Brew Club" with brewing stand on crafting table, water supply, Nether wart farm, furnace for creating glass bottles, and a chest for storing the results.

TIP

Plant Those Nether Warts First

Nether wart only grows in soul sand, but it doesn't have irrigation or light requirements. Given the challenge in collecting Nether wart, use any Nether wart and soul sand you collected from your trip to build a Nether wart farm. Do this *before* you start using the Nether wart for brewing. The simplicity of growing Nether wart means you can put the farm just about anywhere, including inside a small chamber reserved for your potable magic.

Brewing Up a Storm

Brewing up a batch of potions is actually quite easy and will continuously deliver rewarding results. You've already done the hard part: getting the initial ingredients together. The rest is easy, making the creation of potions a useful, easily replicated exercise.

Follow these steps to get started:

1 Craft a brewing stand from three cobblestone blocks and a blaze rod. Place it somewhere convenient.

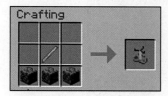

2 Create at least a few glass bottles from three glass blocks. Fill the bottles from your water supply.

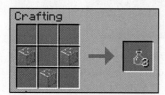

3 Right-click the base of the brewing stand to open the brewing window, and then place the glass bottles in the output slots shown in Figure 10.11. (You can place from one to three bottles, depending on how much of any potion you'd like to create. In this first instance, we're creating the base *awkward potion*. Because this potion is required for most others, it's efficient to create three of these at a time.)

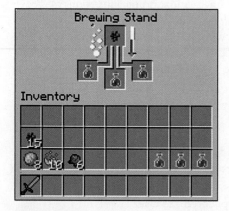

FIGURE 10.11   Drag the brewing ingredient to the top slot and the bottles (water or another potion) to the three output slots.

4 Place one Nether wart in the top of the stand. After a short while, and a brief brewing animation, the three water bottles are converted into three bottles of *awkward potion*. There's no visual change to the bottles, but hovering your mouse over them shows their new name in the tooltip.

NOTE

That Was Awkward...

Awkward potion is inert. It's the wallflower of potions. Turn it into something more out-going by adding one of the secondary ingredients to create the potions in Table 10.4. These potions are usually referred to as *positive potions* because they have a benefi-cial effect on the player's character. There are also negative variants of most of these that you can throw at other mobs to cause damaging effects, with some caveats dis-cussed in the Note, "When Positive Becomes Negative."

TABLE 10.4   Positive Effect Potions

Potion	Effect	Secondary Ingredient	Obtained From
Swiftness	+20% speed for 3 minutes.	Sugar	Sugar cane
Strength	+130% damage for 3 minutes.	Blaze powder	Blaze rods—each will make two blaze powders
Healing	Instantly restore two hearts.	Glistering melon	Melon+eight gold nugget (one gold ingot produces nine gold nuggets)
Regeneration	Restores 9 hearts over 45 seconds.	Ghast tear	Ghast drops
Fire Resistance	Complete protection from fire and lava for 3 minutes. You can even swim across a lake of lava as long as you get to the other side in time! Also provides protection from ranged blaze attacks.	Magma cream	Magma cube drops or by combining blaze powder with a slime ball
Night Vision	See perfectly at night and underwater for 3 minutes.	Golden carrot	Carrot+eight gold nuggets
Invisibility	Become invisible to all mobs for 3 minutes.	Potion of Night Vision	

Use the potions the same way you eat food: select the potion and hold down the right-mouse button to drink it. The potion of healing takes immediate effect, while others last for the specified duration. Open your inventory screen to see all the active potions and their remaining duration, as shown in Figure 10.12. You'll also see a bubble effect come up in the view through the main gameplay window while any potions are in effect.

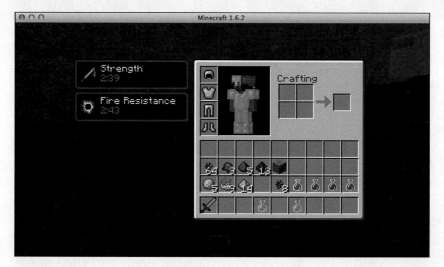

FIGURE 10.12 Active potions show their remaining duration in a box to the left of the inventory window.

Enhancing Potions

Potions provide a particular boost over a specified duration. Add a third brewing cycle to modify their boost *or* their duration, and convert them into a throwable *splash potion,* or a negative potion:

- **Glowstone dust**—Doubles the effectiveness of the potion where possible, typically at the expense of duration. Applies to Swiftness, Healing, Regeneration, and Strength. Replaces the use of redstone dust, as discussed next.

- **Redstone dust**—Doubles the duration of the potion but replaces the use of glowstone dust.

- **Gunpowder**—Converts the potion into a splash potion at the cost of a 25% weaker effect. You'll see the shape of the bottle change, looking a little like it's grown a small hand-grenade pin on the side. Throw splash potions at mobs or down at your feet if you want to get an immediate effect from the potion without taking the time to drink it.

- **Fermented spider eye**—Add this curious crafting to transform the potion into a negative potion. Table 10.5 lists all those available along with other negative effect potions that can be brewed without using a positive effect potion as the base. Craft this ingredient from a spider eye (dropped by spiders), a brown mushroom, and sugar.

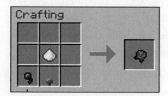

Glowstone and redstone cannot be combined through additional brewing cycles; only the last one used takes effect. However, gunpowder and fermented spider eye definitely are often used together to create a throwable version of a potion that will have negative effects on the enemy. You can add them after glowstone or redstone dust to enhance the effects of any throwable positive or negative potion.

TABLE 10.5 Negative Effect Potions

Potion	Initial Potion	Effect
Slowness	Swiftness	−15% speed for 1.5 minutes
Weakness	Strength (or brew a base potion using a water bottle and add a fermented spider eye)	Reduces melee damage by half a heart for 1.5 minutes
Harming	Healing	Cause 3 hearts immediate damage
Invisibility	Night Vision	Become invisible to all mobs for 3 minutes
Poison	Awkward Potion (add a normal spider eye through brewing)	Causes up to 18 points damage over 45 seconds but does not cause death

NOTE

When Positive Becomes Negative

Not all negative potions have deleterious effects on mobs. Throwing a potion of harming at the undead (zombies and skeletons) helps them heal. Whoops! Throw potions of healing instead to cause them harm. This is particularly useful when you're in a tight battle with these particular mobs because you can just toss a potion of healing at your feet and improve your health while causing harm to any of those currently in close combat.

The Bottom Line

Minecraft's magical effects are potent and powerful.

Start with enchantments because their toughest barrier to entry is a natural by-product of cooking, smelting, and taking care of mobs. You'll gain XP step by step.

Use the anvil to manage your enchantment inventory by storing them in books, repair items when needed, and combine enchantments for even more powerful results.

Potions provide your final boost, and they are the most powerful enhancements in Minecraft.

The next chapter is a small step back from combat preparedness but is important nonetheless. Your world contains numerous villages and a host of hidden structures containing items and resources that will help your push into the game's other dimensions.

Villages and Other Structures

In This Chapter

- Meet the village people, and trade your way up in the game.
- Learn about their professions and the different trades they'll offer.
- Learn a disarming charm, and raid the chests inside.
- Discover witches, warts, and all.
- Craft a map.
- Clock on and off. It's easy!

In Minecraft, you are never truly alone. There are villagers teeming with people, mysterious temples containing hidden treasures, and gigantic structures buried deep in the ground. Besides the bonanza of finding a chest or three packed with useful items, the villagers are more than happy to strike deals for certain resources and items. This chapter takes you on an exploration of the structures in the Overworld and their eccentric inhabitants.

Village Life

Villages are a haven for useful resources. Finding a good-sized one early on can provide a useful leg-up with chests containing numerous items; rows of wheat, carrots, and potatoes; and the opportunity to trade emeralds for other items from the proboscisally endowed villagers. (Okay, that's not a real word, but you'll understand when you see the villagers.)

The only problem with villages is that they are not too common. They only appear in the desert and plains biomes, and not too often at that. They are a lot more prevalent in any world with the **Large Biomes** option turned on during initial generation, as long as **Generate Structures** is selected under **More World Options**. By the way, the villages that appear in the two biomes use construction materials native to those biomes, so you'll see a lot of wood and cobblestone in a village located in the plains (see Figure 11.1) and a lot more sandstone in one village situated in a desert.

FIGURE 11.1 Villages spawn with a varying number of buildings and inhabitants. This one is located in a plains biome.

Villages add a useful dynamic to the game. They're not essential, and you can get by just fine without them, but knowing how to make use of them will help.

Here are the essentials:

■ Villages can appear in almost any form from a single dwelling (or even just a sad lonely well) to a dozen buildings or more. The buildings are any of 10 different designs from small huts to large taverns and churches.

■ Your interaction with the village's inhabitants affects your popularity within that village, and attacking a few—or, even worse, killing them—can result in your being attacked by an iron golem, although golems only appear in larger villages. Villagers won't attack you back, no matter how mean you are to them.

■ Villagers manage their population by producing children. As long as two adult villagers are present, you can increase the population and therefore the trading opportunities by adding doors to any structure, where one side of the door is in a clear space able to receive sunlight. The most efficient method is to add numerous doors side by side to a simple box structure. (The formula built into the software results in one villager per 3.5 doors.)

■ Villages are a lodestone for zombies, resulting in a possible zombie siege where hordes of zombies swarm the village at night. The zombies spawn anywhere in the village itself, including inside rooms, and attack any villagers present. Dead villagers can then turn into zombie villagers, increasing the havoc (see Figure 11.2). Cure a zombie villager by throwing a weakness potion at them, followed by a golden apple, and try to keep them segregated because the cure takes a few minutes to complete. Fortunately, as night falls you'll see most villagers scurry for cover to their favored village building. They'll also do this if it starts to rain. Iron golems fight the good fight by attacking zombies, and they get rid of them very quickly, but iron golems only spawn in villages with a population of 10 villagers and at least 21 houses (although really you just need doors, not complete houses, as described earlier). That's another good reason to increase the population!

TIP

Sleep Through the Siege

Beds don't occur naturally in villages, but if you place one and ensure you sleep through the night, you'll spare your villagers from a zombie siege. It's a neat way to keep zombie infections to a minimum.

FIGURE 11.2   Zombies can spawn in and around a village at night in large numbers, resulting in scenes like that shown here—a zombie siege in full swing!

- Villagers trade goods, and this is the real reason for a village's usefulness. Look for a trade where you can obtain emeralds by harvesting wheat, and then use the emeralds to pay for other types of items or services. Talk to as many villages as you can to find the best trade. Some offer rare Minecraft items such as saddles and horse armor. You can also deconstruct bookshelves in a library to obtain books, and you can happily loot any chests you find without dinging your popularity with the villagers.

- There's no particular technique for finding a village, but if you haven't found one yet in your world, despite substantial exploration, you can get a taste of the experience by searching for a game seed online. Search for something like "Minecraft village seed." It should match your version of Minecraft to ensure the terrain generates correctly. Even though villages can be hard to find, you will find one eventually in your own world. It may just be a small clutch of houses, but there is always the chance you can stumble upon one much larger. If you need a quick refresher on seeds, see "Seeding Your World" in Chapter 1, "Getting Started."

Emerald City: Your Ticket to Trade

Villages contain up to five types of villagers (see Figure 11.3), with each offering a particular set of items for trade, according to their profession, using emeralds as the currency. You can recognize each by their attire. Here's a quick guide:

- Farmers, dressed in brown, specialize in food products and most often offer up an emerald for 18–21 sheaves of wheat.

- Librarians wear a white coat and offer to buy paper, books, and gold. They sell, among other things, bookshelves, enchanted books, compasses, and clocks.

- Priests are recognizable by their purple robes. They buy gold and sell Eyes of Ender (pricey at 7 to 10 emeralds), redstone, and glowstone, and they are the only source in the game for the Bottle o' Enchanting, which generates experience orbs when thrown. Priests can also enchant swords, axes, pickaxes, and armor chestplates.

- Blacksmiths wear brown clothes with a black apron. They buy coal, iron, gold, and diamonds and offer all the metallic items for sale including chainmail armor, which can't otherwise be crafted.

- Butchers have a white apron. They buy raw pork chops and beef, as well as coal and gold, and they sell saddles, leather armor, cooked pork chops, and steak.

FIGURE 11.3 The Village People: from left to right: blacksmith, priest, librarian (this one's a little shy), butcher, and farmer.

You may also spot some villager children running around, but they don't participate in trading.

Right-click on a villager to open the trading window shown in Figure 11.4. Each villager starts with a single trade, either offering to sell you something for emeralds or offering to buy something from you in return for a payment of emeralds. You can't change the trade; villagers stick with their offer until you've performed the trade once and then open additional offers.

Villagers are rock-hard hagglers, so their offers won't budge. However, every unique villager represents another possible trading opportunity, so increasing the overall population can lead to a much more useful set of offers and a better price.

To make a trade, just place the goods or emeralds requested in the empty slot on the left and pick up the payment or goods purchased from the empty one on the right.

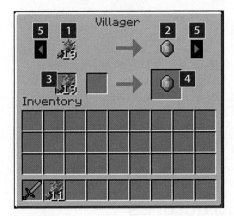

FIGURE 11.4   The goods or payment you need to supply are shown at the top left, and the goods or payment you'll received from the villager are shown on the right with the drop-off and pick-up slots for the trade items directly below.

1. Goods or payment required

2. Payment or goods to be received

3. Drop matching items for the goods or payment here

4. Pick up the reward here

5. Use the arrow keys to cycle through available offers

The additional slot in the middle is used for trading with priests. Place the item to be enchanted in the leftmost slot and the payment in the middle; then pick up the enchanted item from the right.

TIP

Emerald Farming

You can find emeralds in the ground, but the easiest way to get a decent quantity is to either take over the wheat farm in a village or build an even larger farm nearby. There are usually a few farmers about willing to buy the wheat you collect in return for emeralds. However, take extra care at night so you don't get caught on the wrong side of the door if a zombie siege begins. The villagers don't mind if you move into one of their houses to stay safe or build your own nearby, and you could do them a favor by fortifying their village to help alleviate the effects of a zombie siege and keep other mobs away.

CAUTION

Not All's Well with the Well

Village wells are deep, with a lip too high for a standard jump. If you plan to spend a lot of time in a village, consider placing some blocks below the first layer of water in the well. Also, knock out one block from the wall so you can climb out if you happen to fall in. Alternatively, leave the block in place and use the well as a zombie trap. Plenty can fall in during a siege, and the shade from the roof prevents them from burning up during the day, so you can then attack them at your leisure.

Hidden Temples and Other Structures

Villages usually have a chest or two tucked away, but your Minecraft world also contains other buildings that provide a more valuable treasure trove.

NOTE

Structures Within

Minecraft has many types of structures that are the result of specific programming code that is separate to the general terrain generation. Some of these (caverns, ravines, and basins, I'm looking at you!) are a negative structure, adding space to the terrain in ways that expose different types of ore and often provide a geological gasp of wonder. Others, such as the rivers that flow between biomes, are a clever combination of several techniques that both add and remove particular blocks, blurring what would otherwise look like jarring edges between the biomes. This Note serves no other purpose except to say that this is rather clever coding, particularly the rivers. Cajoling software to create apparently natural geology is tremendously difficult. So, here's to you, Mojang, for your natural beaches, soaring overhangs, and delightful waterways!

Most of these structures contain chests with all sorts of juicy loot, but they also often contain hostile mob spawners of different types. Disable the spawner by placing a few torches nearby to raise the light level above that required for mob spawning. You can also attack the spawner with a pickaxe to break it apart. With the spawner disabled, you're now free to loot in peace!

Desert Temples

Desert temples appear in the desert biome, looking like a stone pyramid with two turrets out front, although they are often partially buried under sand dunes. Although architecturally interesting, it's their four chests hidden beneath the floor of the main chamber that make them useful.

Head toward the central chamber. In the middle, you'll see a block of blue wool. The chamber with the chests sits directly beneath this, but so does this structure's biggest danger: a pressure plate connected to nine TNT blocks. Go back a few blocks and dig out a block to see the chamber. Then dig down one of the walls to get to the base shown in Figure 11.6, break the pressure plate to make the chamber safe, and raid the chests. While you're there, you might also want to dig up the floor and retrieve the TNT blocks.

FIGURE 11.5 A desert temple in its full glory. You're as likely to find them partially or even almost completely buried, so keep an eye out for any orange-colored blocks while traipsing through the deserts.

FIGURE 11.6   The treasure room of a desert temple. Be careful of that pressure plate! You may find some such rooms already blown up, typically caused by a mob spawning inside and trampling on the plate.

Jungle Temples

Indiana Jones faced a trap-laden jungle temple in *Raiders of the Lost Ark*, and you can too! The jungle temple is a mossy vine-laden structure that, for obvious reasons, occurs in jungle biomes (see Figure 11.7). Each contains two chests, one hidden behind a set of levers, and, on the lower level, another protected by two sets of tripwire connected to a couple of arrow-shooting, face-piercing dispensers. Use shears to cut the tripwire and access the first chest. Then head back to the levers. These form part of a puzzle that opens a sliding block beside the stairs in the entry level. Jump down to get to the next chest. Alternatively, just smash through the wall behind the levers to get to the chest.

Even if the chests don't contain anything particularly valuable, the jungle temple's construction provides many useful blocks and items, including three sticky pistons, two dispensers, arrows, tripwire hooks, redstone, string, and more. Unlike Indy, you won't need to deal with any giant rolling boulders as you plunder the temple. Bring in the wrecking crew and have a ball!

Witch Huts

Witch huts spawn in swamps and aren't particularly useful on their own because they don't contain chests (see Figure 11.8. However, they do sometimes host a witch complete with prominent wart. You need to take care with these witches, because they're no Glinda the Good. They'll hurl various potions your way and use other potions to counteract your own. But on death, they can drop a few useful goodies such as glowstone dust, bottles, spider eyes, and so on, as well as an occasional potion.

Fight the witches from a distance, out of potion-tossing range, using a bow.

FIGURE 11.7 The treasure room of a desert temple. Be careful of that pressure plate! You may find some such rooms already blown up, typically caused by a mob spawning inside and trampling on the plate.

FIGURE 11.8 A witch and her hut.

Dungeons

Dungeons are smaller rooms buried underground that house a mob spawner and usually one or two chests. Although they can appear anywhere, they're most easily spotted when their wall intersects with the side of a large cavern or abandoned mineshaft. Look out for the greenish moss stone shown in Figure 11.9.

The chests can hold a lot of useful loot, so disable the spawner and enjoy.

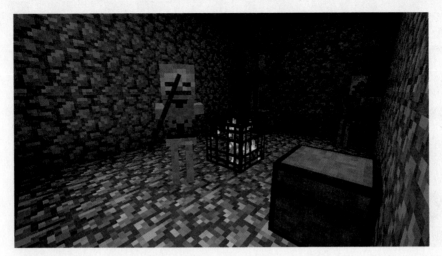

FIGURE 11.9 A dungeon connected to a cave system. Some are more useful than others. This one's chests contained enchanted books, a saddle, lots of gunpowder, and more.

Abandoned Mineshafts

I first mentioned mineshafts in Chapter 5, "Combat School," (see page 88 ["Cave Spiders,"]). They are quite liberally scattered underground and often intersect caves, making them easy to find. Each is different, often sprawling across huge multilayered levels (see Figure 11.10). Explore them for their chests, rails, and timber, but look out for cave spiders while you do so. One small bonus: you'll find lots of cobwebs near cave spider spawners. (Deactivate a spider by placing a torch on or nearby to raise the light level above the spawning threshold.)

Harvest the webs with a sword or shears to obtain string, or use shears enchanted with silk touch to pull in the actual cobweb. Cobwebs slow down all mobs except cave spiders, so they are useful in traps. However, they won't slow you down if you're riding a minecart, so you can use them to defend tunnels by slowing down other mobs while you speed ahead.

Strongholds

Strongholds are large underground structures. They come in a variety of sizes, often with numerous rooms and chests. More importantly, they also contain the End portal needed to reach The End region. The portal is protected by a silverfish spawner and must be activated first with Eyes of Ender.

Strongholds are tough to find. They're usually buried deep, although I have seen them in an ocean biome where their structure could be seen looking through the water.

Finding strongholds takes a specific technique. I'll cover this and the portal in Chapter 12, "Playing Through: The Nether and The End."

FIGURE 11.10 Abandoned mineshafts are renowned for their cave spiders but can contain all the other Overworld's hostile mobs, along with water and lava hazards. They're a great source of rails and wood, as well as other finds from chests.

Nether Fortresses

These huge structures feature exclusively in The Nether region and contain unique ingredients for brewing potions and finding strongholds. They're packed with chests that can hold some powerful items, but getting to The Nether and surviving The Nether long enough to find a fortress is a journey in itself. As with strongholds, I'll show you how in Chapter 12.

Mapping, or There and Back Again

You'll likely make some significant tracks as you journey across the Overworld finding its different structures. One handy tool can help you (if pressing F3—or fn+F3 on OS X—to constantly check coordinates seems a little like cheating): maps, in a word. If you're playing the Xbox Edition, you'll have a map in your inventory when you start a new world, and that one map with a little coercion through zooming (see below) can display the entire world. That's not so on the PC, where the world is so much larger. Follow these steps to start mapping:

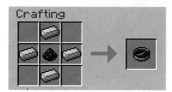

1 Create a compass. The compass on its own isn't too useful—it *always* points to your world's original spawn point. This never changes, even after you change your own spawn

point by sleeping in a bed, but if you've built your base quite close to that original spawn, it could be useful. Just keep it in a quick access slot and follow the red needle. But let's continue on our current path and use the compass instead to make a map.

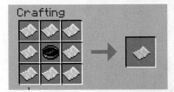

2 Place the compass in the middle of the crafting table and surround it with eight pieces of paper. (Remember: Paper is obtained from sugar cane, so it's quite easy to make.) Drag the map to a quick access slot.

3 The map hasn't yet been used, so it shows up as empty. Select the map and right-click it to activate it. The map gradually fills in to show the landscape around you as well as structures such as villages (see Figure 11.11), although you may need to wander a little toward the edges of the map to complete the cartography because they only show territory you've explored. Move your mouse up and down to bring the map to eye level, or sink it down again so you can still hold it but see the territory ahead. Your approximate location at the time of activation becomes the permanent center of the map. It's approximate because maps align to an overall world grid, making it possible to create a series of maps whose edges align. Place them in a grid of item frames on a wall to create a much larger overall view of the world. Any other maps placed in frames elsewhere show up as a green dot on every map covering that location, providing a way to *pin* locations for later reference.

FIGURE 11.11 A map showing a village and the surrounding landscape. Your location is shown as the white-arrowed rectangle, in this case located in the upper-left corner.

4 The white arrow shows your current location, changing to a white dot if you move off the map. This won't take long because the current map is quite small, covering an area of just 128×128 blocks mapped as one block per pixel, or a scale of 1:1.

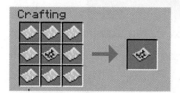

5 You'll probably want to make a larger map to gain more benefit. Maps can zoom out to a scale of 16:1, doubling each time. To do so, place the map back on the crafting table and then add another eight sheets of paper and pick up the new map. Note that this process is not reversible. In other words, you can't zoom in a zoomed-out map.

Crafting a Clock

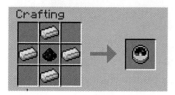

Clocks can help you keep track of time, so you know if it's safe to surface while exploring structures underground or working in your mine. Craft a clock with four gold ingots and one piece of redstone.

A clock works anywhere—in your inventory, in a quick access slot. It even tells the time before you pick it up from the crafting table.

A clock works in a simple manner rotating clockwise (appropriately enough) between night and day phases represented by black and blue hemispheres. At midnight you see the moon located at the 12 o'clock position. The sun rotates to the same location by noon. Figure 11.12 shows a clock mounted in an item frame with sunrise starting to approach, shown by the border between the blue hemisphere starting to push the night disk aside.

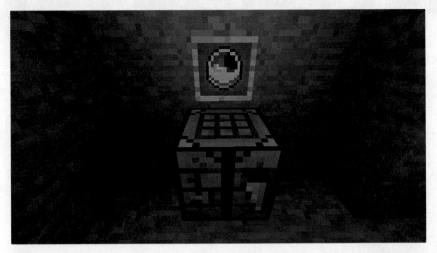

FIGURE 11.12 Time to down tools and get back to the surface; morning has broken.

The Bottom Line

Minecraft's worlds are riddled with dungeons, abandoned mineshafts, and strongholds, as well as intricate, lengthy natural cave systems. You've probably seen some of this if you've done any flying around in Creative mode, where the landscape generates in real time in front of you, starting from the bottom up. Structures are much thinner, literally, on the ground, but the temples do hold some useful bits and pieces, and trading with villages adds a whole new dynamic to the game. You can even treat the trading offers as a quest-generation system, heading out to gather the requirements for any given trade, no matter what, and without breaking the order in which they're received. Actually, as you'll see in the next chapter, the trading system can even let you skip the entire Nether region and jump straight to that epic battle pending with the Ender Dragon. It all depends on the villager priests and their precious Eyes of Ender. Read on to learn how.

Playing Through: The Nether and The End

In This Chapter

- Get kitted up and head to The Nether.
- Find your way through a region of plummeting lava falls, endless fiery lakes, and precipitous cliffs.
- Locate the nether fortress, defeat its mobs, and take home its horde.
- Set course for a stronghold, and activate its portal.
- Travel to The End and defeat the dragon.

Pack your bags—we're off on another field trip. You won't need your winter woolies because you'll be heading to Hell and back. In this chapter, you explore Minecraft's other worlds: The Nether and The End. They're a little like Dante's vision of the seventh and ninth circles of Hell: flaming rivers in one, an icy core in the other. Defeating the Ender Dragon also completes your journey through the official game structure, earning your passage back to The Overworld. You'll bring home countless treasures, valuable experience, and the priceless achievement of having won the toughest battle in Minecraft. Think of it as going from Hell 9 to Cloud 9.

Alternate Dimensions

The Nether and End regions are not fun places to hang out (see Figure 12.1 and 12.2). You need to go in with specific goals; don't dawdle too long. Both places are hazardous to your health, and any time you die, you respawn in The Overworld and lose anything you haven't been able to put away in a chest for safekeeping.

TIP

Nether Here and There

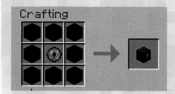

Ender chests transport the same items between all dimensions, so they are incredibly useful for stashing valuable finds when traveling in the more dangerous regions. Die in The Nether, and you can pick up anything you've already stored back in The Overworld when you respawn. Create an Ender chest with one eye of Ender and eight obsidian blocks. (Of course, you need at least two chests—one at each end—to make this useful.) See "The End Game," later in the chapter, for more on creating those elusive eyes.

FIGURE 12.1 Seeing red? It's just The Nether: a cavernous, unforgiving place filled with more lava pools than a Krakatoan conference.

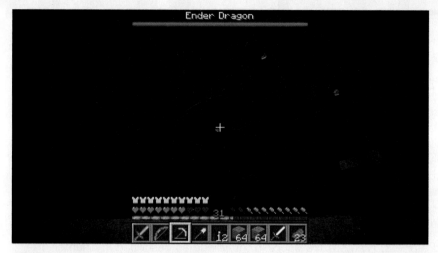

FIGURE 12.2   The End region is a dark dimension inhabited by a large dragon. It's probably high time to swap that pickaxe for something significantly sharper.

Getting through both dimensions and playing through to the end of the game takes a bit of work, but you can definitely get lucky. Although your experience will vary as much as it does in any unique Minecraft world, it will run something like this:

1 Take your time to build up your resources in The Overworld and become combat ready—you're heading into a heck of a fight, and it's going to take a lot more than just a couple of swords and some light armor to get through.

2 Build an obsidian portal to travel to The Nether.

3 Find a Nether Fortress and defeat a dozen or so blaze mobs, collecting their dropped blaze rods.

4 Return to The Overworld and craft Eyes of Ender. You'll also need to defeat about 15 Endermen in The Overworld to gain Ender pearls for this recipe, but also see the tip "Trade Your Way to The End," which follows this list.

5 Use the eyes to find a stronghold and activate its end portal.

6 Defeat the Ender Dragon and travel through the exit portal back to The Overworld. In Minecraft's rather spare tradition, you won't see a fancy end game sequence, but you'll get to read the existential "End Poem" and see the credits roll, followed by a final score that is equal to your current experience points.

Try to be patient as you complete these six steps. This is not a first-person shooter that takes a day, some pizza, and a rack of energy drinks to finish off, although you certainly could. It also isn't an impossible challenge, and you'll see some great sights along the way.

> **TIP**
>
> **Trade Your Way to The End**
>
> Traveling to The Nether is not an actual prerequisite for completing the game. You really only need to go there to obtain the blaze rods that supply blaze powder. These, when combined with an Ender pearl dropped by Endermen, become an Eye of Ender. If you've found a village or two, look for the purple-garbed priest villager. There's about a 16% probability they'll offer to sell you an Eye of Ender for 7 to 10 emeralds a pop. Even if the initial trade isn't useful, you can use it to open additional trades until you have the one you want. This is actually a great way to get to the end of the game if you're not so much into hardcore combat. It will still take quite a bit of time, though, because you'll be extremely busy doing different tasks to complete other trades until you've amassed sufficient Eyes of Ender.
>
> If you can't find a priest, create extra doors in the village as described in Chapter 11, "Villages and Other Structures," to spawn more villagers until one springs into existence.

Getting to The Nether

Most of a successful trip to The Nether is really about being prepared. Start by gathering the items on this survival checklist:

- **A full set of iron armor**—When it comes to armor, diamond is best, but given the scarcity of diamond blocks, and accepting the fact that you'll almost certainly die and respawn without it, just stick with iron. If you can, apply an enchantment of feather falling to your boots so you can jump down cliffs, and any other protection enchantments you can summon up. Remember, though, that when you die your armor doesn't come back with you, so don't go overboard. Be utilitarian rather than trying to become invincible.

- **A couple of iron pickaxes and a few swords**—Make one of the swords diamond—it will help in a difficult fight.

- **An iron shovel and a full stack of gravel (64 blocks)**—You'll need this stuff for pillar-jumping. The Nether has a lot of crazy-tall cliffs you'll need to get up and down.

- **Two full stacks of cobblestone**—You'll need this to create temporary shelters, bridges, and barricades.

NOTE

Forget the Water

Don't worry about bringing water with you. There's no way to place it, so you can't convert any of the numerous, enormous lava lakes to cobblestone or obsidian for easier passage.

- **A bow and a full stack of arrows**—Use these to shoot down ghasts, or a bow with the infinity enchantment to save on arrows.

- **Snow blocks**—Turn these into snowballs to help fight blaze mobs.

- **10 obsidian blocks and a flint and steel**—Gather these in case you need to build another portal to return to The Overworld. (You'll also need 10 blocks to build the portal to get to The Nether, so aim for 20 in all.) See Chapter 10, "Enchanting, Anvils, and Brewing," page 195 if you need help in finding obsidian.

- **Lots of torches!**—As many as a full stack if you can. The torches are mostly useful for creating a trail of breadcrumbs so you can find your way back to your portal. (It's ridiculously easy to become lost down there.) Also consider bringing some jack-o'-lanterns because these are easily spotted across a longer distance.

- **A stack of wood blocks of any kind and around 20 iron ingots**—You can use these to create a crafting table and additional weapons, tools, and ladders as needed.

- **An iron door and some iron bars**—Use these to create a temporary shelter for crafting, healing, taking a breather, and so on. Wooden doors can burn when hit by fireballs in The Nether, even though they are immune to fire in The Overworld. Don't forget to bring some iron buttons so you can open the door.

- **Food**—Aim for bread and cooked meats, at least half a stack of each. You need to keep your hunger bar full so that your health continually regenerates.

- **A chest**—An Ender Chest is fantastic, but you may not have been able to make one yet. Any other chest will do.

Arrange one of each weapon in the quick access slots, along with the torches, shovel, gravel, cobblestone, and a couple of food stacks. You can leave the rest in the upper section of the inventory.

Ready? Let's go. The first order of business is to put up a portal.

Portal Magic

The Nether Portal acts as an interdimensional transport between The Overworld and The Nether. Follow these steps:

1 Create an obsidian frame with an inner dimension that is three blocks high by two blocks wide (see Figure 12.3). The corner blocks can be made from any material. The frame must be vertical, either free-standing, or built directly into any type of wall including a natural cliff face.

FIGURE 12.3 Build your gateway to the underworld (I mean The Nether) with an obsidian frame.

CAUTION

Portals Are a Double-Edged Sword

Once you've built a portal, a second appears in The Nether. Neither belongs to you exclusively, and they allow other mobs to travel back and forth, so expect to see quite a few more zombie pigmen in The Overworld in the near future. (They can even spawn near them in The Overworld without coming from The Nether.)

2 Use a flint and steel to light the top of either of the two bottom blocks. You see the interior spring to life with a shimmering blue and purple transparent texture, as shown in Figure 12.4.

FIGURE 12.4   Once lit, the frame stays that way unless hit by a ghast's fireball, but you only need to worry about that with the companion frame in The Nether.

3 Okay, take a last long look at The Overworld and hope that you won't see it for a while because that probably just means you respawned. Now, jump into that frame!

4 Minecraft may need to download some terrain files the first time you travel through the portal. Wait until you see a wavy animation that covers the whole screen, then step through the portal to enter The Nether.

Now that you're here, you've got some work to do. Remember, your main goal is to find a nether fortress.

The Nether has some very extreme terrain, so you may need to make use of any of the following techniques:

■ Dig tunnels and stairs by mining the netherrack with your pickaxe to move up and down cliffs. Fortunately, netherrack breaks extremely fast so it's easy to get around.

■ Remember to place torches or Jack o'Lanterns as you go, always ensuring you can see the last one placed from the next position. If you do become hopelessly lost, consider building another portal to take you back to The Overworld. You may pop up quite some distance away as every block traveled in The Nether is the equivalent of eight blocks traveled in The Overworld.

■ Deal with mobs carefully, and don't attack zombie pigmen as this will bring an entire horde of them down on you. Your biggest risk as you explore comes from ghasts and their fireballs, but the fireballs are slow, and you can knock them straight back at the ghast with a well-timed sword-swing or arrow. Zig-zag if you decide to retreat so they don't keep a bearing on you with the next volley. See "Nether Mobs" later in the chapter for specific strategies.

- Use the Sneak key (Left Shift) when close to any cliffs and lava lakes to avoid taking a tumble.

- Crank the screen's **Brightness** slider all the way to the right in the game's **Options-->Video Settings...** menu, and ensure **Render Distance** is set to **Far**. This will help you spot nether fortresses.

- Stop to pick up a few things as you go. The bright glowstone, red and brown mushrooms, soul sand, and nether quartz all exist in abundance and are all useful crafting and brewing ingredients.

- Pause every so often to take a good look for the fortress. They're recognizable at a distance by their wide expanses of netherbrick, long exposed walkways and bridges, rows of windows and, often, tall walls. You're looking for any straight-geometric structure within the geological randomness of the cave system. Figure 12.5 shows the ramparts of a netherbrick wall signifying a fortress. How quickly you find one is where the luck comes in. It might take just a few minutes, in which case you can rush in, get things done, head back and have almost all your possessions intact. Or it could take hours of hard slog. Nether fortresses generate along the north/south axis in long lines, so the easiest way to find one is to try to head east or west. A compass won't help as they spin randomly in the Nether, but you can use the F3 coordinate system in a pinch. The x-axis is aligned east/west, and the y-axis north/south. If you don't see one after travelling 160 blocks or so, head about 40 blocks north or south and try again.

FIGURE 12.5   You can spot fortresses from below by the walls that extend down to the lowest levels of a cave. When looking down from above you'll see long straight walkways and rows of window spaces.

■ If you enter a fortress from below, use your pickaxe to dig out the netherbrick and ascend until you reach a corridor. If coming from above just work your way down to a walkway and enter the fortress, or come in through a sidewall. You may need to navigate around broken walkways or cave-ins, but fortresses are massive; so if a viable entry isn't obvious at first, just look around until you can find a way in.

Now you're almost done. There is a bit of combat ahead, and then you can head back out to The Overworld.

Surviving the Nether Fortress

Every fortress presents a similar experience: traipsing long mazes of corridors before stumbling into a moment of extreme terror! Actually, it's not that bad. You will find many long corridors. You'll also find numerous chests filled with some of the most valuable and rare items in the game. Then, once in a while, you'll probably find a small balcony containing a spawner churning out blaze mobs, (see Figure 12.6), wandering wither skeletons, and magma cubes.

Follow these tips to survive:

■ Place torches on the ground as you pass intersections so you can find your way back to your original entry point and then back to the portal.

■ Use blocks to create temporary barricades when attacking or being pursued by mobs. This is particularly useful in long corridors where it's impossible to dodge away from an arrow-wielding wither skeleton, or when ducking out to attack the blazes springing from a spawner.

■ Loot every chest you find. It's always worthwhile!

■ Avoid spending too long on open walkways as you'll be vulnerable to ghast attacks.

■ Look for the bright red nether wart growing around the base of wide stairways. It's the base of all potions, and a few potions will help you complete the final part of the game.

■ When you find a blaze spawner, put up a two-block high barricade nearby, then wait just behind the nearest corner to attack blazes as they approach from the other side. You can duck in and out, timing your attacks for when they've finished throwing their fireballs. If all goes south, retreat back to the barricade and rebuild your health.

■ Remember, you're here mainly for the blaze rods. Collect them from each killed blaze until you have 10 or so, then head back to the portal and the bright, sunny, verdant Overworld.

■ Place your spoils of victory in a chest near the fortress entry point now and then, just in case you die. You can come back and pick them up later, or grab them on the way out after you've hit your quota.

FIGURE 12.6 Try not to pause in this position: there's a blaze spawner in the middle and a floating blaze on the left emitting smoke during its cool-down period.

That's all there is to it, really. It's not so difficult on Normal difficulty, and becomes quite easy once you've done it a few times.

Nether Mobs

You'll meet an interesting mix of mobs while exploring The Nether. If you're properly equipped, they won't present too much of a problem:

- **Zombie pigmen**—I first introduced these in Chapter 5, "Combat School," page 83. Avoid fighting them because, as with zombies, you'll get rushed by a mob. Their drops aren't really worth the risk, and you'll find a lot more swag in a fortress.

- **Ghasts**—With a fittingly ghastly moan, these huge floating mobs attack you from a long distance (see Figure 12.5). They're quite slow moving but spit out dangerous fireballs that can cause as much damage by an indirect hit, setting the netherrack around you on fire, as they do directly. Take care of them with two to three fully charged arrows, and dodge the fireballs by moving just a few blocks out of the line of fire. If you're brave enough, you can also fish them in with a fishing rod and hack at them with a sword. Ghasts drop magma cream and ghast tears, both useful for brewing, but you'll need to find one over land or pull it in with a fishing rod so the drops don't burn up in lava.

FIGURE 12.7 Ghasts typically float through The Nether's sulphurous air, but they can also sink into a lava lake and take pot-shots at you sniper-style.

- **Blazes**—You might find blazes floating down the corridors of a fortress, but they're usually near a spawner. They have a distinctive attack pattern, spinning up for a few seconds while emitting a fire effect, and then shooting three quick fireballs at you. They then cool off for a while. Attack them while they're chilling down, or early on when they're spinning up. Swords work well if one separates from the pack; otherwise, use arrows and then make a dash past the entryway to the spawner to pick up the blaze rod drops.

- **Magma cubes**—These burning cubes split like slime mobs in The Overworld. They're slower but far more dangerous and harder to kill. Attack the large cubes and middle-sized cubes from a distance with arrows, and then finish off the small ones with your sword. You pick up a lot of experience points and the handy magma cream.

- **Wither skeleton**—These tall versions of the regular skeleton stalk the hallways of fortresses. They usually use swords but occasionally can pick up a bow, and getting hit by one causes the Wither effect, a type of soul-destroying poison that darkens your health bar for 10 seconds while causing additional damage. They're best attacked with an arrow from a distance. You can also turn the odds in your favor by creating a bolt hole that's just two blocks high. The wither skeleton is a little taller than the regular skeleton and can't follow you through.

NOTE

Dante's Dimensions

It's probably all just coincidence, but there are some interesting parallels between Minecraft's other dimensions and Dante's own. Dante treated the levels of Hell as concentric spheres, each becoming smaller, like the layers of an onion (with plenty of associated weeping, and a lot of gnashing). The seventh level, the closest corresponding with the nature of The Nether, falls eight layers beneath the earth. In Minecraft, The Nether has a scale 1/8 that of The Overworld, so traveling 100 blocks in The Nether and then taking a portal back to the surface will have taken you 800 blocks in The Overworld. This is exactly how it would work if The Nether was a smaller sphere beneath The Overworld, and, of course, "nether" does mean *lower*, or *under*.

Dante's ninth and final circle is a small frozen region protected by a winged Satan. Minecraft's End region is a similarly barren, tiny region protected by a winged dragon. While Dante's Satan was trapped in the ice and Dante and Virgil didn't have to defeat him, they nevertheless found their way back to the surface of the earth by climbing down through a hole in the center. In Minecraft you'll jump through a portal in the middle of The End to find your way back to the sunny side.

CAUTION

Chores Are Over...Don't Make Your Bed

Sleeping in a bed in either The Nether or The End regions is definitely not a good idea. Settle in for a quick nap, and the bed explodes faster than a creeper on final fuse.

With some blaze rods in hand, you have what you need for the final journey. The End, as they say, is nigh.

The End Game

Are you ready to start the final phase? Just as you prepared for The Nether, you'll need to gather a few items for The End. There are two parts to the conclusion: finding a stronghold and finding The End portal; then defeating the Ender Dragon. You don't need to get everything on this list, but it will give you an idea of the level of preparation:

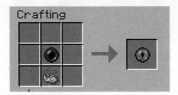

- **Eyes of Ender**—You'll need about 15, either by trading with priest villagers or by crafting. You may need up to 12 to activate The End portal, and the rest to find the stronghold. If crafting the eyes, spend some time defeating 15 Endermen to collect 15 Ender pearls. Endermen are easiest to find at night. Now place the blaze rods you collected from The Nether on the crafting grid (saving at least one for a brewing stand if you plan to concoct some potions), and collect the blaze powder. Combine that with the Ender pearls to create the Eyes of Ender.

- **Weapons**—Bring a diamond sword (hopefully with a sharpness enchantment) and a couple of bows with infinity enchantments or at least two stacks of arrows. Also bring some string in case you need to build additional bows.

- **Armor**—Diamond armor is ideal, including boots with a feather fall enchantment because you'll probably suffer a couple of long drops while fighting the dragon. Bring a helmet and a pumpkin, and consider using the latter so you don't antagonize the numerous Endermen into a fight.

- **Potions**—Brew up potions of regeneration and healing. Strength potions can help, but only when you can attack the dragon with a sword. You'll mostly use a bow and arrows. See Chapter 10 if you aren't familiar with enchanting and brewing.

- **Food**—Pack about half that recommended for The Nether expedition.

- **Tools**—Bring a couple of stacks of dirt or gravel, and of course an iron shovel because there will be some pillar jumping involved. Also bring two iron pickaxes because you'll need to dig down to the stronghold, and they'll help you in The End region.

- **Ladders**—They're an alternative to pillar jumping. Just bring whichever you prefer.

- **Obsidian**—Twelve blocks should do, just in case you need to build a bridge that the Ender Dragon can't destroy.

- **Bed**—You can't use it in The End region, but you may need it while finding the stronghold. Once you have a bed, you can set it up in the portal room to create a new spawn point.

- **The Kitchen Sink**—Bring anything else you can think of to set up a small shelter in the stronghold to act as your base, such as wood and iron blocks for tools, additional diamonds, a crafting table, a furnace, a brewing stand, and so on. At least be prepared to make a small shelter in case you need to spend a night on your way to the stronghold.

Finding a Stronghold

Each Overworld generates with three strongholds located between 640 and 1152 blocks from the world's original spawn point. You might be lucky and find the stronghold in just a few minutes, and it shouldn't take any longer than 20. They're spaced at equidistant angles from the spawn, 120 degrees apart, with no part rising above the general terrain. They are, however, cut by natural terrain features such as ravines and valleys, so while in most cases they're buried deep underground, there's a chance you could stumble across an exposed section. You may even find just a stronghold's portal room sitting on its own in water.

Follow these steps to find your first stronghold:

1 Climb to a high spot, hopefully with some clear space around, and then throw an Eye of Ender. It will float into the air and zoom off in the direction of the nearest stronghold.

2 In four out of five cases the eye floats to the ground a short distance away. Pick it up to use again, and you're already on your way to the stronghold. In some cases the eye just explodes instead. Don't worry; just head in the same direction.

3 Keep travelling for quite some way so you don't use too many eyes; then throw another. The eyes float high when the stronghold is distant and float quickly to the ground when you're close or over the top of the stronghold. In the PC edition, the eye homes in on The End portal room, whereas in the Xbox edition it takes you to the center of the dungeon and you need to explore the dungeon from there.

4 When you think you have the dungeon's location zeroed down, start digging. Use normal mining techniques to create a staircase, turning regularly so that you stay in the same general area. You'll know you're there when you start to dig up stone or mossy bricks. Keep going until you break through into the portal room or a corridor, but don't dig straight down because you could fall into a lava pool (see Figure 12.8). If you do need to work your way down into the room, open the roof a little and sneak-place blocks against the wall to create steps.

FIGURE 12.8 Eureka! Breaking through into The End portal room.

The portal room contains a silverfish spawner. These mobs are best defeated in one blow (requires a diamond sword with at least a sharpness level 1 enchantment). Taking more than one blow alerts others, and you could end up with a swarm, but they're not impossible to handle without an enchanted sword. Just try to dispatch them as quickly as possible.

Once you've cleared the room, there are just a few more preparatory steps:

1 Destroy the spawner with a pickaxe.

2 Block up the entrance you used to enter the portal chamber, assuming you didn't saunter in through the iron door in the anteroom.

3 Place a bed and sleep in it to reset your spawn. If you die in The End (which is very likely), you'll come straight back here, saving an overland trek.

4 Place a torch in the anteroom to prevent other mobs spawning.

5 Check the chest that's in the anteroom to see if there's anything useful there, and then dump almost everything else you're carrying in the chest. You only want to take with you the armor you're wearing (including the pumpkin that you should place on your head), one of each weapon, about two dozen food items, a pickaxe, some potions, and a shovel.

6 If you want to just take a look at The End region first, store everything you have in the chest except for a dozen or so dirt blocks or obsidian, a pickaxe, and a cheap bow and half a dozen arrows. This approach can help if you spawn in an awkward position and need to first build a bridge out of obsidian to the main island. If you get swept into the void by the Ender Dragon, you'll be able to come back and complete the job bringing a complete set of tools once you're sure you can get across. Any dropped items are not recoverable after respawning, although items placed in a chest in The End will survive. When you're ready to return, just die in some convenient way, pick up the main set of supplies stashed in the stronghold, and head back through the portal.

CAUTION

Don't Destroy the Portal!

Be extra careful not to destroy any of The End portal blocks. There's no way to repair them, and you'll then have to find another dungeon to continue your journey.

Now the final magic moment: activating the portal. Climb the steps and place Eyes of Ender into any of the empty slots on top of the stones surrounding the portal. You'll see it spring into deep black life, as shown in Figure 12.9.

FIGURE 12.9 The End portal, activated.

Ready for action? That dragon has no idea what's coming. Go ahead and jump in! Then press Esc to pause, and read on.

Defeating the Ender Dragon

The End region generates as a fairly small island floating in an endless void, dotted with obsidian towers and numerous Endermen. Your actual spawn point is probably located on this island, but it can also be underground (in which case you can use your pickaxe to dig out a staircase to the surface) or on an even smaller platform floating a small distance away from the mainland. If that's the case, you'll need to build a platform across using your dirt blocks or obsidian and keep your bow handy so you can shoot the Ender Dragon if it attacks so it doesn't push you into the void.

The Ender Dragon is no quick kill. With 200 hit points and the ability to knock out up to half your health in a single blow, its wings are not easily clipped, but it's also no Smaug.

Defeat the dragon following these steps. It's actually not difficult but can take a few attempts. Always keep your hunger bar topped up so your health can continually regenerate:

1 The dragon draws healing power from the ender crystals located atop the obsidian tow-ers (see Figure 12.10). You won't defeat it without knocking out every one of them.

2 Put the pumpkin on your head so you don't annoy any Endermen. They'll needlessly sap your health, so it's worth having a reduced field of view, shown in Figure 12.11.

FIGURE 12.10 You'll probably first spot the Ender Dragon in the distance. Look for the line of shimmering power as it passes by an ender crystal.

FIGURE 12.11 Wearing the pumpkin requires a bit more scanning to get the full picture, but it doesn't take too long to get used to it.

3 Head toward the nearest pillar. You'll be able to shoot out the ender crystal on top with a single arrow shot if the pillar is low enough; otherwise, you need to pillar jump to climb to the top. Seeing the dragon's health bar appear means its close by. Take a look around and try to fire an arrow into its head (its most sensitive part) if it's on an attack run heading straight for you. Otherwise, continue pillar jumping a few more seconds and then look again. Keep in mind that you can also get knocked off by the dragon's wing when it's just flying by, and that will destroy the nearby dirt blocks of your pillar. In that case just start another pillar from ground level.

4 Try to hit the crystal with an arrow when you're a block or two from the top, keeping as much distance as possible because the resulting explosion can cause substantial damage. (That explosion can also knock out other nearby crystals, so it may benefit you.) Also, if you have diamond armor with a high-level protection enchantment, just whack the crystal with impunity.

5 Take a good look around from the top of the tower and shoot out any other crystals that are within range.

6 Head back to the ground using your shovel to dig out the dirt blocks you placed, and repeat until you've taken out every crystal. You should be able to spot any you've missed by looking for the white beams that show up as the dragon draws power.

Now it's dragon time. Follow these steps to deal it a deathly blow:

1 Position yourself on any raised area of ground. It's easier to spot the dragon this way because it can actually dive through surrounding hills if you're in a valley, catching you by surprise. For the same reason, burrowing into the ground to find shelter doesn't work. The dragon can dive through and hit you just as hard—you just won't see it coming!

2 Keep your bow fully charged with the arrow ready to fly with a critical hit.

3 Take your time waiting for the dragon to start its attack run. It flaps around in the distance for a while. Don't waste arrows firing at the dragon until you see it turn and head directly toward you. Figure 12.12 shows the moment you should unleash the arrow. Aim your crosshairs directly at the dragon's head. (My aim is a little off in that screenshot. Let me just say that it can be quite difficult to fight an Ender Dragon *and* take screen shots at the same time!)

FIGURE 12.12 The Ender Dragon on the final stage of its attack run.

4 A hit directly into the head causes maximum damage. You'll see the dragon flash red and quickly change direction. With correct timing, you can repeatedly hit the dragon without taking any damage.

5 Keep track of the dragon through the gaps in the pumpkin helmet. You don't need to worry about looking out for anything else *except* its position. It should take your full focus.

6 Stand your ground and repeat until you've knocked the dragon's health down to zero. Then stand by for a striking purple-strobed explosion of splendid proportion (see Figure 12.13).

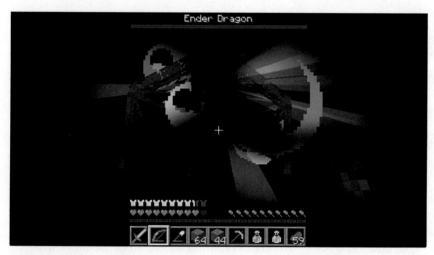

FIGURE 12.13 The final moments of the Ender Dragon.

Congratulations! Notch yourself up as a dragon slayer, because you've just defeated the toughest mob in Minecraft! Enjoy the spectacle—it's probably been a long time coming and is over far too fast.

Watch for a portal to appear directly beneath the dragon's last position as soon as the fireworks finish. It will have a dragon egg perched atop—a shrine, if you like, to the dragon's defeat, or a celebration of your victory. Maybe both?

Before you take the fast route home by jumping into the portal, stop to pick up the numerous experience orbs dropped by the dragon. You'll collect up to 70 XP levels. You can also keep the pumpkin helmet on and start wailing on Endermen to gather experience, but you'll need to do so without the pumpkin for them to drop Ender pearls. You can always return through any stronghold portal to do that later.

TIP

Wanna Grab That Egg?

It's a little tricky and doesn't serve any purpose except as a trophy piece to put in an item frame back home, but why not? Build a small platform up to the egg and hit it with any tool to knock it to the ground. (Actually, it teleports, but not too far.) There's only one way to crack this egg, and that's by digging two blocks under it, placing a torch on the lowest block, and then knocking out the one directly under the egg. Jump in to pick up the dropped egg and scramble out of there.

And that, as they say, is that. When you're ready, jump feet-first into the portal to view the End Poem (it's worth a read) and game credits—or press Esc to skip. You'll return to your last spawn point in The Overworld.

Well done!

The Bottom Line

With The End game complete, you may be wondering what to do next. You've probably got a stronghold to explore, and at some point you may want to get home, but in any case, I have some good news. The end of *Minecraft* is actually just the beginning. Build, explore, survive, and thrive. Then dramatically expand the experience in Chapter 13, "Mods and Multiplayer." Customize your experience, modify Minecraft to the hilt, and join a multitude of servers with worlds, options, trading systems, combat scenarios, and a whole host of extraordinary things to do. The possibilities are as endless as The Overworld itself.

Mods and Multiplayer

In This Chapter

- Go skin deep: switch-up your threads, grab a guise and give Steve the slip
- Adopt a mod and give yourself superhero capabilities, add more creatures, or get an invaluable radar system
- Sharing is caring: create a multiplayer game on your LAN
- Beam yourself and others around the world with command blocks
- Expand your Minecraft universe with multiplayer gaming
- Set up your own server and host a permanent world you, your family, and friends can all enjoy

Customizing Your Experience

You can customize Minecraft in three main ways:

- Change the main character's skin so it looks like someone, or something, else. You can choose from hundreds of thousands of skins, including variations on the in-game mobs, superheroes (although this won't give you any additional powers), and characters from other games and movies—it's an endless list. Or you can design your own.

- Change the in-game textures and sounds, fonts, and menus with a resource pack. Resource packs dramatically improve the world's look with higher-resolution textures that smooth out the rough bitmaps (although not the actual blocks) of the default world or give it an ambience more befitting your own aesthetics—for example, getting a medieval, modern, cartoon, sci-fi, or dungeon look and feel. Thousands are available.

- Include a mod to add in-game functionality, new tools, items, mobs, and more.

These changes can add a lot of excitement to a Singleplayer game, but they're also required at times to get the most from particular Multiplayer worlds.

I'll walk you through each now.

Changing the Skin You're In

I haven't mentioned this before, and you may know it already, but your character in Minecraft actually has a name. Sort of. The original developer, Markus "Notch" Persson, was asked one time if the character had a name, and he jokingly dubbed him *Steve*. The moniker seems to have stuck, a little like Herobrine, the character that doesn't actually exist in the game but has become the stuff of legend through mods, Internet memes, and so on.

NOTE

Who Is Herobrine?

Herobrine is supposed to be a somewhat spooky character who haunts the game, building strange structures and tunnels and doing all manner of dastardly things to the player. He looks the same as Steve, but with eyes lacking pupils, and has become a favorite discussion point for Minecraft-playing kids. Mojang, the makers of Minecraft, have stoked the fires several times in version release notes by including among the usual list of bullet points about things that have changed, a not entirely innocent nod to the meme that they have "Removed Herobrine". Add that to the hoax videos, the actual mods that do add a Herobrine character, and talk among kids, and Herobrine has become as real as the Slender Man, that other Internet spook.

It's all in good fun, of course, especially at Halloween when Herobrine comes knocking at your door.

So, anyway, back to Steve. Want to spruce him up? Maybe change his look entirely? Make him a her? It's nice to be distinctive, especially in a Multiplayer world. You can, and it's quite easy to do. The Xbox edition has eight skins by default, and additional Skin Packs are released now and then as paid downloadable content.

On a PC there's just one skin initially, standard Steve, but you can find multitudes more online. Alternatively, you can create your own using a number of editing tools or even start from scratch if your graphical skills are up to the task.

The first thing you need is a skin file. Figure 13.1 shows the default skin splayed out. Each section corresponds to a particular facet of the character, the top half dealing with the head and the lower half, from left to right, the legs, torso, and arms. Each section wraps around the 3D model file generated by the game.

Fortunately, you don't need to know too much about the specifics of the mapping because there are a number of excellent skin editors available online as well as on iOS and Android devices, and there are abundant preexisting community-created skin files available for easy customization.

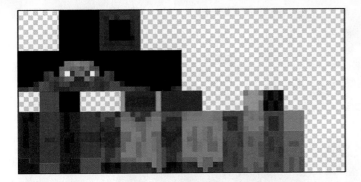

FIGURE 13.1   Steve's skin file, splayed out so that it shows every surface.

The basic steps are unusual because you'll need to use an external editor to adjust the file, and then, rather than loading it into the game, you'll instead load it up to your online Minecraft account as detailed below.

All of the external editors I've listed below come with many thousands of sample skins produced by their community of users.

Minecraft Skin Editors

There's been something of an explosion recently in the number of skin editors available online, as downloadable applications for PC and mobile devices. Some of the iOS and Android apps work extremely well. Most cost a few dollars, and it takes just a few taps to upload the skin so you can view it on the PC edition of Minecraft. (Minecraft Pocket Edition doesn't support custom skins.)

However, you'll find a better collection of editors online. Next, I go into the best three I've found so far.

Skincraft

Skincraft, at www.silvergames.com/minecraft-skin-editor, is an editor (see Figure 13.2) that provides a range of prebuilt components that are built up in layers—everything from ears and eyebrows to coats, vests, pants, skirts, and so on. Yes, you can even have your character running around in little more than a Speedo. It's a quick way to get started, although you'll need to load the skin into another editor to get down to individual pixel adjustments.

Minecraftskins

Minecraftskins, at www.minecraftskins.com, is one of the easier-to-use free-form skin editors. It shows the skin wrapped around a 3D model (see Figure 13.3), so you can easily rotate and adjust the skin one pixel at a time. It also has extensive community integration. Visit the site, select a skin, and then click **Editor** to adjust.

FIGURE 13.2 Skincraft has a straightforward interface with a unique layering approach that makes it easy to quickly create a customized character.

FIGURE 13.3 Men In Black, or any color you like. Minecraftskin's editor is one of the easiest to use with pixel-level adjustments on a 3D rotating model.

Novaskin

Novaskin, at http://minecraft.novaskin.me, provides a comprehensive editing system, although with an at-times daunting interface. However, the integrated search system makes it easy to find existing skins and edit them with precision. Novaskin has a huge community with an easy search interface to find the one you want. See Figure 13.4.

FIGURE 13.4 One of the many Sonic the Hedgehog skins loaded into the Novaskin editor.

These editors create a new skin file that you can save to your PC. You may also be able to load them directly to your Minecraft account, but if you'd prefer to do that later or can't do so directly, follow these steps to load a saved file:

1 Log into your account at http://minecraft.net.

2 Click the **Profile** link at the top of the screen.

3 Click on the **Choose File** button, and select the skin file you previously saved.

4 Click **Upload**.

5 Relaunch Minecraft to download the new skin. Press **F5** to toggle between the different view modes.

Resource Packs: Change Your World

Resource packs replace the default textures, sounds, menus, icons, and even the clouds, sun, and moon, although some are more complete than others. Figure 13.5 shows one example. The packs come in all shapes and sizes. Some are ambitious, whereas others are quite simple in scope. All, however, are easy to install.

FIGURE 13.5   The Dokucraft resource pack, like many of the better ones, changes the default textures and also the styling of all the interface elements and menus.

NOTE

Under Construction, Pardon the Dust

As of this writing, during the release of Minecraft v1.6.2, resource packs do not yet have full functionality. In the future, resource packs will include mod installation, so a single resource pack could have an effect not just on Minecraft's appearance, menus, and soundscape, but on gameplay mechanics. In addition, at present you can activate only one resource pack at a time. Minecraft v1.7 will introduce multiple packs, so you can use the mods in one pack, the textures in another, and the sounds from a third, and also arrange the loaded packs by priority to resolve issues where each pack has similar resources. Always match the resource pack to your version of Minecraft. In case you are wondering, you're Minecraft version is always displayed in the title bar.

Installing a resource pack is easy:

1 First download the pack. Try these three:

   ■ **Planet Minecraft**—www.planetminecraft.com

   ■ **Minecraft Texture Packs**—www.minecrafttexturepacks.com

   ■ **MinecraftDL**—www.minecraftdl.com

2 Open the **Options** menu and click **Resource Packs** to open the resource pack management window.

3 Select **Open resource pack folder** to open the directory where the game accesses resource packs.

4 Move the downloaded resource pack file to that folder.

TIP

Are You Packing? Try This

Among the many thousands of resource packs, there are a few that you should try. They're carefully constructed, go beyond being just derivative, and provide a complete overhaul that's gleefully lacking glaring errors. Just remember that you'll get best results by finding the version of the resource pack that is an exact match to your current version of Minecraft so search from them on the sites above and then select the most appropriate link.

- **Dokucraft**—A swords and sorcery pack with animated textures that enliven the game.

- **Faithful 32**—Faithful because it replicates Minecraft's default textures but in a higher-resolution format. I highly recommended it if you just want to improve the standard look.

- **Ovo's Rustic**—Beautifully designed to look like the Wild West. Once you install it, you'll love the new pickaxe.

The default Minecraft textures use a grid of 16x16 pixels. Consider this the size of the pattern placed on each side of a standard block such as cobblestone. Custom resource packs allow this to increase from 16 to 32, to 64, to as high as 128x128 pixels per texture. However, the higher the resolution the more of a hit it will take on your computer. Typically any system can handle a texture of 32x32 and this tends to be where most of the resource packs fall, but switching to 128x128 may well make Minecraft unplayable due to the additional demands those textures place on your PC. If that happens, just restart Minecraft, open the Options menu before starting a game, and switch back to a lower-resolution resource pack.

5 Switch back to Minecraft, and you should see the pack's information appear in the list. If it doesn't, chances are it's not compatible, so just delete it.

6 Click to select it. You may not see anything happen for a few seconds or more as Minecraft extracts the contents of the pack and then reloads its resources. Once it has, you'll typically see some subtle or major changes to the window, including the styling of buttons and usually a change in fonts, although this does depend on the contents of the pack.

7 Press **Esc** to return to the game. (There's no need to go back through all the menus.)

8 Voilà! You've just installed your first resource pack.

Now, a caveat. There's a lot of confusing information in some of the downloads. You'll see references to MCPatcher and Optifine, complex file paths, and more. You can feel free to ignore these. They're old news, left over from earlier versions of Minecraft.

CAUTION

Beware the Pop-Ups

Downloading resource packs, and mods for that matter, can be a tricky business. Most creators try to make some funds from their efforts, which is no problem at all—they've often put thousands of hours into them—but it does lead to one of those first world problems: pop-ups. You can quickly become lost in a sea of spring-loaded pages, interspersed misleading download buttons, strange captcha entries, and, at times, downright duplicity. Unfortunately, there's no real way around this. Websites such as AdFly and MediaFire offer a way for the creators to make a bit of a return for their efforts, at the expense of forcing adviews on everyone downloading that pack. Pop-up blockers provide varied results, sometimes working, other times preventing the download from taking place. Just take care out there, never enter your credit card details, and watch out for misleading links.

Mind My Mods

Mods are the marvel of Minecraft because they can change almost every aspect of the game. Fancy the ability to fire arrows that explode on impact like a block of TNT? Why, certainly. Want a radar that shows every nearby mob overlaid on a map? No problem. Explored your way through every biome there is and, gosh, just want a bit more variety? There's a mod for that, too, and it can generate worlds of fantastic variety.

So what, exactly, is a mod?

In a word, programming. Mods change the way Minecraft works by replacing parts of Minecraft's own program code with their own routines, and by adding additional functionality that goes beyond the original program's design. And herein lies the danger. Mods are the equivalent of the Wild West living within the ordered confines of Minecraft's civilized releases. They are not officially supported by Mojang, and every time a new version, or even a small update to Minecraft comes out, there's a very real risk that the new code will be sufficiently different to the previous version to turn perfectly working mods into piles of binary mush. In turn, installing a mod designed to work with a previous version of Minecraft into a new version may break Minecraft itself, forcing a complete reinstallation of the core game files.

Things become even hairier when mods try to co-exist. One may change a routine upon which another relies, breaking it, and so on. It's a fragile existence. I've even heard of one user, and perhaps there are many more, who continues to use Minecraft v1.4 because they daren't lose compatibility with the 90+ mods they have installed. I'm not exactly sure why anyone needs that many mods, but as you can see, it can become a real problem.

CAUTION

Mods Change Worlds

Mods can add new items, block types, and all sorts of additional data to a world's saved game file. This can have a permanent effect on any world that you open in a modded version of Minecraft. If you just want to test a mod, do so by creating a new world when you have the mod loaded rather than a world to which you may want to return so you don't break a favored world's data. Alternatively, create a backup of that world or your entire saved game folder. See "Adding Mods to Forge" later in this chapter for details on locating this folder. Copy the folder to any convenient location outside the Minecraft directory. Restore it later by copying it back over the original folder.

The good news? Modding Minecraft is no longer the minefield it used to be. There is a solution coming. Mojang have committed to releasing an official programming interface that will ensure mods have a way to work with Minecraft without actually trampling all over the program's code. But there is no release date as yet. However, there is a similar alternative that you can use right now. It's called *Forge*.

Forge acts as a layer between Minecraft and mods. Mods designed to work with Forge talk to it instead of trying to insert themselves into Minecraft. Forge then handles the Minecraft side of the discussion. Forge is, in its way, just another mod, but it ensures all the others that use it "play nice." It also simplifies the installation of mods. You'll see how this works later in this chapter.

Installing Forge Mods

Forge makes mods easy, so don't leave home without it. Follow these steps to install:

1. First download the Forge installer from http://files.minecraftforge.net. Look for the recommended file for your version of Minecraft under the Promotions list at the top of the page. (In this case, *promotions* simply means that it's a promoted file, and has nothing to do with advertising.) Then click "(installer)" under the Downloads column.

2. You'll pass briefly through the AdFly network. Wait 5 seconds and then click SKIP AD in the top-right corner of the web page to download the file.

3. Open the downloaded file to install. Usually everything is correctly set by default, but ensure **Install Client** is selected. You'll also see a file path to your Minecraft application folder. I've never seen the installer get it wrong, but you can adjust it if you see a problem. Then click **OK**.

4. Within a second or two you'll see a window confirming Forge was successfully installed.

The installer obviously installs its own files, but it does so in a clever way by creating a new profile in the Minecraft Launcher. Select the Forge profile or your standard profile to quickly switch between the modded and un-modded versions of Minecraft.

To test the installation, open your Minecraft Launcher and click the **Profile** drop-down menu. You'll see a new profile called *Forge*. Select this and click **Play**. If your Forge installation was successful, you'll see some additional information on the title screen in the lower-left corner, as shown in Figure 13.6.

FIGURE 13.6   Forging ahead: look for the additional text in the title screen to confirm an active Forge.

Forge on its own doesn't add any visible functionality to Minecraft. For that you need to install an actual mod.

Forge makes adding and removing mods as easy as drag and drop, although you'll first need to get to the actual mods folder. Follow these steps:

1 Click **Options** from Minecraft's title screen.

2 Select **Resource Packs**.

3 Click on **Open resource pack folder** and use your standard file system controls to go up one folder or directory level to the main Minecraft folder. Within there you'll see the *mods* folder. Forge adds this folder on installation, so you won't see it if you haven't yet installed.

4 Copy or move any forge-compatible mods into this folder.

5 Restart Minecraft to load the mod and start testing it out.

NOTE

No Need to Decompress

Mods are usually found inside a .jar file or a .zip. Either works just fine—there's no need to decompress the zip before placing it in the mods folder.

Here's a small list of mods you can try to get started. Remember to always download the version that corresponds to your Minecraft version—Forge doesn't remove that particular requirement.

Too Many Items

http://goo.gl/vyE3JG

Too Many Items is one of the most popular and useful mods, providing an incredible enhancement to the inventory window. (FYI, everyone calls it *TMI*.)

TMI adds a host of controls to the window for quickly setting up stacks of inventory items, enchanting items up to any level, brewing potions, and controlling other aspects of the game such as the time, weather, and difficulty level. It also supports saving and reloading of stored inventory configurations.

While a mod such as TMI makes it ridiculously easy to get through the game in Survival mode, the ability to quickly load a particular configuration of items or blocks makes it quite useful for construction projects in Creative.

FIGURE 13.7   Too Many Items greatly expands the inventory screen.

More Explosives

http://moreexplosives.com

From too many items to not enough mayhem! I like this mod. It's a bit of fun, especially on multiplayer. *More Explosives* adds an arsenal of modern weaponry to Minecraft, including landmines, hand grenades, Molotov cocktails, and other things that go kaboom all the way up to nuclear (see Figure 13.8). It even includes targeted missiles and a radar!

On the more utilitarian side this mod adds a handy tunneling explosive that will knock out a 3x3x20 hole in the direction the explosive is facing.

In the true spirit of Minecraft every item can be crafted from raw ingredients, adding some very interesting options to a multiplayer game on Survival.

FIGURE 13.8   Going thermo: a dramatic nuclear crater courtesy of More Explosives.

Super Heroes

http://goo.gl/gEICO4

This is another fun mod that's perfect for multiplayer. Superheroes! Iron Man, Thor, Hulk, and Captain America complete with customized armor suits and, of course, their core capabilities. For example, Iron Man can fly (if you have crafted the rocket fuel), shoot bullets, launch rockets, and do a few other interesting things. Thor, as you'd expect, puts an Olympian's hammer throw to shame, and the Hulk is, essentially, indestructible and capable of smashing through everything except bedrock.

REI's MiniMap

http://goo.gl/U5m8MY

This is another community favorite, adding a very handy and highly configurable map to the top-right corner of the screen (see Figure 13.9). The map is switchable between a surface display, a second that helps highlight biomes, and a third that is optimized for underground exploration. The map window is expandable to the full size of the Minecraft display and also acts as an entity radar showing nearby passive and hostile mobs.

FIGURE 13.9 The highly-configurable REI's minimap (with main menu shown) can quickly become indispensable.

Legendary Beasts

http://goo.gl/rypxlw

Now that you have super heroes and a map, it's time to balance the equation with Legendary Beasts. This mod adds new boss characters to the game: the Elf Hunter, Lightning Spirit, Ender Lord, Fire Demon, and the huge Snow Beast (see Figure 13.10). Each has its own vulnerability and they drop incredibly powerful weapons upon defeat. Some of the mobs live in giant pyramids while others, such as the Elf Hunter, camp out. They're not easily defeated, but it's worth the fight.

FIGURE 13.10 New boss mobs: the Snow Beast on the left and the Lightning Spirit on the right.

More Mobs

http://goo.gl/40q0rl

The More Mobs mod adds dozens of new creatures to Minecraft, from human entities to all kinds of species including new hostile mobs specific to The Nether and End regions. It's nothing short of the Minecraft equivalent of the Galapagos Islands and is a fabulous piece of work. In fact, the author of this mod contributed substantially to the horse models used in the Minecraft v1.6 update.

Unfortunately, at this writing, the mod's developer has embedded the installation into an adware-ridden utility that only works on Windows PCs. I wouldn't usually include a mod that does that because one must take extra care to decline all offers during installation, but it really is a splendid mod so if you do go ahead and download, just be super careful as you install to ensure your browser isn't hijacked by another search engine, or similar. If you use Linux or OS X you're out of luck with this one unless you can persuade someone who has installed it on Windows to give you a copy of the actual mod that's placed in their *mods* folder. The mod itself is cross-platform so the same file will work anywhere without any additional risk.

TIP

Finding More Mods

There's no go-to list of mods, but Planet Minecraft does have a very comprehensive offering (http://goo.gl/1folnq). For best results look for mods that include [FORGE] in their title, and remember to match the displayed version to your own Minecraft version. The mods listed in this section provide just the tiniest glimpse into what is quite an amazing amount of custom development. Mods exist that can change the tiniest detail, or alter the entire experience. Just remember to tread carefully when downloading or going through a custom install, and install the mods one at a time, launching Minecraft in-between to ensure the mod hasn't broken the main game. If it has, just delete the mod and move onto the next.

Multiplayer Madness

Playing Minecraft alone is all well and good ("sniff"), and there's plenty to keep one occupied. But playing as part of a group can be a lot more fun and, if creative builds are your goal, hugely more productive.

Minecraft provides several ways to party up:

- **LAN**—Share your world on your local network and anyone on the same wired or wireless connection can join.

- **Join a Multiplayer Server**—Jump into any server to join other players. Some servers support hundreds of players at the same time, engaged in acts both creative and combative. More on these later.

- **Host a Multiplayer Server**—Start up your own server, punch a hole through your firewall, and share your Minecraft world with the rest of the actual world.

- **Join Realms**—See the "Minecraft Realms" Note in the following pages.

There are a few pre-requisites to joining any multiplayer game, no matter the connection method. First, each player needs his or her own Mojang account (a Minecraft license), even on a LAN. Second, the Minecraft client has to match the server's version. This means a v1.7 client can't talk to a 1.6.2 server. Finally, some servers will ban players for using mods, and on a LAN game all the mods that change blocks or add new items must match between the client and server. Once resource packs support mods, this will probably be a much simpler requirement: just install the recommended resource pack and you'll be ready to go. For now, though, ensure the contents of your mods directory match across all PCs if playing on LAN.

Sharing and Joining on LAN

To set up a LAN server, open any Minecraft world:

1 Press Esc to open the options window.

2 Select **Open to LAN**.

3 Join a LAN server by clicking **Multiplayer** on the title screen and look for a server called *LAN World*, as shown in Figure 13.11. You'll also see the account name of the user hosting the session, and the name given to that world.

4 Double-click to join the server.

FIGURE 13.11 Joining a LAN server.

That's all there is to it. In a few moments you'll appear at the world's spawn point.

TIP

Teleporting Other Players

Bring other players to your location quickly and easily with the teleport command. It's a sort of "beam me up, Scotty" for Minecraft. Make sure you start a multiplayer game with cheats enabled, then type /tp playername, replacing *playername*] with the name of the player you want to teleport. Hit Enter and you'll zap them direct to your location. See http://www.minecraftwiki.net/wiki/Commands for a complete list of multiplayer commands.

NOTE

Command Blocks

Minecraft has a special block designed specifically for multiplayer, although you can also place it in a single player world. It's called the Command Block, and it can't be crafted, and you won't even find it in the inventory in creative mode. However, if your world has cheats enabled, or you're running a server, you can give it to yourself or another player. Type /give [playername] 137 to make a command block appear in their or your inventory. When placed, a right-click on the block open a command window. From here you can type in and store any of the available commands to cause that action to occur to the player. Just set a lever, pressure plate, or button on or near the block to send a redstone pulse that triggers the command. For example, setting /tp @p 0,0,0 will teleport the player to location coordinates 0,0,0. Substitute the 0's for more specific coordinates, put a pressure plate next to the command block, and you can create an instant transport system between different bases, hubs, mines and so on in your world.

Joining a Multiplayer Server

Just as mods expand Minecraft's functionality in any number of useful and imaginative ways, multiplayer servers create whole new worlds that can take the experience even further. These servers allow you to communicate with other players either co-operatively or combatively, depending on the server's rules. Some are plain-vanilla, meaning there's not a lot of difference between them and a standard Minecraft world besides it being multiplayer, but many others are carefully constructed, elaborate masterpieces with special code that provides a heavily customized experience for their players. The Shotbow Network shown in Figure 13.12 is one such example.

FIGURE 13.12 Shotbow's game lobby showing just a few of the game types as well as other players.

NOTE

Minecraft Realms

By the time you read this, the new Minecraft Realms service should be online. Realms is a subscription service that provides an easy way for families or groups of friends to host small co-operative servers of up to 20 players. While it's easy enough to set up a LAN game if you're all on the same network, Realms works across the broader internet so players can get together from all over the world. Interestingly, the Pocket Edition also supports Realms with the goal of supporting up to 10 players per server, but PE cannot join other multiplayer servers.

The first thing you should do is to locate an actual server. There are literally thousands to choose from, and sites such as planetminecraft.com and minecraftservers.org do a great job of keeping a complete database running. Some servers are open to one and all while others require registration. Most are free to some extent, although paid subscriptions may provide access to use otherwise full servers and give you other benefits.

Join a multiplayer server with these steps:

1 Click on **Multiplayer** in the title screen.

2 Select **Add server**.

3 Type in a **Server Name** (it can be anything you like that will help you identify that server in the future).

4 Type in the **Server Address** and click **Done**.

5 Select the server from the list (see the earlier Figure 13.11) and click **Join Server**, or just double-click the server's name to do so automatically.

Most servers drop you into a game lobby where you can see the different game types and read the server's rules. Typically these include information on permitted mods, so make sure you read the signs or any books dropped into your inventory as this can help you from getting banned.

To get started, try any of these—the server's address is shown in parentheses:

- **Shotbow (us.shotbow.net)**—The shotbow network hosts a huge range of game types, each with their own particular rules. Visit http://shotbow.net to learn more. Make sure your skills are up as it tends to have some hardcore players.

- **The Hive (eu.hivemc.com)**—The Hive is full of games that are great for kids, and anyone who wants to have a bit of fun. There's an arcade with paintball, hide 'n' seek, survivor maps, and a Herobrine game.

- **Supercraft Brothers (1.cbga.me)**—Supercraft Brothers is something of a riot. Fast-paced player versus player (PvP) gaming. They have a range of servers well beyond 1.cbga.me so check supercraftbrothers.com to register and find the rest in case the one shown here is full.

- **Phanatic (play.phanaticmc.com)**—A busy server with creative-mode, a host of mini-games, and a hunger games mode based on the premise from the popular film.

- **BeastsMC (c.beastsmc.com)**—Don't let the name perturb you, this is an excellent server for creative builds. The same host also offers survival and hardcore multiplayer. See http://www.beastsmc.com for more information.

There is a huge range of impressive servers out there, some with incredibly extensive worlds and gigantic creative builds. Look through the server lists to find one that suits you. There is, truly, something for everyone.

Hosting a Multiplayer Server

Hosting your own server is a rewarding way to create a consistent, stable world that you and others can connect to from anywhere. It does require a little technical knowledge, especially if you want to be able to access the server externally, but nothing insurmountable.

The basic steps are fairly simple, and you can use a *whitelist* to ensure that only you and your trusted family or friends can join. For now, we'll set up the server on the local network. You can actually do this even if you have just one PC hosting the server and accessing it from the Minecraft client simultaneously.

Follow these steps and you'll be up and running in no time:

1 First download the server software from http://minecraft.net/download. Choose the .exe file if you're running Windows, or the .jar file for any other platform.

2 Create a new folder and move the downloaded software to it.

3 Double-click or open the downloaded file to launch the server. You'll see a window similar to that shown in Figure 13.13.

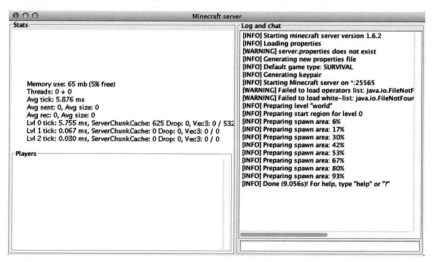

FIGURE 13.13 The Minecraft Server provides a clean interface for managing players and should run well in the background on all but very low specification PCs.

The server does a few things on first run, generating a new world and also creating a number of configuration files. The world generates into a folder called, appropriately enough, *world*, in the same directory as the server software. Its format is the same as those the Minecraft client creates, so if you'd like to share out a world you've already created, shut down the server and copy that world from the *saves* directory of your Minecraft application into the server directory, and then rename the folder *world*. Restart the server to share it.

TIP

Host With the Most

If hosting with your own hardware doesn't appeal for security or other reasons, but you still have the urge to share a world for collaborative creation or otherwise, consider using a paid hosting provider. There are numerous providers online who specialize in Minecraft hosting and will provide you with all you need, including configuration and customization tools. Mcprohosting.com starts for as little as $2.50 per month for five players.

At this point you should have a server running on your local network. You'll need its IP address to connect. The IP is the address on your local network, usually looking like 192.168.0.*x* or 90.0.0.*x*, where *x* is the final IP number assigned to your computer.

Discovering the IP depends on the server's operating system. On Windows you'll find it under the network card or wi-fi connection in the Network and Sharing Center in the Control Panel. Select the active connection and click **Details** to see the IP address. On OS X, open **System Preferences...** under the Apple menu, click **Network** and then the active connection. You will see the IP address under the Status line in the right-panel of the window. If you're using Linux, I'm just going to go right ahead and assume you already know or know how to discover the address.

Connect to the server using the same steps as connecting to a multiplayer server using the IP address as the Server Address in the Add Server window.

Opening the server up to the broader world requires a few more steps, and it is not without its risks as you'll have to expose your server through the firewall to the untethered wilds of the Internet. I can't provide specific steps as this is all about router configuration, and they're all different, but here are some pointers that should help:

1 Assign a permanent local IP to your server. You want to ensure, for example, that if your server is addressed on your local network as 192.168.0.4, that it stays that way. Typically IP addresses are dynamically assigned within the local network, but if your router supports IP reservation then you can use the MAC address of the server to assign a permanent local address.

2 Use the router's port forwarding to send all traffic it receives on port 25565 to the server's local IP address.

3 In almost all cases, your Internet provider assigns you a dynamic IP address—an address that can change without notice. Static IP addresses cost extra, sometimes hundreds of dollars, so I'd recommend using a dynamic DNS service instead. I prefer dyndns.org, but there are many available. A dynamic IP ensures that you or others can reach the server from anywhere with a standard address such as "mcserver.mydyndns.org". You then type that address into Minecraft's Add Server page rather than an IP address. In many cases it's possible to configure the router to talk to one of the more common dynamic DNS providers, but if not then you will be able to download a small piece of software from the provider that will keep the domain-name version of the address up to date and running smoothly even if your Internet provider changes your external numerical IP address.

Finally, you should take some steps to protect the Minecraft server application to prevent just anyone logging in:

1 There's a small chat bar just below the main window log in the server's display. Type in "/whitelist on". This ensures only those people specifically approved to access the server can log in. If anyone else tries they'll simply be disconnected.

2 Add the account name (the Mojang or Minecraft account used to log in to the game) for everyone you want to grant access to the server. Do this by typing "/whitelist add [playername]", replacing [playername] with the actual name. The whitelist is a file contained in the server's directory. If you need to add a lot of names you can do so just by typing them into the file itself using a plain text editor, each name on a single line. You may need to type "/whitelist reload" to force the server to recognize the changes to the file when you're done.

3 Add yourself as an operator so that you can control the server from any Minecraft client by typing "op [yourname]". Again, replace the latter part with your actual account name.

4 Create a startup script that will automatically restart the Minecraft server if the power goes down or the server hardware resets.

That's the essence of a Minecraft server. You can do a lot more besides, including setting up a texture pack that will automatically download to anyone who joins, adding Bukkit mods (see wiki.bukkit.org), and more, but I'll leave you to discover these on your own. There is a wealth of material online and a large number of game configuration settings stored in the server properties file in the server's main directory.

Hosting a customized Minecraft server is, perhaps, the ultimate expression of not just playing, but also optimizing the Minecraft gaming experience and sharing it with others.

The Bottom Line

Minecraft is one of the most open games on the market. From skins to mods to hosting a server, it's a malleable ball of clay waiting to be shaped by your deft hands.

Fortunately, you don't need to start from scratch. Many dedicated developers, artists, and designers have traveled this road before. Thousands of mods, tens of thousands of servers, and hundreds of thousands of skins are already there.

The ultimate player is not the one who simply finishes the game, but the one who takes it ever further. From fantastic constructions to amazing redstone contraptions, from ludicrously complicated automated farms to tricks (the TNT cannon comes to mind) that go far beyond any of the game's original intentions. Minecraft is fertile ground, an endless expanse of possibility both within gameplay and also deep within its code. Multiple mods can ensue in something like programmatic chaos, but when well orchestrated result in an experience that sings.

Enjoy, and if you ever think you've gone as far as you can go, take another look. There's a new experience just around the corner. I hope to see you there.

INDEX

NUMBERS

A

D

F

J - K

L

Q - R

S

FREE
Online Edition

Your purchase of *The Ultimate Player's Guide to Minecraft* includes access to a free online edition for 45 days through the **Safari Books Online** subscription service. Nearly every Que book is available online through **Safari Books Online**, along with thousands of books and videos from publishers such as Addison-Wesley Professional, Cisco Press, Exam Cram, IBM Press, O'Reilly Media, Prentice Hall, Sams, and VMware Press.

Safari Books Online is a digital library providing searchable, on-demand access to thousands of technology, digital media, and professional development books and videos from leading publishers. With one monthly or yearly subscription price, you get unlimited access to learning tools and information on topics including mobile app and software development, tips and tricks on using your favorite gadgets, networking, project management, graphic design, and much more.

Activate your FREE Online Edition at
informit.com/safarifree

STEP 1:   Enter the coupon code: LGEQXAA.

STEP 2:   New Safari users, complete the brief registration form.
Safari subscribers, just log in.

If you have difficulty registering on Safari or accessing the online edition,
please e-mail customer-service@safaribooksonline.com